The I-Series

Microsoft® Excel 2002

Brief

Stephen Haag
University of Denver

James T. Perry
University of San Diego

Boston   Burr Ridge, IL   Dubuque, IA   Madison, WI   New York   San Francisco   St. Louis
Bangkok   Bogotá   Caracas   Kuala Lumpur   Lisbon   London   Madrid   Mexico City
Milan   Montreal   New Delhi   Santiago   Seoul   Singapore   Sydney   Taipei   Toronto

McGraw-Hill Higher Education

A Division of The **McGraw-Hill** *Companies*

The I-Series: Microsoft Excel 2002, Brief

Published by McGraw-Hill/Irwin, an imprint of The McGraw-Hill Companies, Inc. 1221 Avenue of the Americas, New York, NY 10020. Copyright © 2002 by The McGraw-Hill Companies, Inc. All rights reserved. No part of this publication may be reproduced or distributed in any form or by any means, or stored in a database or retrieval system, without the prior written consent of The McGraw-Hill Companies, Inc., including, but not limited to, in any network or other electronic storage or transmission, or broadcast for distance learning.

Some ancillaries, including electronic and print components, may not be available to customers outside the United States.

This book is printed on acid-free paper.

1 2 3 4 5 6 7 8 9 0 WEB/WEB 0 9 8 7 6 5 4 3 2 1

ISBN 0-07-247031-3

Publisher: *George Werthman*
Sponsoring editor: *Dan Silverburg*
Developmental editor: *Melissa Forte*
Manager, Marketing and Sales: *Paul Murphy*
Senior project manager: *Jean Hamilton*
Production supervisor: *Rose Hepburn*
Coordinator freelance design: *Mary L. Christianson and Jennifer McQueen*
Lead supplement producer: *Marc Mattson*
Senior producer, Media technology: *David Barrick*
Interior freelance design: *Asylum Studios*
Cover freelance design/illustration: *Asylum Studios*
Compositor: *GAC Indianapolis*
Typeface: *10/12 New Aster*
Printer: *Webcrafters, Inc.*

Library of Congress Cataloging-in-Publication Data
Haag, Stephen.
    Microsoft Excel 2002: brief / Stephen Haag, James T. Perry.—1st edition
      p. cm.   (I-series)
    Includes index.
    ISBN 0-07-247031-3 (alk. paper)
    1. Microsoft Excel for Windows. 2. Business—Computer programs. 3. Electronic spreadsheets. I. Perry, James T. II. Title. III. Series.
HF5548.4.M523 H3 2002
  005.369—dc21
                                                    2001054417

http://www.mhhe.com

InformationTechnology

INFORMATION TECHNOLOGY AT MCGRAW-HILL/IRWIN

At McGraw-Hill Higher Education, we publish instructional materials targeted at the higher education market. In an effort to expand the tools of higher learning, we publish texts, lab manuals, study guides, testing materials, software, and multimedia products.

At McGraw-Hill/Irwin (a division of McGraw-Hill Higher Education), we realize that technology has created and will continue to create new mediums for professors and students to use in managing resources and communicating information to one another. We strive to provide the most flexible and complete teaching and learning tools available as well as offer solutions to the changing world of teaching and learning.

McGraw-Hill/Irwin is dedicated to providing the tools for today's instructors and students to successfully navigate the world of Information Technology.

- **SEMINAR SERIES**—McGraw-Hill/Irwin's Technology Connection seminar series offered across the country every year demonstrates the latest technology products and encourages collaboration among teaching professionals.

- **MCGRAW-HILL/OSBORNE**—This division of The McGraw-Hill Companies is known for its best-selling Internet titles, *Internet & Web Yellow Pages* and the *Internet Complete Reference*. For more information, visit Osborne at www.osborne.com.

- **DIGITAL SOLUTIONS**—McGraw-Hill/Irwin is committed to publishing digital solutions. Taking your course online doesn't have to be a solitary adventure, nor does it have to be a difficult one. We offer several solutions that will allow you to enjoy all the benefits of having your course material online.

- **PACKAGING OPTIONS**—For more information about our discount options, contact your McGraw-Hill/Irwin sales representative at 1-800-338-3987 or visit our Web site at www.mhhe.com/it.

THE I-SERIES PAGE

By using the I-Series, students will be able to learn and master applications skills by being actively engaged—by *doing*. The "I" in I-Series demonstrates Insightful tasks that will not only Inform students, but also Involve them while learning the applications.

How will The I-Series accomplish this for you?

Through relevant, real-world chapter opening cases.

Through tasks throughout each chapter that incorporate steps and tips for easy reference.

Through alternative methods and styles of learning to keep the student involved.

Through rich, end-of-chapter materials that support what the student has learned.

I-Series titles include:

- Microsoft Office XP, Volume I
- Microsoft Office XP, Volume I Expanded
- Microsoft Office XP, Volume II
- Microsoft Word 2002 (Brief, Introductory, Complete Versions) 12 Chapters
- Microsoft Excel 2002 (Brief, Introductory, Complete Versions) 12 Chapters
- Microsoft Access 2002 (Brief, Introductory, Complete Versions) 12 Chapters
- Microsoft PowerPoint 2002 (Brief, Introductory Versions) 8 Chapters
- Microsoft Windows 2000 (Brief, Introductory, Complete Versions) 12 Chapters
- Microsoft Windows XP and Bonus Books to come!

To accompany the series: The I-Series Computing Concepts text (Introductory, Complete Versions)

For additional resources, visit the I-Series Online Learning Center at www.mhhe.com/i-series/

GOALS/PHILOSOPHY

The I-Series applications textbooks strongly emphasize that students learn and master applications skills by being actively engaged—by *doing*. We made the decision that teaching how to accomplish tasks is not enough for complete understanding and mastery. Students must understand the importance of each of the tasks that lead to a finished product at the end of each chapter.

Approach

The I-Series chapters are subdivided into sessions that contain related groups of tasks with active, hands-on components. The session tasks containing numbered steps collectively result in a completed project at the end of each session. Prior to introducing numbered steps that show how to accomplish a particular task, we discuss why the steps are important. We discuss the role that the collective steps play in the overall plan for creating or modifying a document or object, answering students' often-heard questions, "Why are we doing these steps? Why are these steps important?" Without an explanation of why an activity is important and what it accomplishes, students can easily find themselves following the steps but not registering the big picture of what the steps accomplish and why they are executing them.

I-Series Applications for 2002

The I-Series offers three levels of instruction. Each level builds upon knowledge from the previous level. With the exception of the running project that is the last exercise of every chapter, chapter cases and end-of-chapter exercises are independent from one chapter to the next, with the exception of Access. The three levels available are

Brief Covers the basics of the Microsoft application and contains Chapters 1 through 4. The Brief textbooks are typically 200 pages long.

Introductory Includes chapters in the Brief textbook plus Chapters 5 through 8. Introductory textbooks typically are 400 pages long and prepare students for the Microsoft Office User Specialist (MOUS) Core Exam.

Complete Includes the Introductory textbook plus Chapters 9 through 12. The four additional chapters cover advanced level content and are typically 600 pages long. Complete textbooks prepare students for the Microsoft Office User Specialist (MOUS) Expert Exam. The Microsoft Office User Specialist program is recognized around the world as the standard for demonstrating proficiency using Microsoft Office applications.

In addition, there are two compilation volumes available.

Office I Includes introductory chapters on Windows and Computing Concepts followed by Chapters 1 through 4 (Brief textbook) of Word, Excel, Access, and PowerPoint. In addition, material from the companion Computing Concepts book is integrated into the first few chapters to provide students an understanding of the relationship between Microsoft Office applications and computer information systems.

Office II Includes introductory chapters on Windows and Computing Concepts followed by Chapters 5 through 8 from each of the Introductory-level textbooks including Word, Excel, Access, and PowerPoint. In addition, material from the companion Computing Concepts book is integrated into the introductory chapters to provide students a deeper understanding of the relationship between Microsoft Office applications and computer information systems. An introduction to Visual Basic for Applications (VBA) completes the Office II textbook.

Approved Microsoft Courseware

Use of the Microsoft Office User Specialist Approved Courseware logo on this product signifies that it has been independently reviewed and approved to comply with the following standards: Acceptable coverage of all content related to the Microsoft Office Exams entitled Microsoft Access 2002, Microsoft Excel 2002, Microsoft PowerPoint 2002, and Microsoft Word 2002, and sufficient performance-based exercises that relate closely to all required content, based on sampling of the textbooks. For further information on Microsoft's MOUS certification program, please visit Microsoft's Web site at www.microsoft.com.

STEPHEN HAAG

Stephen Haag is a professor and Chair of Information Technology and Electronic Commerce and the Director of Technology in the University of Denver's Daniels College of Business. Stephen holds a B.B.A. and an M.B.A. from West Texas State University and a Ph.D. from the University of Texas at Arlington. Stephen has published numerous articles appearing in such journals as *Communications of the ACM*, *The International Journal of Systems Science*, *Applied Economics*, *Managerial and Decision Economics*, *Socio-Economic Planning Sciences*, and the *Australian Journal of Management*.

Stephen is also the author of 13 other books including *Interactions: Teaching English as a Second Language* (with his mother and father), *Case Studies in Information Technology, Information Technology: Tomorrow's Advantage Today* (with Peter Keen), and *Excelling in Finance*. Stephen is also the lead author of the accompanying *I-Series: Computing Concepts* text, released in both an Introductory and Complete version. Stephen lives with his wife, Pam, and their four sons, Indiana, Darian, Trevor, and Elvis, in Highlands Ranch, Colorado.

JAMES PERRY

James Perry is a professor of Management Information Systems at the University of San Diego's School of Business. Jim is an active instructor who teaches both undergraduate and graduate courses. He holds a B.S. in mathematics from Purdue University and a Ph.D. in computer science from The Pennsylvania State University. He has published several journal and conference papers. He is the co-author of 56 textbooks and trade books such as *Using Access with Accounting Systems, Building Accounting Systems, Understanding Oracle, The Internet,* and *Electronic Commerce*. His books have been translated into Dutch, French, and Chinese. Jim worked as a computer security consultant to various private and governmental organizations including the Jet Propulsion Laboratory. He was a consultant on the Strategic Defense Initiative ("Star Wars") project and served as a member of the computer security oversight committee.

RICK PARKER

Rick Parker received his bachelor's degree from Brigham Young University. He received his Ph.D. in animal physiology at Iowa State University. After completing his Ph.D., he and his wife, Marilyn, and their children moved to Edmonton, Alberta, Canada, where he completed a post-doctorate at the University of Alberta. He accepted a position as a research and teaching associate at the University of Wyoming, Laramie, Wyoming.

Rick developed a love for the power and creativity unleashed by computers and software. After arriving at the College of Southern Idaho, Twin Falls, in 1984, he guided the creation and development of numerous college software courses and software training programs for business and industry. He also led the conversion of an old office occupations technical program into a business computer applications program, which evolved into an information technology program. During the early adoption of computers and software by the college, Rick wrote in-house training manuals and taught computer/software courses.

Rick currently works as a professional-technical division director at the College of Southern Idaho. As director, he supervises faculty in agriculture, information technology and drafting, and electronics programs. He is the author of four other textbooks.

MERRILL WELLS

The caption next to **Merrill Wells'** eighth grade yearbook picture noted that her career goal was to teach college and write books. She completed an MBA at Indiana University and began a career as a programmer. After several years of progressive positions in business and industry, she returned to academia, spending 10 years as a computer technology faculty member at Red Rocks Community College and then becoming an information technology professor at the University of Denver, Daniels College of Business. She completed her first published book in 1993 and began presenting at educational seminars in 1997. Other publications include *An Introduction to Computers, Introduction to Visual Basic,* and *Programming Logic and Design*.

Each textbook features the following:

Did You Know Each chapter has six or seven interesting facts—both about high tech and other topics.

Sessions Each chapter is divided into two or three sessions.

Chapter Outline Provides students with a quick map of the major headings in the chapter.

Chapter and MOUS Objectives At the beginning of each chapter is a list of 5 to 10 action-oriented objectives. Any chapter objectives that are also MOUS objectives indicate the MOUS objective number also.

Chapter Opening Case Each chapter begins with a case. Cases describe a mixture of fictitious and real people and companies and the needs of the people and companies. Throughout the chapter, the student gains the skills and knowledge to solve the problem stated in the case.

Introduction The chapter introduction establishes the overview of the chapter's activities in the context of the case problem.

Another Way and Another Word Another Way is a highlighted feature providing a bulleted list of steps to accomplish a task, or best practices—that is, a better or faster way to accomplish a task such as pasting a format onto an Excel cell. Another Word, another highlighted box, briefly explains more about a topic or highlights a potential pitfall.

Step-by-Step Instructions Numbered step-by-step instructions for all hands-on activities appear in a distinctive color. Keyboard characters and menu selections appear in a **special format** to emphasize what the user should press or type. Steps make clear to the student the exact sequence of keystrokes and mouse clicks needed to complete a task such as formatting a Word paragraph.

Tips Tips appear within a numbered sequence of steps and warn the student of possible missteps or provide alternatives to the step that precedes the tip.

Task Reference and Task Reference Round-Up Task References appear throughout the textbook. Set in a distinctive design, each Task Reference contains a bulleted list of steps showing a generic way to accomplish activities that are especially important or significant. A Task Reference Round-Up at the end of each chapter summarizes a chapter's Task References.

MOUS Objectives Summary A list of MOUS objectives covered in a chapter appears in the chapter objectives and the chapter summary.

Making the Grade Short answer questions appear at the end of each chapter's sessions. They test a student's grasp of each session's contents, and Making the Grade answers appear at the end of each book so students can check their answers.

Rich End-of-Chapter Materials End-of-chapter materials incorporating a three-level approach reinforce learning and help students take ownership of the chapter. Level One, review of terminology, contains a fun crossword puzzle that enforces review of a chapter's key terms. Level Two, review of concepts, contains fill-in-the blank questions, review questions, and a Jeopardy-style create-a-question exercise. Level Three is Hands-on Projects.

Hands-on Projects Extensive hands-on projects engage the student in a problem-solving exercise from start to finish. There are six clearly labeled categories that each contain one or two questions. Categories are Practice, Challenge!, On the Web, E-Business, Around the World, and a Running Project that carries throughout all the chapters.

We understand that, in today's teaching environment, offering a textbook alone is not sufficient to meet the needs of the many instructors who use our books. To teach effectively, instructors must have a full complement of supplemental resources to assist them in every facet of teaching, from preparing for class to conducting a lecture to assessing students' comprehension. The **I-Series** offers a complete supplements package and Web site that is briefly described below.

INSTRUCTOR'S RESOURCE KIT

The Instructor's Resource Kit is a CD-ROM containing the Instructor's Manual in both MS Word and .pdf formats, PowerPoint Slides with Presentation Software, Brownstone test-generating software, and accompanying test item files in both MS Word and .pdf formats for each chapter. The CD also contains figure files from the text, student data files, and solutions files. The features of each of the three main components of the Instructor's Resource Kit are highlighted below.

Instructor's Manual Featuring:

- Chapter learning objectives per chapter
- Chapter outline with teaching tips
- Annotated Solutions Diagram to provide Troubleshooting Tips, Tricks, and Traps
- Lecture Notes, illustrating key concepts and ideas
- Annotated Syllabus, depicting a time table and schedule for covering chapter content
- Additional end-of-chapter projects
- Answers to all Making the Grade and end-of-chapter questions

PowerPoint Presentation

The PowerPoint presentation is designed to provide instructors with comprehensive lecture and teaching resources that will include

- Chapter learning objectives followed by source content that illustrates key terms and key facts per chapter

- FAQ (frequently asked questions) to show key concepts throughout the chapter; also, lecture notes, to illustrate these key concepts and ideas
- End-of-chapter exercises and activities per chapter, as taken from the end-of-chapter materials in the text
- Speaker's Notes, to be incorporated throughout the slides per chapter
- Figures/screen shots, to be incorporated throughout the slides per chapter

PowerPoint includes presentation software for instructors to design their own presentation for their course.

Test Bank

The I-Series Test Bank, using Diploma Network Testing Software by Brownstone, contains over 3,000 questions (both objective and interactive) categorized by topic, page reference to the text, and difficulty level of learning. Each question is assigned a learning category:

- Level 1: Key Terms and Facts
- Level 2: Key Concepts
- Level 3: Application and Problem-Solving

The types of questions consist of 40 percent Identifying/Interactive Lab Questions, 20 percent Multiple Choice, 20 percent True/False, and 20 percent Fill-in/Short Answer Questions.

ONLINE LEARNING CENTER/ WEB SITE

The Online Learning Center that accompanies the I-Series is accessible through our Information Technology Supersite at http://www.mhhe.com/ catalogs/irwin/it/. This site provides additional review and learning tools developed using the same three-level approach found in the text and supplements. To locate the I-Series OLC/Web site directly, go to www.mhhe.com/i-series. The site is divided into three key areas:

- **Information Center** Contains core information about the text, the authors, and a guide to our additional features and benefits of the series, including the supplements.

- **Instructor Center**   Offers instructional materials, downloads, additional activities and answers to additional projects, answers to chapter troubleshooting exercises, answers to chapter preparation/post exercises posed to students, relevant links for professors, and more.

- **Student Center**   Contains chapter objectives and outlines, self-quizzes, chapter troubleshooting exercises, chapter preparation/post exercises, additional projects, simulations, student data files and solutions files, Web links, and more.

RESOURCES FOR STUDENTS

Interactive Companion CD   This student CD-ROM can be packaged with this text. It is designed for use in class, in the lab, or at home by students and professors and combines video, interactive exercises, and animation to cover the most difficult and popular topics in Computing Concepts. By combining video, interactive exercises, animation, additional content, and actual "lab" tutorials, we expand the reach and scope of the textbook.

SimNet XPert   SimNet XPert is a simulated assessment and learning tool. It allows students to study MS Office XP skills and computer concepts, and professors to test and evaluate students' proficiency within MS Office XP applications and concepts. Students can practice and study their skills at home or in the school lab using SimNet XPert, which does not require the purchase of Office XP software. SimNet XPert will contain new features and enhancements for Office XP, including:

NEW! **Live Assessments! SimNet *XPert*** now includes live-in-the-application assessments! One for each skill set for Core MOUS objectives in Word 2002, Excel 2002, Access 2002, and PowerPoint 2002 (total of 29 Live-in-the-Application Assessments). Multiple tasks are required to complete each live assessment (about 100 tasks covered).

NEW! **Computer Concepts Coverage!** **SimNet *XPert*** now includes coverage of computer concepts in both the Learning and the Assessment sides.

NEW! **Practice or Pretest Questions!** **SimNet *XPert*** has a separate pool of 600 questions for practice tests or pretests.

NEW! **Comprehensive Exercises! SimNet *XPert*** offers comprehensive exercises for each application. These exercises require the student to use multiple skills to solve one exercise in the simulated environment.

ENHANCED! **More Assessment Questions!** **SimNet *XPert*** includes over 1,400 assessment questions.

ENHANCED! **Simulated Interface!** The simulated environment in **SimNet *XPert*** has been substantially deepened to more realistically simulate the real applications. Now students are not graded incorrect just because they chose the wrong sub-menu or dialog box. The student is not graded until he or she does something that immediately invokes an action.

DIGITAL SOLUTIONS FOR INSTRUCTORS AND STUDENTS

PageOut   PageOut is our Course Web Site Development Center that offers a syllabus page, URL, McGraw-Hill Online Learning Center content, online exercises and quizzes, gradebook, discussion board, and an area for student Web pages. For more information, visit the PageOut Web site at www.pageout.net.

Online Courses Available   OLCs are your perfect solutions for Internet-based content. Simply put, these Centers are "digital cartridges" that contain a book's pedagogy and supplements. As students read the book, they can go online and take self-grading quizzes or work through interactive exercises.

Online Learning Centers can be delivered through any of these platforms:

McGraw-Hill Learning Architecture (TopClass)

Blackboard.com

College.com (formerly Real Education)

WebCT (a product of Universal Learning Technology)

Did You Know?

A unique presentation of text and graphics introduce interesting and little-known facts.

Chapter Objectives

Each chapter begins with a list of competencies covered in the chapter.

---

did you
know?

the *Penny is the only coin currently minted in the United States with a profile that faces to the right. All other U.S. coins feature profiles that face to the left.*

the *world's largest wind generator is on the island of Oahu, Hawaii. The windmill has two blades 400 feet long on the top of a tower, twenty stories high.*

the *only house in England that the Queen may not enter is the House of Commons, because she is not a commoner. She is also the only person in England who does not need a license plate on her vehicle.*

former *U.S. Vice President Al Gore and Oscar-winning actor Tommy Lee Jones were roommates at Harvard.*

Chapter Objectives

- Plan and document a workbook
- Create formulas containing cell references and mathematical operators (MOUS Ex2002-5-1)
- Write functions including Sum, Average, Max, and Min (MOUS Ex2002-5-2)
- Use Excel's AutoSum feature to automatically write Sum functions
- Learn several ways to copy a formula from one cell to many other cells
- Differentiate between absolute, mixed, and relative cell reference (MOUS Ex2002-5-1)
- Adjust column widths (MOUS Ex2002-3-2)
- Set a print area (MOUS Ex2002-3-7)
- Move text, values, and formulas (MOUS Ex2002-1-1)
- Insert and delete rows and columns (MOUS Ex2002-3-2)
- Format cells (MOUS Ex2002-3-1)
- Create cell comments (MOUS Ex2002-7-3)

CHAPTER

2

two

Planning and Creating a Worksheet

Task Reference

Provides steps to accomplish an especially important task.

reference

Changing Relative References to Absolute or Mixed References

- Double-click the cell containing the formula that you want to edit or click the cell and then press **F2**
- Move the insertion point, a vertical bar, to the left of the cell reference you want to alter
- Press function key **F4** repeatedly until the absolute or mixed reference you want appears
- Press **Enter** to complete the cell edit procedure

Making the Grade

Short-answer questions appear at the end of each session and answers appear at the end of the book.

SESSION 2.1

making the grade

1. Explain how AutoSum works and what it does.

2. Suppose you select cell A14 and type D5+F5. What is stored in cell A14: text, a value, or a formula?

3. You can drag the _____, which is a small black square in the lower-right corner of the active cell, to copy the cell's contents.

4. Evaluation of a formula such as =D4+D5*D6 is governed by order of precedence. Explain what that means in general and then indicate the order in which Excel calculates the preceding expression.

5. Suppose Excel did not provide an AVERAGE function. Show an alternative way to compute the average of cell range A1:B25 using the other Excel statistical functions.

Copying a formula from one cell to many cells:

1. Click cell **G4** to make it the active cell. The cell's formula, =F4/B4, appears in the formula bar

2. Click **Edit** on the menu bar and then click **Copy** to copy the cell's contents to the Clipboard. Notice that a dashed line encloses the cell whose contents are on the Clipboard

tip: *You can press **Ctrl+C** instead of using the Copy command. Those of you who keep your hands on the keyboard may favor this keyboard shortcut.*

3. Click and drag cells **G5** through **G8** to select them. They are the target range into which you will paste the cell G4's contents

4. Click **Edit** on the menu bar and then click **Paste**. Excel copies the Clipboard's contents into each of the cells in the selected range and then adjusts each cell's formula to correspond to its new location. Notice that the Paste Options Smart Tag appears below and to the right of cell G8 (see Figure 2.16). The Paste Options Smart Tag provides several formatting and copying options in its list. You can access the options by clicking the Smart Tag list arrow

FIGURE 2.16
Copied formulas' results

	A	B	C	D	E	F	G	H
1	Aluminum Can Recycling Contest							
2								
3	City	Population	Jan	Feb	Mar	Total	Per Capita	
4	Arcata	15855	10505	24556	12567	47628	3.003974	
5	Los Gatos	28951	24567	21777	26719	73063	2.523678	
6	Pasadena	142547	10					
7	San Diego	2801561	271					
8	Sunnyvale	1689908	152					
9	Total		437					
10	Minimum							
11	Average		875					
12	Maximum		271					
13								
14								

tip: You can press Ctrl+ paste the Clipboard's conte

5. Press **Escape** to cl line from the sourc and view the formu

Step-by-Step Instruction

Numbered steps guide you through the exact sequence of keystrokes to accomplish the task.

Tips

Tips appear within steps and either indicate possible missteps or provide alternatives to a step.

Screen Shots

Screen shots show you what to expect at critical points.

hands-on projects

LEVEL THREE

practice

r Work Hours

r Wexler's Tool and age a group of five r group has a differ- record on a weekly ch employee works, , and percentage of at each employee's ing the information icient way to record Alan Gin, the com- r, wants you to pre- report your group's ges. You create a nd wages.

Wages.xls and

n sheet and then ove to that work-

all the employees'

ve row 1: Click cell , and release the e Menu bar and

he range and type

click cell **C1**, type e Wages, click cell

12. Click cell **E3** and type the formula that represents the employee's percentage of the total wages: **=D3/D$8*100**
13. Copy the formula in cell E3 to the cell range **E4:E7**
14. Select cell range **A1:E8**, click **Format**, click **AutoFormat**, select the **Simple** format, and click **OK**
15. Select cell range **E3:E7** and click the **Decrease Decimal** button enough times to reduce the displayed percentages to two decimal places
16. Click cell **A10** and type your first and last names
17. Set the left, right, top, and bottom margins to two inches
18. Either execute **Print** or execute **Save As**, according to your instructor's direction

2. Creating an Invoice

As office manager of Randy's Foreign Cars, one of your duties is to produce and mail invoices to customers who have arranged to pay for their automobile repairs up to 30 days after mechanics perform the work. Randy's invoices include parts, sales tax on parts, and labor charges. State law stipulates that customers do not pay sales tax on the labor charges. Only parts are subject to state sales tax. State sales tax is 6 percent. Create and print an invoice whose details appear below.

End-of-Chapter Hands-on Projects

A rich variety of projects introduced by a case lets you put into practice what you have learned. Categories include Practice, Challenge, On the Web, E-Business, Around the World, and a running case project.

*another*word

. . . about Smart Tags

Microsoft Office Smart Tags are a set of buttons that are shared across the Office applications. The buttons appear when needed, such as when Excel detects you may have made an error in an Excel formula, and gives the user appropriate options to change the given action or error.

Another Way/ Another Word

Another Way highlights an alternative way to accomplish a task; Another Word explains more about a topic.

task reference roundup

Task	Location	Preferred Method
Writing formulas	EX 2.00	• Select a cell, type **5**, type the formula, press **Enter**
Modifying an AutoSum cell range by pointing	EX 2.00	• Press an arrow key repeatedly to select leftmost or topmost cell in range, press and hold **Shift**, select cell range with arrow keys, release **Shift**, press **Enter**
Writing a function using the Paste Function button	EX 2.00	• Select a cell, click **Paste Function**, click a function category, click a function name, click **OK**, complete the Formula Palette dialog box, click **OK**
Copying and pasting a cell or range of cells	EX 2.00	• Select source cell(s), click **Edit**, click **Copy**, select target cell(s), click **Edit**, click **Paste**
Copying cell contents using a cell's fill handle	EX 2.00	• Select source cell(s), drag the fill handle to the source cell(s) range, release the mouse button

Task Reference RoundUp

Provides a quick reference and summary of a chapter's task references.

APPROVED COURSEWARE

What does this logo mean?

It means this courseware has been approved by the Microsoft® Office User Specialist Program to be among the finest available for learning _Microsoft Word 2002, Microsoft Excel 2002, Microsoft Access 2002, and Microsoft PowerPoint 2002_. It also means that upon completion of this courseware, you may be prepared to become a Microsoft Office User Specialist. The I-Series Microsoft Office XP books are available in three levels of coverage: Brief level, Intro level, and the Complete level. The I-Series Introductory books are approved courseware to prepare you for the MOUS level 1 exam. The I-Series Complete books will prepare you for the expert level exam.

What is a Microsoft Office User Specialist?

A Microsoft Office User Specialist is an individual who has certified his or her skills in one or more of the Microsoft Office desktop applications of Microsoft Word, Microsoft Excel, Microsoft PowerPoint®, Microsoft Outlook® or Microsoft Access, or in Microsoft Project. The Microsoft Office User Specialist Program typically offers certification exams at the "Core" and "Expert" skill levels. * The Microsoft Office User Specialist Program is the only Microsoft approved program in the world for certifying proficiency in Microsoft Office desktop applications and Microsoft Project. This certification can be a valuable asset in any job search or career advancement.

More Information:

To learn more about becoming a Microsoft Office User Specialist, visit www.mous.net

To purchase a Microsoft Office User Specialist certification exam, visit www.DesktopIQ.co

To learn about other Microsoft Office User Specialist approved courseware from McGraw-Hill/Irwin, visit http://www.mhhe.com/catalogs/irwin/cit/mous/index.mhtml

.

---

* The availability of Microsoft Office User Specialist certification exams varies by application, application version and language. Visit www.mous.net for exam availability.

Microsoft, the Microsoft Office User Specialist Logo, PowerPoint and Outlook are either registered trademarks or trademarks of Microsoft Corporation in the United States and/or other countries.

acknowledgments

The authors want to acknowledge the work and support of the seasoned professionals at McGraw-Hill. Thank you to George Werthman, publisher, for his strong leadership and a management style that fosters innovation and creativity. Thank you to Dan Silverburg, sponsoring editor, who is an experienced editor and recent recruit to the I-Series. Dan quickly absorbed a month's worth of information in days and guided the authors through the sometimes-difficult publishing maze. Our special thanks go to Melissa Forte, developmental editor, who served, unofficially, as a cheerleader for the authors. The hub of our editorial "wheel," Melissa shouldered more than her share of work in the many months from prelaunch boot camp to bound book date. We are grateful to Gina Huck, developmental editor, for her dedication to this project. From the project's inception, Gina has guided us and kept us on track. Sarah Wood, developmental editor, paid attention to all the details that required her special care.

Thank you to Valerie Bolch, a University of San Diego graduate student, who did a wonderful job of creating some of the end-of-chapter exercises and tech editing the Excel manuscript. Ron Tariga, also a graduate student at the University of San Diego, helped categorize and display several Office XP toolbar buttons. Stirling Perry, a University of San Diego undergraduate student, took screen shots of all of the Office XP toolbar buttons and organized them into logical groups. Wendi Whitmore, a University of San Diego undergraduate student, provided screen shots of Office 2000 toolbars, prior to the release of Office XP. Many thanks to Linda Dillon, who provided creative input and feedback for the PowerPoint end-of-chapter materials. Also, the labor of Carolla McCammack in tech editing many of the Access chapters has been invaluable.

Thank you to Marilyn Parker, Rick's partner for 32 years, for her help, support, and tolerance. She helped with some of the manuscript details, supported Rick's need for time, and tolerated his emotional absence. Rick's sons, Cole, Morgan, Spence, and Sam, were patient and helpful during the time required for all the steps in the production of this book. All of them filled in and did "his" chores at times as they tolerated his distractions. Also, thanks to Mali Jones for her excellent technical editing.

We all wish to thank all of our schools for providing support, including time off to dedicate to writing: University of San Diego, University of Denver, and the College of Southern Idaho.

If you would like to contact us about any of the books in the I-Series, we would enjoy hearing from you. We welcome comments and suggestions that we might incorporate into future editions of the books. You can e-mail book-related messages to us at i-series@mcgraw-hill.com. For the latest information about the I-Series textbooks and related resources, please visit our Web site at www.mhhe.com/i-series.

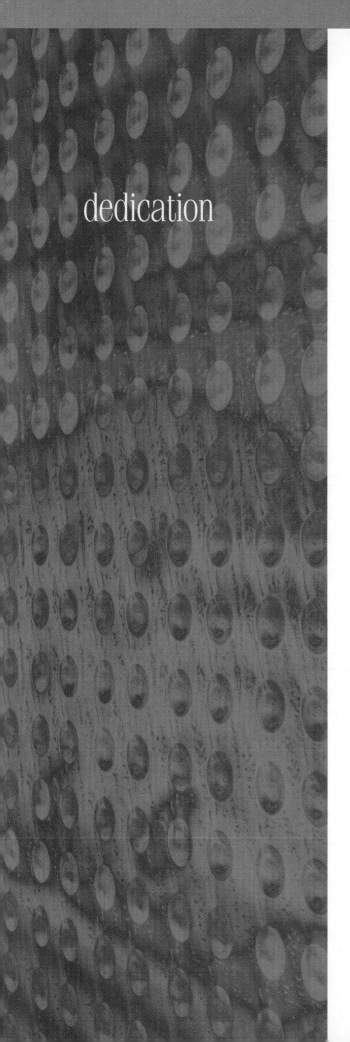

dedication

TO my daughter, Kelly Allison Perry

You say "I will do that," and then you do! What an amazing, bright, and lovely young woman you are. You have taught me more than you realize.

J.T.P.

brief contents

table of contents

CHAPTER 3

CHAPTER 4

Common Microsoft Office XP Features

Chapter Objectives

In this chapter you will:

- Be introduced to the Office XP suite

- Find out what new features exist in Office XP

- Become familiar with the different versions of Office XP and which four applications are included in all versions

- Learn about the common screen elements such as the title bar, menu bar, and toolbars

- Learn how to switch between two or more open applications

- Learn how to use Office XP's newest features: the task pane and smart tags

- Become familiar with how to get help in an application

- Learn how to customize your Office Assistant

- Learn about the newest Help features: Answer Wizard and Ask a Question

INTRODUCTION

Office XP is the newest version of the popular Microsoft integrated application suite series that has helped personal computer users around the world to be productive and creative. Specifically, an *application* is a program that is designed to help you accomplish a particular task, such as creating a slide-show presentation using PowerPoint. An *integrated application suite,* like Office XP, is a collection of application programs bundled together and designed to allow the user to effortlessly share information from one application to the next.

SESSION 1.1 INTRODUCING MICROSOFT OFFICE XP

There are several versions of Office XP available to users with a diversity of personal and business needs. They include the Standard edition, the Professional edition, the Professional Special edition, and the Developer edition. Each edition comes with a collection of different programs, but all include the basic applications of Word, Excel, Outlook, and PowerPoint, which is the collection known as the *Standard edition*. The *Professional edition* adds Access to the collection, whereas the *Professional Special edition* includes Access, FrontPage, and Publisher. A summary of some of the more popular applications available in Office XP is listed in Figure 1.1.

FIGURE 1.1

Application programs available in Microsoft Office XP

Office XP Application	Summary of What the Program Does
Word 2002	Word is a general-purpose word-processing tool that allows users to create primarily text-based documents, such as letters, résumés, research papers, and even Web pages.
Excel 2002	Excel is an electronic spreadsheet tool that can be used to input, organize, calculate, analyze, and display business data.
PowerPoint 2002	PowerPoint is a popular presentation tool that allows users to create overhead transparencies and powerful multimedia slide shows.
Access 2002	Access is a relational database tool that can be used to collect, organize, and retrieve large amounts of data. With a database you can manipulate the data into useful information using tables, forms, queries, and reports.
Outlook 2002	Outlook is a desktop information management tool that allows you to send and receive e-mail, maintain a personal calendar of appointments, schedule meetings with co-workers, create to-do lists, and store address information about business/personal contacts.
FrontPage 2002	FrontPage is a powerful Web publishing tool that provides everything needed to create, edit, and manage a personal or corporate Web site, without having to learn HTML.
Publisher 2002	Publisher is a desktop publishing tool that provides individual users the capability to create professional-looking flyers, brochures, and newsletters.

FIGURE 1.2

A blank document in Word 2002

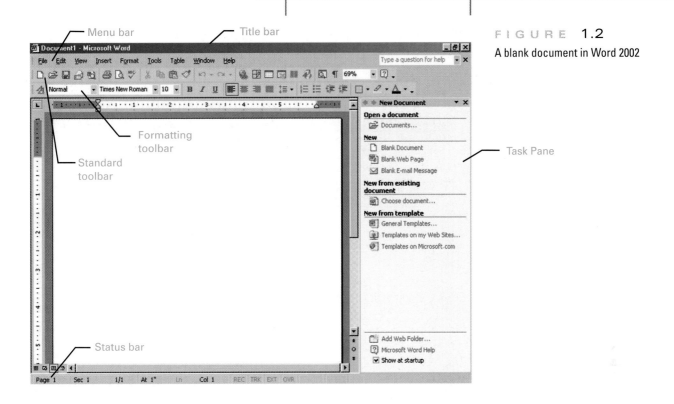

Menu bar

Title bar

Formatting
toolbar

Standard
toolbar

Task Pane

Status bar

Identifying Common Screen Elements

When you open two or more of the Microsoft applications, you will notice the similarities in the programs. This design is done intentionally so that as you learn to use one application, you will be able to quickly navigate through the remaining Office XP programs. When you first open Word, you will find a blank document as seen in Figure 1.2. In this exercise you will get to preview a blank document in Word and a blank workbook in Excel. Notice the common features of the two programs as you work with them. These features will be explained over the next few pages.

another word

. . . on the Office XP Suite

Collectively, the programs are officially referred to as **Microsoft Office XP,** but individually each application is referred to as version 2002.

Opening multiple applications in Office XP:

1. Click the **Start** ![Start] button on the taskbar to display the pop-up menu

2. Move your cursor up the menu and stop on **Programs.** Another menu will appear listing all the programs available on your computer

3. Locate **Microsoft Word** in the program list and click it. After a few seconds you should see a blank document as previously seen in Figure 1.2. Now compare the screen layout with that found in Excel

4. Click the **Start** button, then point to **Programs,** once again

FIGURE 1.3

A blank workbook in
Microsoft Excel

5. This time locate and click **Microsoft Excel** in the program list. After a few seconds you will see a blank workbook, similar to the one found in Figure 1.3

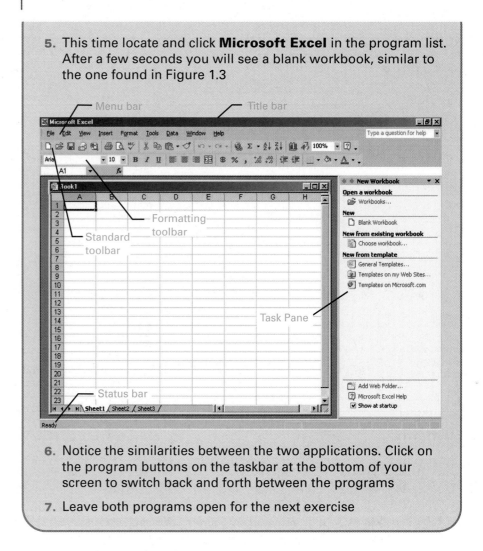

6. Notice the similarities between the two applications. Click on the program buttons on the taskbar at the bottom of your screen to switch back and forth between the programs

7. Leave both programs open for the next exercise

Title Bar, Menu Bar, and Toolbars

As you examine the Word and Excel programs, you will notice that each application contains similar elements such as a title bar, a menu bar, a toolbar, and a status bar. The ***title bar*** at the top of each screen displays the application's icon, the title of the document you are working on, and the name of the application program you are using.

The ***menu bar*** displays a list of key menu options available to you for that particular program. In addition to a few program-specific menu items, all of the Office XP applications generally will contain the identical menu options of File, Edit, View, Insert, Tools, Window, and Help. To use these menus, you simply click one time on the desired menu, and a submenu will then appear with additional options.

On the third row of each application is the ***toolbar,*** which is a collection of commonly used shortcut buttons. A single click on a toolbar button activates a program feature that also can be found in one of the menu options. Most office applications will display the ***Standard toolbar,*** which contains the popular icons such as Cut, Copy, and Paste. The table displayed in Figure 1.4 shows a list of these common buttons and their functions.

Another popular toolbar found in Office XP applications is the ***Formatting toolbar,*** which allows you to change the appearance of text,

*another*way

. . . . to switch
between
applications

You also can switch between applications by using what is known as the Alt+Tab sequence. Press and hold the **Alt** key, then press **Tab** one time. Let go of both keys when you see the gray box in the middle of your screen displaying program icons. This will allow you to quickly cycle back and forth through any open programs.

FIGURE 1.4
Standard toolbar buttons and their function

New	Opens a new blank document, workbook, presentation, or database.
Open	Opens a previously created document, workbook, presentation, or database.
Save	Allows you to quickly save your work. The first time you save, you will be prompted for a file name and location.
E-mail	New to Office XP, this button lets you quickly send the existing document as an email message.
Print	Prints a document.
Cut	Removes selected information from your document and temporarily places it on the Clipboard.
Copy	Duplicates selected information and places it on the Clipboard.
Paste	Copies information on the Clipboard to the current document.
Undo Typing	Reverses the last action or keystroke taken. This is a great safety net for those uh-oh type mistakes!

such as bold, italicize, or underline. There are many toolbars available to display and some will appear as you use certain features in Office applications.

Task Panes, Clipboard, and Smart Tags

Most of the Office XP applications include a new feature known as the *Task Pane* as shown in Figure 1.5. This window allows you to access important tasks from a single, convenient location, while still working on your document. With the Task Pane window you can open files, view your clipboard, perform searches, and much more. By default, when you open an Office XP application, the Task Pane window is displayed to allow the user to open a file. As you select various functions of the application, the contents of the task pane will automatically change. You can close the task pane at any time by clicking on the close button, and redisplay the window by selecting it from the View menu.

One of the options available on the task pane is the *Clipboard,* which is a temporary storage location for selected text. In Office XP, you can actually view the contents of up to 24 items that have been cut or copied to the clipboard. This is a very powerful tool that will allow you to collect 24 sets of data and then let you quickly paste those data to a new location or document. When you paste any of the clipboard contents to your document, a Smart Tag button will appear next to the text. This smart tag, known as the *Paste Options button,* will prompt the user (when clicked) with additional features such as allowing you to paste with or without the original text formatting. There are additional *smart tag buttons* that appear as needed to provide options for completing a task quickly. In this next exercise you will get to practice using the Task Pane, Clipboard, and Paste Options smart tag button.

anotherway

. . . to activate a menu option

You also can activate a menu option by using shortcut key strokes. In the menu you will notice that one letter of each option is underlined. These designated letters can be used in conjunction with the Alt key to quickly access a menu task. For example, you can press **Alt+F+S** to save your file.

anotherword

. . . on the Clipboard

It is important to note that the Clipboard contents are available to all applications and not just the original application from where it was extracted.

OFFICE

FIGURE 1.5

Task Pane in Microsoft Word

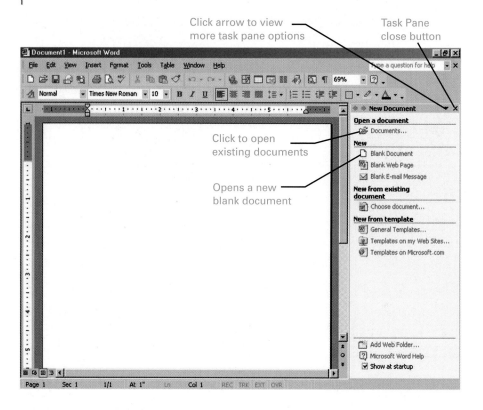

Click arrow to view more task pane options

Task Pane close button

Click to open existing documents

Opens a new blank document

Working with the Task Pane

1. In the Excel application, type **Hello Office XP!** in cell A1 and press **Enter**

2. Click cell A1 and then change the font size of the text to size **22.** Click the **Italic** button on the Formatting toolbar to italicize your text as shown in Figure 1.6

3. Click the **Copy** button on the Standard toolbar. This will copy the contents of cell A1 to the clipboard

4. Press **Alt+Tab** to switch back to the Word program

5. Click the **Paste** button and press **Enter.** The text should appear in the blank document exactly as it was typed and italicized

6. At the top of the Task Pane window, click the **drop-down menu arrow** and select **Clipboard** from the drop-down list. You can now view the Clipboard task pane and the text that was copied to it

7. In the Clipboard Contents task pane, click on the **Hello Office XP!** item as indicated in Figure 1.7. This will paste the text a second time into your document

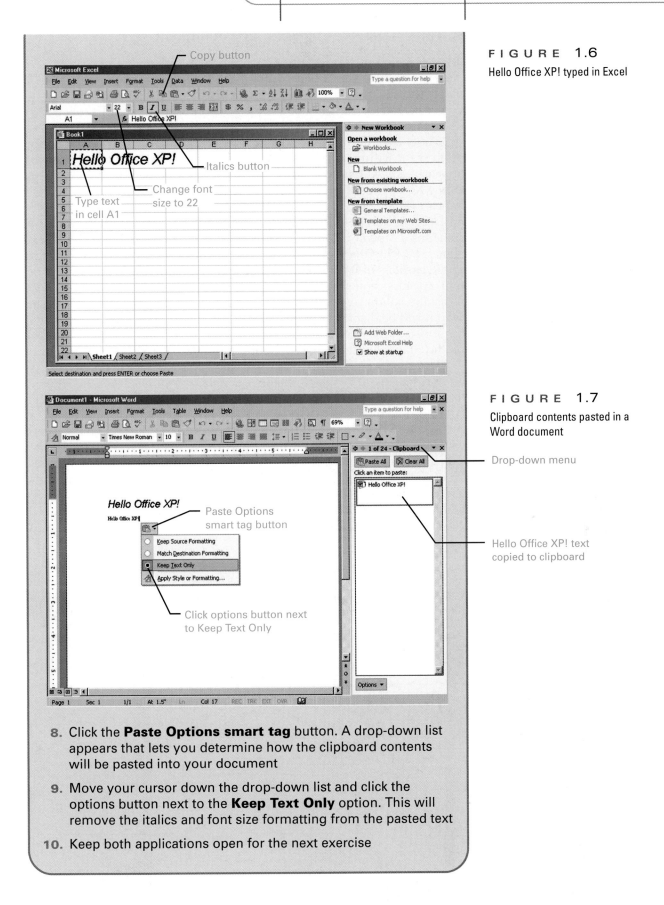

FIGURE 1.6

Hello Office XP! typed in Excel

FIGURE 1.7

Clipboard contents pasted in a
Word document

Drop-down menu

Hello Office XP! text
copied to clipboard

8. Click the **Paste Options smart tag** button. A drop-down list
   appears that lets you determine how the clipboard contents
   will be pasted into your document

9. Move your cursor down the drop-down list and click the
   options button next to the **Keep Text Only** option. This will
   remove the italics and font size formatting from the pasted text

10. Keep both applications open for the next exercise

Getting Help

When you use any of the Office XP applications, you may find yourself in need of some assistance. There are several ways to obtain help, and fortunately for the user, they are once again consistent across the applications. To get help, the user can use the Help menu option, press F1, or use the Office Assistant, Answer Wizard, or Ask a Question text box.

The most common way of getting help is to use the Help menu option or press the F1 function key. If you do ask for help, an ***Office Assistant*** will appear ready to help you with your question as shown in Figure 1.8. In Office XP applications, the Office Assistant is hidden by default and only appears when Help is activated. One of the fun aspects about the Office Assistant is that you can select your favorite character to help you. The standard assistant is known as ***Clippit*** (the paper clip), but you also can choose ***F1*** (the robot), ***Links*** (the cat), or ***Rocky*** (the dog), among others.

Regardless of which one you use, once you request help and your assistant appears, you must then type in your help question in the Office Assistant balloon and click on the Search button. The results of your search will be displayed in a Help window for you to review or print. For those users who prefer not to use an Office Assistant, you can right-click on the character and choose the option to hide the assistant.

The ***Answer Wizard,*** located in the Microsoft Help dialog box, is another means of requesting help through your application. In order to use the Answer Wizard, you must first hide the Office Assistant and then click on Help menu. Once the Help dialog box is displayed, simply click on the Answer Wizard tab and type in your question in the text box. Another way to get help without using the Office Assistant is to use the new feature called ***Ask a Question.*** Located in the top-right corner of your window, this is perhaps the most convenient method for getting help because the user simply has to key in a search topic in the text box and press enter, without having to launch the Answer Wizard or Office Assistant. You will get to practice requesting help in the next exercise.

FIGURE 1.8

The Office Assistant appears when you ask for help

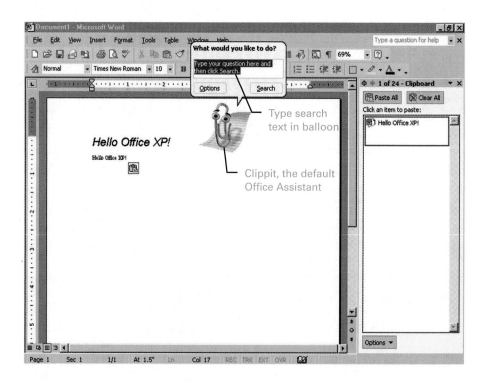

To get help:

1. In your Word document or Excel workbook, press the **F1** function key. This should activate your Office Assistant to the screen

   tip: *If the office assistant does not appear, click on the* **Help** *menu and select* **Show the Office Assistant**

2. In the Office Assistant balloon, type **Speech Recognition,** then click the **Search button**

3. In the next balloon that appears, click the **About Speech Recognition** bullet. This will open up the Microsoft Help window with the speech recognition search results as shown in Figure 1.9. Press the **ESC** key on your keyboard to remove the Office Assistant balloon

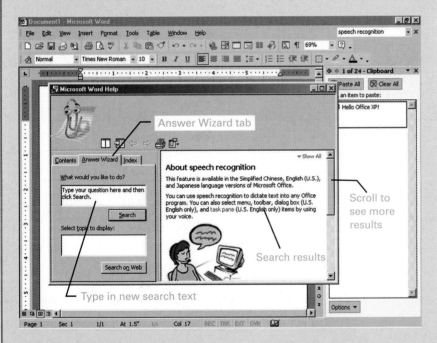

FIGURE 1.9

Results of search displayed in Microsoft help window

4. After looking over your search results, click the **Close** button of the Help window

5. Right-click the **Office Assistant** and, in the menu that pops up, select **Choose Assistant**

6. Click either the **Back** or **Next** button in the Office Assistant dialog box as shown in Figure 1.10 until you find an assistant that you like, and then click **OK**

7. Right-click the **Office Assistant** again, and this time select **Hide.** This will hide the Office Assistant until you request help again

8. **Close** any open documents and programs

FIGURE 1.10
Office Assistant dialog box

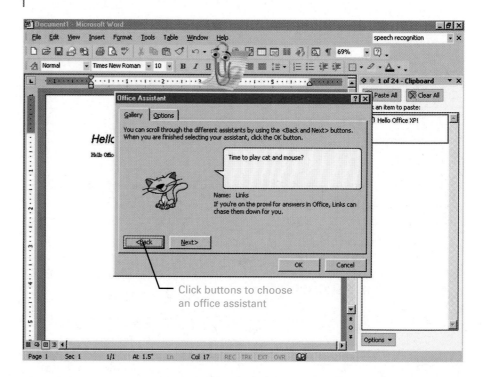

SESSION 1.1   *making the grade*

1. What four application programs are available in all versions of Office XP?

2. What is the default Office Assistant character?

3. How many items can be posted to the clipboard contents?

4. Which two toolbars are the most frequently used in all applications?

5. What is the quickest and most convenient method for getting help in any of the Office XP applications?

SUMMARY

In this chapter you have been introduced to the common elements of Microsoft's newest integrated application suite, known as Office XP. Regardless of which version of the program you are using, you always will have access to the Word, Excel, PowerPoint, and Outlook applications. As you learn to navigate through these applications, you will notice many similarities that allow the user to easily adapt from one application to the next. These common features include the title bar, the menu bar, and toolbars. You learned that the standard and formatting toolbars are the most commonly used toolbars in Office XP, but that there also are many toolbars available for users to select from or that automatically appear when completing a task.

Through the exercises in this chapter, you learned how to use one of Office XP's newest features, the task pane. This window allows the user quick access to various task sequences such as opening a file, viewing the Clipboard contents, performing a search, and inserting clip art. While the

Clipboard is not new to Microsoft products, it is more powerful in this version because it allows the user to post up to 24 different items in its contents. Finally, when in desperate need of answers, the user can always turn to the many help modes of Office XP. You can use one of the customized Office Assistants such as Clippit, use the Answer Wizard in the Help dialog box, or use the Ask a Question text box to find a quick solution to a problem.

task reference roundup

Task	Page #	Preferred Method
Switch between applications	OFF 1.3	• Press **Alt+Tab**
Copy and Paste using Clipboard task pane	OFF 1.5	• Highlight/select text to be copied
		• Click the **Copy** button on the toolbar
		• Place cursor in desired paste location
		• Click on item in Clipboard task pane to paste
Obtaining Help	OFF 1.8	• Press **F1** or click **Office Assistant**

review of terminology

CROSSWORD PUZZLE

Across

2. The dog Office Assistant
6. Office XP version that consists of Word, Excel, PowerPoint, and Outlook
7. Relational database tool that can be used to collect, organize, and retrieve large amounts of data
8. Is located in the Help dialog box and provides another means of requesting help
10. A popular presentation tool that allows users to create multimedia slide shows
11. Temporary storage location for up to 24 items of selected text that has been cut or copied
13. This window allows you to view clipboard contents in addition to other important tasks
14. A collection of commonly used shortcut buttons

Down

1. Toolbar that allows you to change the appearance of your text
3. The cat office assistant
4. Button that appears when you paste into your document
5. Buttons that appear as needed to provide options for completing a task quickly
9. The paper clip Office Assistant
12. Displays a list of key menu options available to you for that particular program

FILL-IN THE BLANKS

1. _____ is the newest version of the popular Microsoft integrated application suite series.

2. An _____ is a program that is designed to help you accomplish a particular task, such as creating a slide-show presentation.

3. By default, when you open an Office XP application, the _____ window is displayed to allow the user to open a file.

4. The standard Office Assistant is known as _____(the paper clip), but you can also choose _____ (the robot), _____ (the Cat), or _____ (the dog).

5. In Office XP, you can actually view the contents of up to _____ items that have been cut or copied to the clipboard.

6. A single click on a toolbar button activates a program feature that also can be found in one of the _____ options.

7. Most office applications will display the _____ toolbar, which contains the popular icons such as Cut, Copy, and Paste.

REVIEW QUESTIONS

1. What are some of the common features found in all Office XP applications?

2. What tools can you use to get help or search for additional information?

3. What is the Task Pane window used for?

4. What are smart tag buttons and when do you have access to them? Give an example of one.

5. What are the four basic applications that are included as part of all versions of Office XP?

MATCHING

Match the term with the related definition.

1. _____ Access 2002

2. _____ Clipboard

3. _____ Excel 2002

4. _____ Formatting toolbar

5. _____ PowerPoint 2002

6. _____ Standard toolbar

7. _____ Task pane

8. _____ Word 2002

a. A temporary storage location for up to 24 items of selected text that has been cut or copied.

b. Collection of buttons that allows you to change the appearance of text, such as bold, italicize, or underline.

c. Collection of buttons that contains the popular icons such as Cut, Copy, and Paste.

d. Electronic spreadsheet tool that can be used to input, organize, calculate, analyze, and display business data.

e. General-purpose word-processing tool that allows users to create primarily text-based documents.

f. A popular presentation tool that allows users to create overhead transparencies and powerful multimedia slide shows.

g. Relational database tool that can be used to collect, organize, and retrieve large amounts of data.

h. This window allows you to access important tasks from a single, convenient location, while still working on your document.

did you know?

one-third *of online shoppers abandon their electronic shopping carts before completing the checkout process.*

goldfish *lose their color if they are kept in a dim light or if they are placed in a body of running water such as a stream.*

electric *eels are not really eels but a type of fish.*

in *1963, baseball pitcher Gaylord Perry said, "They'll put a man on the moon before I hit a home run." Only a few hours after Neil Armstrong set foot on the moon on July 20, 1969, Perry hit the first and only home run of his career.*

Chapter Objectives

- Start Excel
- Open a workbook (MOUS) Ex2002-2-1
- Move around a worksheet using the mouse and arrow keys
- Select a block of cells
- Type into worksheet cells text, values, formulas, and functions (MOUS) Ex2002-1-2
- Edit and clear cell entries (MOUS) Ex2002-2-1
- Save a workbook (MOUS) Ex2002-2-3
- Adding a header and a footer (MOUS) Ex2002-3-6
- Previewing output (MOUS) Ex2002-3-7
- Print a worksheet
- Print worksheet formulas
- Exit Excel

CHAPTER

1

one

Creating
Worksheets for
Decision
Makers

chapter case
Western University Rugby Team

Rugby is a popular sport around the world and is played at many universities in the United States. The sport has a loyal group of people who attend most of the games in the region. Often, U.S. collegiate rugby teams play on open fields that are not fenced. Occasionally, they play in soccer stadiums or on football fields where they can control access of fans and charge a nominal fee—a donation—to view a rugby game.

Western University is a small private school with a rugby team composed of 21 varsity players and 15 freshman and novice players. Stirling Leonard is a senior on the team and one of its co-captains. He is responsible for ensuring that everyone is available for each week's game and for overseeing the athletes' pregame warm-up regimen. He has also taken a lead role in organizing the annual fundraising campaign for the team.

Unlike football or soccer, which are varsity sports at Western University, rugby is a club sport and not eligible to receive financial support from the university. The team's annual costs include transportation to games, replacement of some game uniforms each year, and sundry supplies such as tape and bandages. These costs at Western amount to over $24,000 per year—a small amount compared to the cost of a varsity sport, but a daunting cost for rugby team members to provide. Each team member must pay a fee to offset the projected cost of running the team. Some of Western's rugby team members pay their fees directly, whereas others help with the team's annual fundraising and use the funds they raise to pay their fees.

Past fundraising activities included monthly car washes, club T-shirt sales, and the annual rug-

FIGURE 1.1

Scrip Sales Projection worksheet

	A B	C	D	E	F	G	H	I	J	K
1	**Scrip Sales Projection**									
2				Projected			Detail			
3		Percent	Unit	Unit						
4		Donation	Value	Sales			Donation	Retail		
5	**Specialty Stores**									
6	Circuits West	4.50%	$10	300			$135.00	$3,000.00		
7	Enterprise Electronics	5.00%	20	400			400.00	8,000.00		
8	Radio Hut	6.50%	10	300			195.00	3,000.00		
9	University Bookstore	10.00%	5	900			450.00	4,500.00		
10						Subtotal	$1,180.00	$18,500.00		
11										
12	**Restaurants**									
13	Burgers 'R Us	12.00%	$10	600			$720.00	$6,000.00		
14	Country Cupboard	5.00%	5	670			167.50	3,350.00		
15	McCrackens	6.00%	10	500			300.00	5,000.00		
16	Taco King	8.00%	10	400			320.00	4,000.00		
17						Subtotal	$1,507.50	$18,350.00		
18										
19							Total	Total		
20							Donation	Retail		
21							$2,687.50	$36,850.00		
22										
23										
24										
25										

Documentation \ **Scrip Sales Projection** /

Ready

by alum game. This year, Stirling has devised a new and innovative way to raise money for the team: selling scrip issued by local specialty and fast-food stores near the college. Scrip is special paper issued by various merchants that are evidence of payment for a good or service from that merchant. Similar to a gift certificate, a store's own brand of scrip is the same as cash at the issuing merchant's store. Teams make money on the difference between the wholesale price at which they purchase scrip and the retail price at which they sell the scrip to customers.

Using Microsoft Excel 2002, Stirling has created a worksheet that he and the team can use to calculate the total scrip sold each month as well as the team's profit. He has to complete the worksheet by entering the scrip sales quantities and some formulas to compute the donation value and retail value of the sales this month.

In this chapter, you will learn how to complete the Scrip Report to determine how well the team is doing toward its goal of raising the money it needs to support the team. Figure 1.1 shows the completed Scrip Sales Projection worksheet.

INTRODUCTION

Chapter 1 introduces you to Excel. You start Excel and examine the Standard toolbar, Formatting toolbar, Task Pane, and other features of a new Excel's window. You learn several ways to move around a worksheet, including using arrow keys and the mouse. Select worksheet cells by clicking a cell and then dragging the mouse across a contiguous group of cells.

Excel worksheet cells can contain text, values (constants), formulas, functions, and a combination of these. You enter text into a cell by clicking it and then typing. You enter values, which are numbers, by typing the number preceded by an optional plus or minus sign. Formulas always begin with an equals sign (=). Following the equals sign you can type an arbitrarily complex expression involving values, mathematical operators, and Excel functions. Excel functions are built in or prerecorded formulas that provide a shortcut for complex calculations. Writing Excel functions saves time and trouble. For example, it is far easier to write a SUM function to total several worksheet cell values than it is to write a long formula containing the plus operator and individual cell references to be summed.

Edit a cell that contains an error and then press Enter to complete the work. Alternatively, you can completely replace a cell's contents by typing a new formula. Clear a cell to empty its contents with the Clear command on the Edit menu. Attempting to clear a cell by typing a space usually leads to problems as you develop a worksheet. Specify a worksheet's print area consisting of any rectangular group of cells. When you print the worksheet, Excel remembers each worksheet's print area and prints only cells within the print area.

SESSION 1.1 GETTING STARTED

In this section, you will learn how to start Excel, open a workbook, and observe the anatomy of an Excel worksheet and its window. You will investigate several ways to move around an Excel workbook using the mouse, arrow keys, and combinations of keyboard keys that employ shortcuts to move the worksheet cursor quickly to a particular worksheet cell. Finally, you will learn how to select a block of cells.

INTRODUCTION TO EXCEL

Excel is a computerized spreadsheet—an automated version of an accountant's ledger. A **spreadsheet** is a popular program used to analyze numeric information and help make meaningful business decisions based on the analysis. Spreadsheets are used for a variety of applications ranging from financial analysis of stock portfolios, manufacturing and production quantity assessment, inventory turnover and cost estimation, budgeting, and simple household record keeping.

Dan Bricklin and Bob Frankston invented the electronic spreadsheet in 1979. Bob Frankston joined Dan Bricklin, a Harvard MBA student, to cooperatively write the program for the new electronic spreadsheet. They formed a new company called Software Arts, Inc. and called their spreadsheet product VisiCalc. Bricklin and Frankston later sold VisiCalc to Lotus Development Corporation, where it developed into the PC spreadsheet Lotus 1-2-3. VisiCalc was the first of several spreadsheet programs to develop over the next two decades.

Spreadsheet software has been one of the most popular pieces of software of all time. Why is it so popular? Consider the way people performed a typical spreadsheet task before the advent of the electronic version. A typical application of a hard copy, paper and pencil method of creating and maintaining a spreadsheet is projecting net profit. Prior to the advent of electronic spreadsheets, accountants used paper ledgers and wrote entries in pencil so that they could easily modify various entries in the spreadsheet and then recalculate, using a calculator, the new values. Bricklin once said, "VisiCalc took 20 hours of work per week for some people and turned it out in 15 minutes and let them become much more creative."

Figure 1.2 shows a facsimile of a manual accounting spreadsheet showing projected net profit of a product whose unit price is $200. Expenses for marketing, manufacturing, and overhead are but a few of the

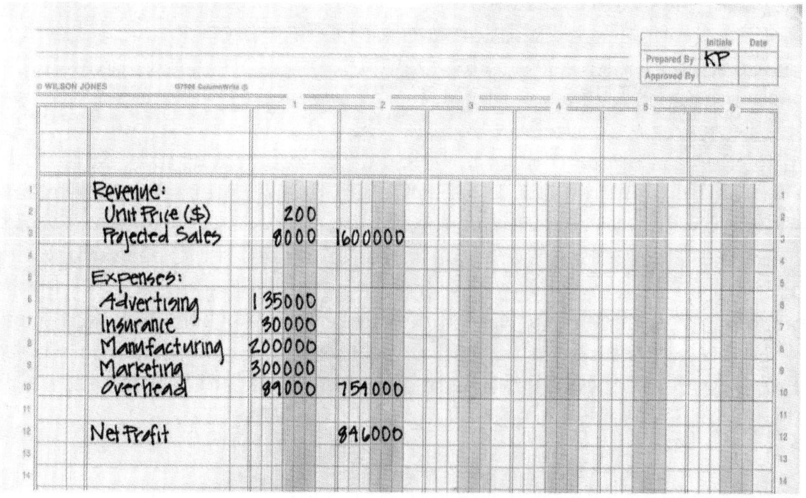

FIGURE **1.2**

Hard copy accounting spreadsheet

expenses needed to advertise the product and bring it to market. People who worked with ledger spreadsheets like the one shown in Figure 1.2 often had to modify projected sales numbers, unit sale prices, and other values and then recalculate values such as net profit. Any change to a hard copy worksheet can take a lot of time for even the simplest alteration because many values that are dependent on the change must be recalculated. Making changes to spreadsheets and reviewing their effect on other values is a classic use of spreadsheets and is called *what-if analysis*—one of the popular uses for today's electronic spreadsheets. With electronic spreadsheets, any changes you make to a spreadsheet automatically recalculate to quickly reveal new values. Formulas give Excel its power.

People refer to spreadsheet programs as electronic spreadsheets or simply spreadsheets. Using Excel 2002, you create a document called a *workbook,* which is a collection of one or more individual *worksheets.* Worksheets are so named because they resemble pages in a spiral-bound workbook like the ones you purchase and use to take class notes. You will probably hear the terms *spreadsheets*, *workbooks*, and *worksheets* used interchangeably.

STARTING EXCEL AND OPENING A WORKSHEET

Stirling's alarm clock wakes him at 6:30 A.M. He's an early riser and wants to get started on the worksheet so that he can show it to his rugby coach, Rod Harrington, for his comments. Stirling has discovered which of the nearby merchants and restaurants offer scrip, and he has learned that he must purchase the scrip through a broker whose warehouse contains scrip from hundreds of stores in the region. After talking to the scrip distribution center manager, Stirling was able to get a special deal: He can request and receive up to $10,000 worth of scrip to be delivered to the university's athletic office and he will have up to 45 days to pay for it.

Start Excel to design the worksheet to calculate the scrip profits and project how many units to order next time.

Starting Microsoft Excel:

1. Make sure Windows is running on your computer and the Windows desktop appears on your computer screen

2. Click the taskbar **Start** [Start] button to display the Start menu, then point to **Programs** to display the Programs menu

3. Point to **Microsoft Excel** on the Programs menu and then click **Microsoft Excel.** Within a few seconds, the Microsoft Excel copyright information page appears. Then the Excel window containing an empty worksheet appears. When both Excel and its worksheet are maximized, your screen should look like Figure 1.3

4. Microsoft Excel should fill the screen and show an empty worksheet. If it does not, then click the **Maximize** [□] button found in the upper-right corner of the Excel window

5. If the empty worksheet is not maximized, then click the worksheet **Maximize** [□] button

EXCEL

F I G U R E   1.3

Excel program window containing an empty worksheet

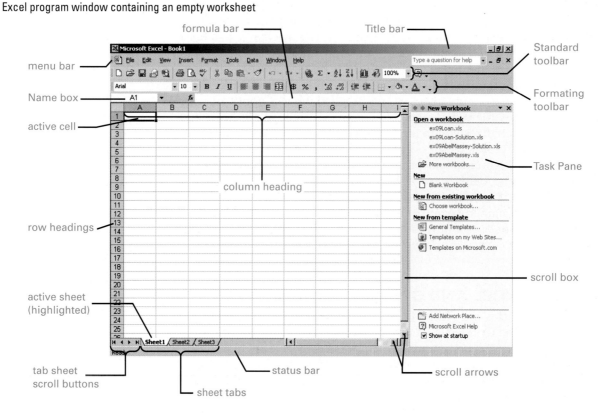

ANATOMY OF THE EXCEL WINDOW

The Excel program window shown in Figure 1.3 is typical of many Microsoft Windows applications. The Excel application is divided into several important areas. These will become very familiar to you as you gain experience with Excel.

Task Pane

A *Task Pane* is a dockable dialog window that provides a convenient way to use commands, gather information, and modify Excel documents. An Excel Task Pane can contain one or more pages, and each page is broken up into sections. The Excel Task Pane in Figure 1.3 contains sections for opening a workbook, creating a new workbook, and creating a workbook from a template. The Task Pane puts relevant features one click away.

Menu Bar

The *menu bar,* which is visible no matter which Excel activity is taking place, contains the Excel menus. Clicking a command on the menu bar reveals the menu's associated commands. Menus are arranged in a familiar way beginning on the left with the File, Edit, and View menus. Clicking the File menu, for example, reveals the New, Open, Close, and Save commands, among others, that are typical of all Windows File menu commands. Normally the menu bar appears just below the Title bar, but you can click the menu handle at the left end of the menu bar and drag the menu bar to any location on the screen, or you can dock it on any of the other three sides of the screen.

Toolbars

Toolbars allow you to execute commands with a single click. Most of the frequently used commands appear in one of the several Excel toolbars. The **Standard toolbar,** which normally appears below the menu bar, contains buttons that execute popular menu bar commands such as Print, Cut, and Insert Table. The **Formatting toolbar** contains buttons that change the appearance of a worksheet. For example, you can set the typeface or underline entries by pressing Formatting toolbar buttons.

Formula Bar

The Formula bar appears below the menu bar and toolbars just above the Workbook window. The **formula bar** displays the active cell's contents, appearing at the top of the screen, in which you can enter cell contents or edit existing contents. **Cell contents** are the text, formulas, or numbers you type into a cell. A cell's contents can look different from the value it calculates and displays in a cell. A discussion of these differences appears later in this chapter. The **name box,** appearing on the left of the formula bar, displays either the active cell's address (A1 in Figure 1.3) or its assigned name. (More information about cell addresses and names appears later in this chapter.)

Workbook Window

The document window is called the **workbook window** or **worksheet window**. It contains the workbook on which you are working. A workbook can contain up to 255 worksheets, and each worksheet contains columns and rows that are labeled with letters and numbers respectively. A worksheet can contain up to 256 columns with labels A through IV to uniquely identify each column. A worksheet contains 65,536 rows with numeric labels from 1 to 65536. A **cell** is located at the intersection of a row and a column and identified by a cell reference, such as A1. The **cell reference,** or cell address, is a cell's identification consisting of its column letter(s) followed by its row number. The cell located at the intersection of column D and row 42 is identified as D42, for example. A worksheet cell contains data that you enter such as text, numbers, or formulas. Each cell is like a small calculator, capable of computing the value of any arbitrarily complex formulas you type. The **active cell** is the cell in which you are currently working. Its name or cell reference appears in the name box, its contents appear in the formula bar, and a dark rectangle surrounds the active cell (see Figure 1.3).

Sheet Tabs

Each of a workbook's sheets has a unique name. That name appears in its **sheet tab.** When you create a new workbook, the number of sheets varies. By default, new sheets are named Sheet1, Sheet2, and so on. You can change the name of any sheet to something more meaningful. Clicking a sheet tab makes the clicked sheet active. The sheet tab of the active sheet—the one into which you are entering data—is bright white whereas inactive sheet tabs are dark gray. If your workbook contains many worksheets, only a few sheet tabs appear just above the status bar. To move to another worksheet whose tab is not shown, click the **sheet tab scroll buttons** to scroll through the sheet tabs until you find the sheet you want. Then click the sheet tab to make the sheet active.

EXCEL

Status Bar

The *status bar* is located at the very bottom of the window—below the sheet tabs and above the Windows task bar. This shows general information about the worksheet and selected keyboard keys. Status indicators on the right side tell you about the current state of selected keys. For instance, one indicator displays NUM whenever the NumLock key is active. Another status indicator displays CAPS when the Caps Lock key is active.

Mouse Pointer

The *mouse pointer* indicates the current position of the mouse as you move it around the screen. It changes shape to indicate what duties you can perform at the location over which the mouse pointer is positioned. When the mouse is over a worksheet, it appears as a white plus sign. Move the mouse to a menu and it changes to an arrow, which indicates that you can select an item by clicking the mouse. When you move the mouse to the formula bar, it changes into an I-beam shape, which indicates that you can click and then type data.

MOVING AROUND A WORKSHEET

In order to enter information into a worksheet, you must first select the cell to make it the active cell. There are a number of ways to select a cell.

Using the Keyboard

Excel provides several ways to move to different cells in your worksheet. Pressing Ctrl+Home always makes cell A1 the active cell. Pressing the right arrow key moves the active cell one cell to the right. Other arrow keys move the active cell corresponding to the arrow's direction (right, left, up, and down). Figure 1.4 shows keys that select different worksheet cells.

FIGURE **1.4**

Keys to move around a worksheet

Keystroke	Action
Up arrow	Moves up one cell
Down arrow	Moves down one cell
Left arrow	Moves left one cell
Right arrow	Moves right one cell
PgUp	Moves active cell up one screen
PgDn	Moves active cell down one screen
Home	Moves active cell to column A of current row
Ctrl+Home	Moves the active cell to cell A1
Ctrl+End	Moves to the lower, rightmost active corner of the worksheet
F5 (function key)	Opens the Go To dialog box in which you can enter any cell address

Using the Mouse

The mouse is a quick and convenient way to select a cell. Simply click the cell you want to make the active cell by placing the pointer over the cell and clicking the left mouse button. Moving to cells not yet visible on the screen is simple too. Use the vertical and horizontal worksheet scroll bars or arrow keys to scroll to the area of the worksheet containing the cell to which you want to move. Then click the cell to select it.

Try moving to different parts of the worksheet. Prepare for this short exercise by ensuring that an empty Excel worksheet is open. Then do the following:

Making a cell the active cell:

1. Close the Task Pane by clicking the **Task Pane Close** button in the New Workbook title bar. Position the mouse pointer over cell C4, then click the **left mouse** button to make cell C4 the active cell

2. Click cell **G7** to make it the active cell

3. Click cell **N53.** (You will have to use the horizontal and vertical scroll bars to bring cell N53 into view on your screen prior to selecting it)

4. Press the **Home** key to move to column A and make cell A53 the active cell

5. Finally, press **Ctrl+Home** to move to cell A1

6. Press the **PgDn** key to scroll the screen down one screen. The active cell is column A and a row below row 20. The exact row that becomes the active cell depends on the size and resolution of your screen. A new, previously hidden set of rows is revealed in any case

7. Press **F5** to open the Go To dialog box

tip: *Ignore any contents in your Go To panel and the Reference text box. If there is already an entry in your Reference text box, simply type over it*

8. Type **CD451** in the Reference text box and click **OK.** Cell CD451 becomes the active cell

9. Press **F5** to open the Go To dialog box again

10. Type **IV65536** and click **OK.** Cell IV65536 becomes the active cell

11. Click the **vertical scroll bar down arrow** three times to move the display up three rows, and then click the **horizontal scroll bar right arrow** two times. Notice that cell IV65536 is located at the highest row and right-most column in the worksheet (see Figure 1.5)

12. Press **Ctrl+Home** to move to cell A1

*another*way

. . . to Move to a Worksheet Cell

Press **Ctrl+G** to display the Go To dialog box

Type in the Reference text box the cell reference to which you want to move

Click the **OK** button

EXCEL

FIGURE 1.5

Moving to the last cell on an Excel worksheet

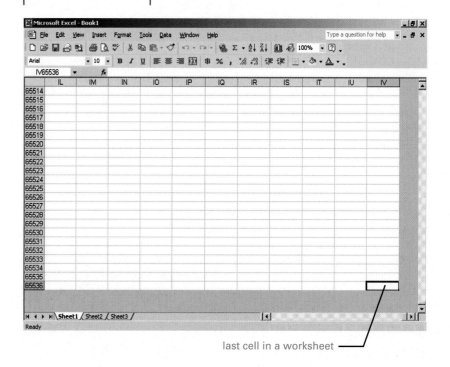

last cell in a worksheet ————

MOVING FROM SHEET TO SHEET

Workbooks can contain more than one worksheet, because worksheets are a convenient way to organize collections of related sheets. An inventory manager might keep each month's raw materials purchases on separate worksheets by month. Similarly, stockbrokers can keep records about their clients' purchases in one Excel workbook, assigning one page per client. You can move from one worksheet to another within one workbook by clicking its sheet tab. The new sheet becomes active. You can use the sheet tab scroll buttons to reveal hidden sheet tabs when necessary.

OPENING AN EXISTING WORKBOOK

When you want to examine, modify, or work with a workbook you or someone else created previously, you must open it first. When you open a workbook, Excel locates the file on your disk, reads it from the disk, and transfers the entire file into your computer's main memory, called Random Access Memory (RAM). The disk-to-memory loading process is complete when the worksheet appears on your computer's monitor. Loading a worksheet from a removable disk takes more time than loading the same worksheet from a hard disk—a time difference you will notice. Once loaded into memory, a worksheet resides both in memory and on disk. Any changes you may make to the worksheet should be saved back to the removable disk. If you maintain your worksheets on a removable disk, remember to first save any worksheet changes before you remove the disk. Otherwise, the worksheet stored on your removable disk may be out of synchronization with the one stored in memory.

Stirling has created a workbook called **ex01Scrip.xls** to help you and the team estimate how much scrip they must sell to raise money for the team.

task reference

Opening an Excel Workbook

- Click **File** and then click **Open**

- Ensure that the Look In list box displays the name of the folder containing your workbook

- Click the workbook's name

- Click the **Open** button

Opening an existing Excel workbook:

1. Place your data disk in the appropriate drive

2. Click **File** on the menu bar and then click **Open**

3. Click the **Look in** list arrow to display a list of available disk drives. Locate the drive containing your data disk and click the drive containing your data disk. The window displays a list of folders and Excel workbook file names

4. Locate and double-click the folder name **Ch01,** then click the Excel file **ex01Scrip.xls** to select it

5. Click the **Open** button located on the Standard toolbar. The first page of the Scrip workbook opens and displays the documentation worksheet. See Figure 1.6

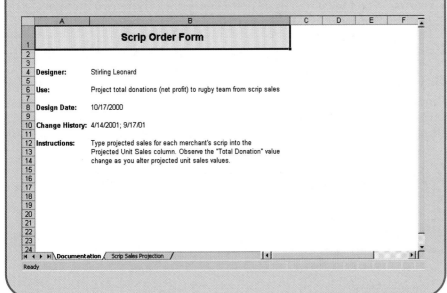

FIGURE 1.6

Scrip workbook documentation worksheet

Scrip Worksheet Design

The Scrip workbook created by Stirling consists of two worksheets, which Stirling name "Documentation" and "Scrip Sales Projection." The first worksheet is labeled Documentation. This sheet name appears on its tab (see Figure 1.6) and contains information about the workbook's designer, its use, when the workbook was created, a list of dates when the workbook was changed, and brief comments. Stirling explains that the Documentation worksheet conveys important information about the Scrip workbook to anyone who works with it. The instructions description is particularly helpful because it provides a reminder of how to use the workbook. That's especially helpful, he explains, when you work with several workbooks and want a quick reminder of how to use this particular workbook. The Documentation worksheet is not typical of most Excel worksheets as it contains no grid lines and no column or row headings. Excel provides options to remove those features. Because the Documentation worksheet is unlike others, removing the gridlines reduces confusion.

After you review the Documentation worksheet with Stirling, he opens the Scrip Sales Projection worksheet by clicking the Scrip Sales Projection worksheet tab. Figure 1.7 shows the Scrip Sales Projection worksheet. Stirling describes the two major parts of the Scrip Sales Projection worksheet. The left half of the sheet contains merchants grouped into the two categories Specialty Stores and Restaurants. Under each category heading are lists of merchants offering scrip—one row for each merchant. The Specialty Stores category contains the three most popular stores near campus: Circuits West, Enterprise Electronics, and Radio Hut. Similarly, beneath the Restaurants category label are four restaurants popular with students and close to campus. Each merchant row contains the percent donation, which is the percentage profit that the club makes on the sale of that merchant's scrip, and the scrip denomination available. The fourth column, Projected Unit Sales, is the column into which you will enter different values, later in this chapter, and the estimate of projected sales, in units, for each merchant. Cells E6 through E16 in that column are a critical part of the worksheet because they contain the assumptions you will be exploring. A change in the projected sales for one or more merchants' scrip causes changes in other worksheet locations.

Under the Donation and Retail columns are the projected values of the revenue that the club keeps—its profit—and the total retail value of the scrip respectively. Cells H6 through H8 display the dollar value that the club receives if they sell the scrip units listed in cells E6 through E8. Similarly, Cells H13 through H16 display projected rugby club profits for restaurant scrip sales for the listed restaurants. To the right, cells I13 through I16 show the total retail value of each merchant's scrip based on

FIGURE **1.7**

Partially complete Scrip Sales Projection worksheet

	A	B	C	D	E	F	G	H	I	J	K
1	**Scrip Sales Projection**										
2					Projected			Detail			
3			Percent	Unit	Unit						
4			Donation	Value	Sales			Donation	Retail		
5	Specialty Stores										
6		Circuits West	4.50%	$10	300			$135.00	$3,000.00		
7		Enterprise Electronics	5.00%	20	400			400.00	8,000.00		
8		Radio Hut	6.50%	10	300			195.00	3,000.00		
9											
10									$14,000.00		
11											
12	Restaurants										
13		Burgers 'R Us	12.00%	$10	600			$720.00	$6,000.00		
14		Country Cupboard	5.00%	5	670			167.50	3,350.00		
15		McCrackens	6.00%	10	500			300.00	5,000.00		
16		Taco King	8.00%	10	400			320.00	4,000.00		
17									$18,350.00		
18											
19								Total	Total		
20								Donation	Retail		
21									$32,350.00		
22											
23											
24											
25											

Documentation \ **Scrip Sales Projection** /

Ready

the projected scrip units sold shown in column E. Likewise, Cell I21 displays the scrip's total face value. You can see that the projected total value of all projected scrip retail sales is $32,350.00, but the club's total profit (Total Donation) on those sales for both specialty stores and restaurants is not yet displayed (under the heading Total Donation).

The percent donation column, representing the profit percentage, or discount, that the rugby club receives, is fixed by the merchant and thus unlikely to change. The single variable in the scrip sales worksheet that most determines the success of the scrip sales effort is the column into which Stirling will type in different numbers to see the effect—the projected unit sales. These are called the worksheet's **assumption cells,** which are cells upon which other formulas depend and whose values can be changed to observe their effect on a worksheet's entries. A change in some or all of these values directly affects the total sales and therefore the profit that the rugby team generates. Under the current assumptions, the best single profit-making scrip is Burgers 'R Us, because their scrip yields 12 percent profit—the highest percentage of any scrip in the current set—and the projected sales of 600 units is the current largest. Of course, the value 600 is an assumption and not a record of actual sales. If Burgers 'R Us proves to be popular, the team may want to focus its efforts on selling more Burgers 'R Us scrip.

Overall, the Scrip Sales Projection worksheet provides Stirling with an estimate of how much scrip the team must sell in order to make a real dent in their team expenses. If the total donation value were very small, then the team might consider alternative fundraising activities. The Scrip Sales Projection worksheet is a valuable decision-making tool because it provides a clear picture of the how scrip sales can translate into team profits.

making the grade   SESSION 1.1

1. A popular program used to analyze numeric information and help make meaningful business decisions is called a _____ program.

2. _____ analysis is observing changes to spreadsheets and reviewing their effect on other values in the spreadsheet.

3. An Excel spreadsheet is called a(n) _____ and consists of individual pages called _____.

4. Beneath Excel's menu bar is the _____ toolbar, which contains button shortcuts for commands such as Print, and the _____ toolbar containing button shortcuts to alter the appearance of worksheets and their cells.

5. The _____ cell is the cell in which you are currently entering data.

SESSION 1.2 ENTERING DATA, SAVING WORKBOOKS, AND PRINTING WORKSHEETS

In this session, you will learn how to enter data into worksheet cells, enter formulas into worksheet cells, save a workbook, and print a worksheet. Stirling wants you to modify the Scrip Sales Projection worksheet by adding another store and modifying projected scrip sales. In particular, you will learn how to enter text entries, values, formulas, and functions. You will learn how to remove information from one or more worksheet cells. You will save your workbook and print the worksheet and its formulas. When you have completed your work on the Scrip Sales Projection worksheet, you will close it and exit Excel.

EXCEL DATA TYPES

You can enter three types of data into Excel worksheet cells: text, formulas, and values. You will learn the difference between these three data types in this session. Each type has a slightly different purpose. First you will learn about text entries, because they are straightforward and yet fundamental to good worksheet design.

ENTERING TEXT, VALUES, FORMULAS, AND FUNCTIONS

Worksheet cells can contain text, value, formula, and function entries. Text entries document and identify important elements in a worksheet. Important worksheet input numbers, such as the Scrip Sales Projection worksheet's projected unit sales, are values. More complicated entries are formulas consisting of mathematical operators, cell references, and Excel functions. Formulas compute and display numeric or text entries that usually change when you alter values upon which the formulas depend. Functions are prerecorded formulas that make calculations easier for you. Each of these types of cell entries has an important role to play, and each one is introduced next.

Text

Text entries are any combination of characters that you can type on the keyboard including symbols ($, #, @, and so on), numbers, letters, and spaces. While text can be used as data, it almost always identifies and documents important worksheet columns, rows, and cells. (Sometimes text entries are called labels.) The Scrip workbook contains many text entries. Text appears in the Documentation sheet shown in Figure 1.6. All the entries in column A are text. Column B contains almost all text, with the exception of cell B8. (Cell B10 contains dates separated by a semicolon and is text.) A payroll worksheet, for example, contains employee names in several rows under a particular column. Expense reports contain the days of the week as column labels.

To enter text into a worksheet cell, first select the cell by clicking it and then type the text. As you type the text, it appears both in the formula bar and the selected cell. Excel aligns text entries on the left. Whenever text is longer than the cell containing it, the text visually spills over into the adjacent cell—if the adjacent cell is empty. If the adjacent cell already contains an entry, then the long text appears to be cut off at the boundary between the two cells. In either case, the text is completely contained within the cell you select, whether you can see all of it or not. Figure 1.8 shows the same long text entered into cells B2 and B4. Cell C2, which is adjacent to cell B2, already has an entry, so the long text in B2 appears cut off. Cell C4 is empty, so the long text in Cell B4 is completely visible.

Just today, Stirling has convinced another merchant that selling their scrip will benefit the merchant and the team. Happily, the new merchant is the university bookstore. Stirling wants you to add the newly recruited merchant's name to the Specialty Stores listed in the Scrip Sales Projection worksheet. Enter the new store in the list.

active cell, containing long
label, is visually truncated at
the cell border

formula bar matches contents
of cell B2, proving long label is
complete

FIGURE   1.8

Long text entries

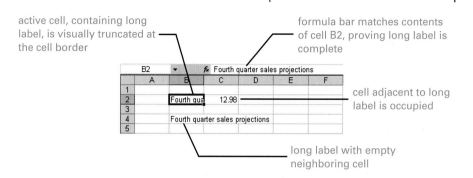

cell adjacent to long
label is occupied

long label with empty
neighboring cell

Entering text labels:

1. If you closed the Scrip workbook following the end of the previous session, make sure Excel is running and that the Scrip Sales Projection worksheet is showing. (Click the Scrip Sales Projection worksheet tab to open it)

2. Click cell **B9** to make it the active cell

3. Type **University Bookstore** and then press the **Enter** key. The text appears in cell B9, and cell B10 becomes the active cell

tip: *If you press a keyboard arrow key instead of pressing the Enter key, you complete entering text into the current cell and control which cell becomes the active cell*

4. Click cell **G10** to make it the active cell, type **Subtotal,** and then press the **Enter** key

tip: *You may notice the text in G10 is right aligned—contrary to what you read earlier about text entries. This is because the cell has been formatted to align text on the right. You will learn about formatting in Chapter 2*

5. Click cell **G17** to make it the active cell and type **Subtotal.** Excel completes the entry because a similar entry already exists in the column. Figure 1.9 shows the worksheet after you have entered the three text values, also called labels

Next, you need to enter the percent donation, scrip unit value, and the projected unit sales.

Values

Values are numbers that represent a quantity, date, or time. A value can be the number of students in a class, the quantity ordered of some vehicle part, the height in meters of a building, and so on. Examples are 15456, −35.8954, and 17. Values can be times and dates, too. For example, if you were to type 10/17/2001, Excel recognizes that value as a date. Similarly, if you were to type 15:32:30, Excel would interpret your entry as a time value. In other words, Excel can determine automatically whether you are entering text or a value based on what you type. For instance, if you were to type −9435, Excel would recognize the entry as a value and, by default,

FIGURE 1.9

Worksheet after entering text

new text entries

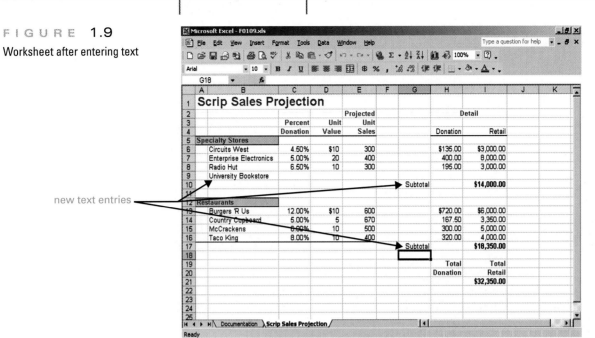

would place it right justified in the cell. Similarly, if you typed <u>28 ways to win</u>, Excel would recognize the entry as text. A number enclosed in parentheses such as (9876) is also a value—a negative value.

Common entries that appear to be values sometimes are not. For example, Excel considers a social security number such as 123-45-6789 to be text, not the value of 123 minus 45 minus 6789. Telephone numbers, with or without area codes or country codes, are text also. The key difference between text and values is that cells containing text cannot be used in a meaningful way in mathematical calculations.

Next, you will enter the values for the University Bookstore's percent donation, and scrip unit values. In addition, Stirling talked to you this morning and asked you to enter 900 for the projected unit sales. While this may be an optimistic figure, Stirling thinks that students will like the idea of spending their scrip on campus.

Entering values:

1. Click cell **C9** to make it the active cell. Type **10%** and press the **right arrow** key. The value 10.00% appears in cell C9 and cell D9 becomes the active cell. By pressing the right arrow key, you save a step because you do not have to use the mouse to select the next cell prior to entering data into the cell—in the step that follows

2. Type **5** into cell D9 and then press the **right arrow** key. The value 5 appears in cell D9 and E9 becomes the active cell

3. Type **900** into cell E9 and press the **Enter** key. See Figure 1.10

Next, you will enter formulas that will calculate the total donation value and total retail value for the newly added University Bookstore row. This row will contribute to the subtotal and grand totals, as you will see after you complete the following steps.

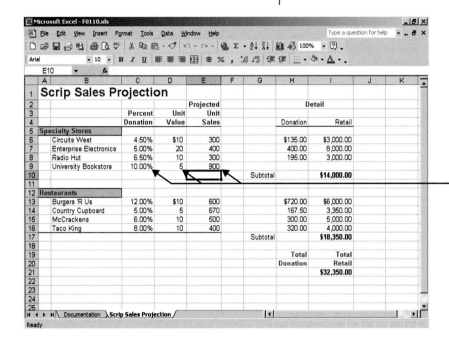

Worksheet after entering values in three cells

three new values entered

Formulas

A *formula* is an expression that begins with an equal sign and can contain cell references, arithmetic operators, values, and Excel built-in functions that result in a calculated value that is displayed in a worksheet cell. Without formulas, Excel would be little more than a word processing program, incapable of producing what-if analysis and not even as capable as an inexpensive calculator. Formulas give Excel its power. Formulas that contain a reference to another cell automatically compute new results whenever you change *any* cell in the worksheet. A formula can be as simple as the sum of two numbers or cells, or it can be as complex as the calculation of the present value of a lottery prize that is paid once a year for 22 years. Formulas contain arithmetic operators such as addition, subtraction, multiplication, and division. Figure 1.11 lists the arithmetic operators available in Excel.

Formulas begin with an equal sign. The equal sign informs Excel that you are entering a formula, not a label. A formula can contain values, arithmetic operators, and cell addresses. For example, the formula $=(C5-C7)/(D43+D28)*54.987$ references cells and contains a constant. The formula mathematically combines the values in cells and the constant using parentheses, division, addition, and multiplication.

task reference

Entering a Formula

- Select the cell in which you want to type a formula

- Type **=** followed by the remainder of the formula

- Type cell references in either uppercase or lower case, or use the mouse or the arrow keys to select cells as you type the formula

- Press the **Enter** key to complete the formula

EXCEL

Arithmetic operators

Arithmetic Operator	Operator Name	Example Formula	Description
( )	Parentheses	=(1+B4)/B52	Alters the way in which the expression is evaluated: Add 1 to the contents of cell B4 and divide the result by the value in cell B52
^	Exponentiation	=E4^6	Raises the value stored in cell E4 to the 6th power
		=17.4^B2	Raises 17.4 to the value stored in cell B2
*	Multiplication	=B4*D4	Multiplies the value in cell B4 by the value in D4
		=A21*B44*C55	Multiples the values of cells A21, B44, and C55
/	Division	=D1/C42	Divides the value in cell D1 by the value in cell C42
		=A53/365.24	Divides the value in cell A53 by the constant 365.24
+	Addition	=A4 + B29	Adds the contents of cell A4 and the contents of cell B29
		=10/17/46	Divides 10 by 17 and then divides that result by 46
-	Subtraction	=A2-A1	Subtract the value of cell A1 from the value of cell A2
		=100-A2	Subtract the value of cell A2 from the constant, 100

Stirling explains that you must enter a formula to compute the donation and retail values for the University Bookstore row. The subtotal and grand totals automatically include the new calculated values you are about to add because the subtotal and grand total formulas have been written to do so. Stirling asks you to complete the University Bookstore row.

Entering formulas to calculate donation and retail amounts:

1. With the Scrip Sales Projection worksheet displayed, click cell **H9** to select it, type the formula **5C9*D9*E9** (remember to type the equal sign first) and then press **Enter** to complete the formula. The formula multiplies the percent donation (C9), unit value (D9), and unit sales value (E9) for the University Bookstore. In this example, the formula calculates 10 percent of 900 units at 5 dollars per unit sold. The value 450.00, the result, appears in cell H9

   tip: *If you make a mistake while typing a formula but <u>before</u> you press Enter or an arrow key, simply press the **Backspace** key to erase the mistake and then type the correction. If you make a mistake <u>after</u> you press Enter or an arrow key, simply select the cell again and retype the formula.*

2. Click cell **H9** again to observe the formula, which appears in the formula bar. See Figure 1.12

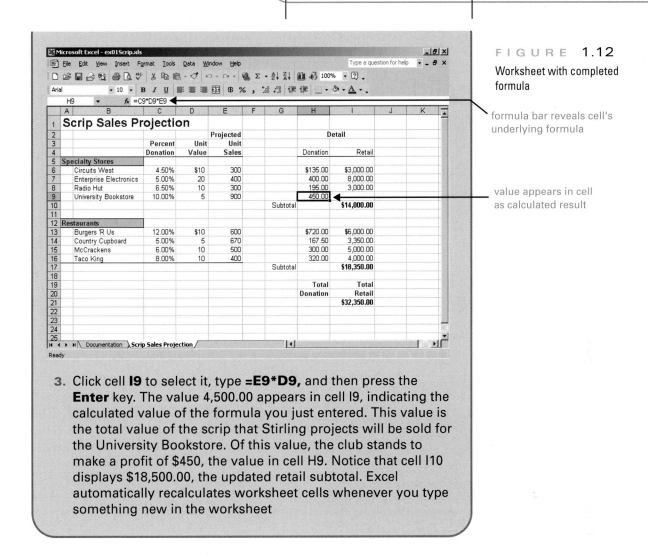

FIGURE 1.12

Worksheet with completed formula

formula bar reveals cell's underlying formula

value appears in cell as calculated result

3. Click cell **I9** to select it, type **=E9*D9,** and then press the **Enter** key. The value 4,500.00 appears in cell I9, indicating the calculated value of the formula you just entered. This value is the total value of the scrip that Stirling projects will be sold for the University Bookstore. Of this value, the club stands to make a profit of $450, the value in cell H9. Notice that cell I10 displays $18,500.00, the updated retail subtotal. Excel automatically recalculates worksheet cells whenever you type something new in the worksheet

Functions

A **function** is a built-in or prerecorded formula that provides a shortcut for complex calculations. Excel has hundreds of functions available for your use. One example is the Excel statistical function SUM. The SUM function is a handy shortcut for summing the contents of any collection of worksheet cells. Instead of writing a long formula such as =A1+A2+A3+A4+A5+A6+A7 to sum the values stored in cells A1 through A7, you can write a shorter equivalent formula =SUM(A1:A7). The SUM function, like all Excel functions, starts with the function's name followed by opening and closing parentheses that optionally contain a list of cells or other expressions upon which the named function operates. In the preceding example, the SUM function adds the values in the cell range designated by A1, which is the upper-left cell in the range, through cell A7, which is the lower rightmost cell in the range. The function calculates and displays the sum in the cell in which the function is written. A *cell range* consists of one or more cells that form a rectangular group. You specify a cell range by typing the name of the upper-left cell, a colon, and the name of the lower-right cell. For example, the cell range B4:C6 consists of the six cells B4, B5, B6, C4, C5, and C6. Because Excel imposes a limit on the size of a formula you can write, the Excel function SUM solves the problem of

F I G U R E   1.13

Cell range examples

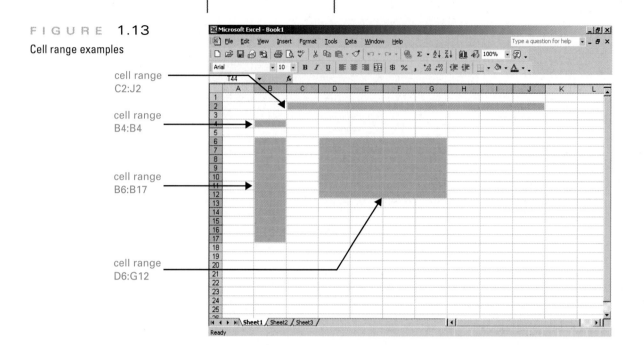

cell range
C2:J2

cell range
B4:B4

cell range
B6:B17

cell range
D6:G12

anotherword

. . . on Cell Ranges

A SUM function can contain more than one cell range. For example, the function =SUM(A1:A5,B42:B51) totals two cell ranges. Place commas between distinct cell ranges within the SUM function. The collection of cells, cell ranges, and values in the comma-separated list between a function's parentheses is its **argument list**

writing an extremely long formula that contains a potentially large number of cell addresses. For example, without the SUM function, adding up a column of 600 retail sales values would be impossible, because a formula consisting of 600 cell references separated by addition operators would exceed Excel's limit on formula size. Figure 1.13 shows several examples of cell ranges.

Stirling points out that there are three cells into which you can place the SUM function. Two of those SUM functions will calculate the subtotal of the donations for each of the two categories of merchants. The third SUM function will add the two donation subtotals to calculate and display the grand total donation value—the projected dollar value that the team can use to underwrite some of its costs.

task reference

Entering the SUM Function

- Select the cell in which you want to type a formula

- Type **=**

- Type **SUM** in either uppercase, lowercase, or a mixture of both, followed by a left parenthesis. Do not place a space between "SUM" and the left parenthesis

- Type the cell range to be summed followed by a right parenthesis

- Press **Enter** to complete the SUM function

Entering SUM functions:

1. With the Scrip Sales Projection worksheet displayed, click cell **H10** to select it, type the formula **=SUM(H6:H9)** and press **Enter** to complete the formula. The SUM function adds the four donation amounts and displays it in cell H10

2. Click cell **H17** to select it. This time, you will type part of the formula, use the mouse to indicate the cell range to sum, and finish the formula by typing the final right parenthesis. Using the mouse to select a cell range while writing a formula is called **pointing**. Pointing has the advantage that you are less likely to type an incorrect cell range

3. With cell H17 the active cell, type **=SUM(**

4. Next, click cell **H13,** drag the mouse pointer down to cell **H16,** and release the mouse. Notice that Excel writes the cell range into the function for you as you drag the mouse. A moving dashed line surrounds the selected cell range. See Figure 1.14

	A	B	C	D	E	F	G	H	I	J
1	**Scrip Sales Projection**									
2					Projected			Detail		
3			Percent	Unit	Unit					
4			Donation	Value	Sales			Donation	Retail	
5	Specialty Stores									
6		Circuits West	4.50%	$10	300			$135.00	$3,000.00	
7		Enterprise Electronics	5.00%	20	400			400.00	8,000.00	
8		Radio Hut	6.50%	10	300			195.00	3,000.00	
9		University Bookstore	10.00%	5	900			450.00	4,500.00	
10							Subtotal	$1,180.00	$18,500.00	
11										
12	Restaurants									
13		Burgers 'R Us	12.00%	$10	600			$720.00	$6,000.00	
14		Country Cupboard	5.00%	5	670			167.50	3,350.00	
15		McCrackens	6.00%	10	500			300.00	5,000.00	
16		Taco King	8.00%	10	400			320.00	4,000.00	
17							Subtotal	=SUM(H13:H16		
18										
19								Total	Total	
20								Donation	Retail	
21									$36,850.00	
22										

FIGURE 1.14

Pointing to specify a cell range

the dashed line highlights the selected cell range

Excel automatically fills in cell references as you drag the mouse

5. Type **)** and press **Enter** to complete the function

tip: *You can click the Enter button, (a green checkmark button appearing on the left end of the formula bar) whenever you enter data into a cell instead of pressing the Enter keyboard key. The difference between the two methods is that pressing the keyboard Enter key makes another cell active, whereas click-ing the Enter button on the formula bar does not make another cell active*

6. Click cell **H21,** type **=SUM(H10,H17)** and press **Enter** to complete the function

tip: *Notice that you place a comma between the two cell references in the SUM function, not a colon. In this formula, SUM is adding two single-cell ranges, not the cell range H10 through H17. Sum can have a large number of cell ranges separated by commas in one function, indicating that all the cells in the several cell ranges are summed.*

EXCEL

You show your nearly complete worksheet to Stirling. He likes the work you have done, but points out that the entry Country Cupboard is incorrect. The merchant's name is Country Kitchen. Stirling asks you to make that correction.

EDITING CELL ENTRIES

Periodically, you may want to make changes to text, values, formulas, or functions. The change may be small and subtle, or you may want to completely replace the contents of a cell. When you modify the contents of a cell, that process is called *editing.*

---

task reference

Editing a Cell

- Select the cell that you want to edit
- Click in the formula bar and make any changes
- Press **Enter** to finalize the changes

or

- Select the cell that you want to edit
- Press **F2** and make changes in the selected cell or in the formula bar
- Press **Enter** to finalize the changes

or

- Double-click the cell and make changes to it
- Press **Enter** to finalize the changes

Editing a text entry by using the F2 edit key:

1. Select cell **B14** and press the **F2** function key
2. Press the **Backspace** key eight times to erase Cupboard
3. Type **Kitchen** and press **Enter** to complete the change and move to cell B15

You notice that McCrackens is misspelled. The correct spelling contains an apostrophe before the letter *s:* McCracken's.

Editing a text entry by typing in the formula bar:

1. Make sure that B15 is the active cell and then click in the formula bar

2. Press the **left arrow** key to move the insertion point between the letters *n* and *s*

3. Type **'** (apostrophe) and press **Enter** to complete the change

Stirling learned that the University Bookstore misquoted their donation percentage. Instead of 10 percent, the correct value is 7.5 percent. Also, he thinks that 900 units is a bit optimistic and asks you to reduce the projection for University Books scrip to 650 units. Stirling asks you to make those changes. When changes to a cell are extensive, you can save time by simply typing a completely new formula, which replaces the original formula when you press Enter or select another cell. Next, you make the changes that Stirling requests.

Replacing worksheet cells with new contents:

1. Click cell **C9** to make it the active cell, type **7.5%**, and press **Enter** to replace the University Bookstore percentage donation value with 7.5%

2. Click cell **E9** and type **650**

3. Press **Enter** to complete the change to cell E9. See Figure 1.15

	A	B	C	D	E	F	G	H	I	J
1	**Scrip Sales Projection**									
2					Projected			Detail		
3			Percent	Unit	Unit					
4			Donation	Value	Sales			Donation	Retail	
5	Specialty Stores									
6		Circuits West	4.50%	$10	300			$135.00	$3,000.00	
7		Enterprise Electronics	5.00%	20	400			400.00	8,000.00	
8		Radio Hut	6.50%	10	300			195.00	3,000.00	
9		University Bookstore	7.50%	5	650			243.75	3,250.00	
10							Subtotal	$973.75	$17,250.00	
11										
12	Restaurants									
13		Burgers 'R Us	12.00%	$10	600			$720.00	$6,000.00	
14		Country Kitchen	5.00%	5	670			167.50	3,350.00	
15		McCracken's	6.00%	10	500			300.00	5,000.00	
16		Taco King	8.00%	10	400			320.00	4,000.00	
17							Subtotal	$1,507.50	$18,350.00	
18										
19								Total	Total	
20								Donation	Retail	
21								$2,481.25	$35,600.00	
22										

FIGURE 1.15

Worksheet with cell edits completed

edited cells

SAVING A WORKBOOK

Whenever you first create a workbook or make extensive changes to a workbook, you should save your work frequently. By storing a workbook as a file on a disk, you can later recall it, make changes to it, and print it without retyping all the cell entries. When you save a workbook, the computer saves the contents of your computer's internal memory holding the entire workbook to a disk file. You can save a workbook under a new file name by selecting Save As in the File menu or, for existing workbooks, you can click Save to replace the workbook with the newer version. If

anotherword

. . . on Saving Workbooks

You can never save your workbook too frequently. If your computer should fail, your current work in memory is lost. Saving your work frequently avoids having to re-enter large amounts of information that was lost as a result of the computer failure.

you save a file under a new name (Save As), the original workbook file remains on disk unchanged. Always choose the Save As command when you create a workbook and save it for the first time. Also choose the Save As command when you want to preserve the original workbook. Use the Save command when you want to replace the original workbook stored on disk with the new one using the same name. The Standard toolbar has a Save button for your convenience, because Excel users save their workbooks frequently.

task reference

Saving a Workbook with a New Name

- Click the **File** menu and then click **Save As**

- Make sure the Save in list box contains the name of the disk and folder in which you want to save your workbook. If not, use the mouse to navigate to the correct disk and folder

- Change the file name in the File name list box

- Click the **Save** button

You have made a number of changes to the Scrip Sales Projection workbook and it is time to preserve those changes.

Saving an altered workbook under a new file name:

1. Click **File** on the menu bar and then click **Save As.** The Save As dialog box opens and displays the current workbook name in the File name text box

2. If necessary, click the **Save in** list box arrow and then select the disk and folder in which you want to save your workbook

3. Click in the **File name** list box, drag across the file name to select the entire name, and type **Scrip2.xls**

4. Ensure that the Save as type list box specifies "Microsoft Excel Workbook (*.xls)" (see Figure 1.16)

5. Click the **Save** 🖫 button to save your Excel workbook under its new file name. After you save a workbook, you will notice that the new workbook name (Scrip2) appears in the Excel title bar

Stirling tells you that the workbook is designed so that anyone using it can change the values in the Projected Unit Sales column and observe the changes to the worksheet. He wants to save the workbook without any assumptions about the values in the Projected Unit Sales column. That

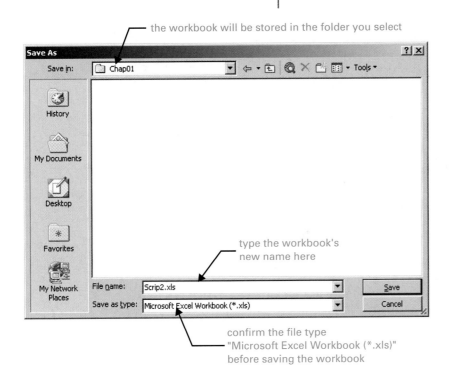

FIGURE 1.16
Saving a workbook under a new file name

way, a new user can load the Scrip Sales Projection workbook and type in a new set of unit sales assumptions without first deleting the previous assumptions. You are not sure how to empty or delete a cell's contents, and you wonder if simply selecting the cell and pressing Spacebar or typing a zero will clear out the cells. You remember Stirling telling you that whenever you have questions and no one is available for help, you can go to online help. You decide to investigate Excel's online help to answer your question.

GETTING HELP

Excel provides online help to answer many of your questions. If you don't know how a function is written, or if you have a question about how to complete an Excel task, use Excel's extensive Help feature. Help in Excel is similar to Help in the other Office products. You can obtain help from the Office Assistant, from the Excel Help menu, or from Microsoft's Web site.

task reference

Obtaining Help

- Click the **Microsoft Excel Help** command from the **Help** menu (or click the Microsoft Excel **Help** button on the Standard toolbar)

- Click the **Answer Wizard** tab

- In the *What would you like to do?* text box, type an English-language question (replacing the words displayed and highlighted in blue) on the topic with which you need help and click the **Search** button

Using Help, you can locate an answer to your question about deleting cells' contents.

EXCEL

Obtaining help:

1. Click **Help** on the menu bar and then click **Microsoft Excel Help.** The Microsoft Excel Help dialog box appears

2. If necessary, click the **Answer Wizard** tab

3. Type **how do I delete cells** in the *What would you like to do?* text box, and then click **Search** to display help alternatives

tip: *You can also press the Enter key instead of clicking the Search key*

4. Click **Clear cell formats or contents** in the *Select topic to display* list to display information about removing cells' contents. See Figure 1.17

5. Read the information and print it out if you wish (click the printer icon on the Help toolbar). Click the **Close** [Close] button on the Microsoft Excel Help Title bar to close the Help dialog box

Now you know how to empty cells' contents. Deleting cells is not quite what Stirling wants. He wants the cells to remain but their contents to be emptied. Now that you have obtained help, you know just what to do.

CLEARING CELLS

Periodically you may want to delete the contents of a cell containing text, a value, a formula, or a function. You have a couple of choices. You can empty a cell by selecting it with the mouse and then pressing the Delete key or by clicking Edit on the menu bar, then clicking Clear, and finally

FIGURE **1.17**

Obtaining help

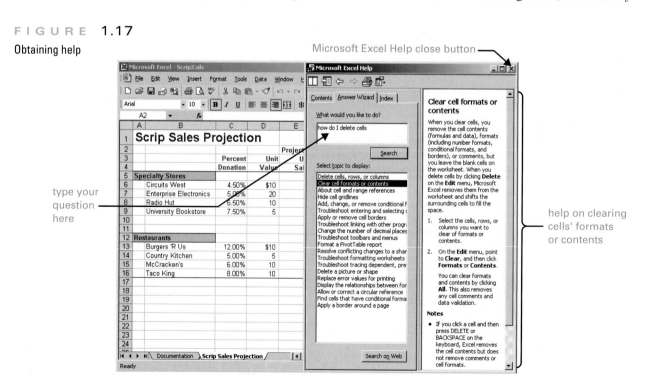

type your question here

help on clearing cells' formats or contents

clicking Contents from the command list. Either way, Excel erases the cell's contents. You might be tempted to simply select the cell and press the Spacebar key in order to clear the cell. While the cell *appears* to be empty, it is not—it contains a space. This is the "colorless, odorless, tasteless gas" that later can harm your worksheet. Cells containing one or more spaces (blanks) are treated differently from those that are empty and they are very difficult to locate.

---

task reference

Clearing Cells' Contents

- Click the cell or cells you want to empty

- Press the **Delete** keyboard key

or

- Click **Edit** on the menu bar, click **Clear,** and then click **Contents** to empty the contents of the cell or cells you selected

---

All the assumptions for the Scrip Sales Projection worksheet are in column E. Cells E6 through E9 contain the assumed unit sales for the group of specialty stores, and cells E13 through E16 contain the assumed unit sales for restaurants. You are ready to clear those cells' contents.

Clearing several cells' contents:

1. Click cell **E6,** drag the mouse down through cell **E9,** and release the mouse. This selects the cell range E6:E9

   tip: *If you select the wrong cells, simply repeat the click-and-drag sequence in step 1.*

2. Press the **Delete** keyboard key to clear the contents of the selected cells

   tip: *If you delete the wrong cells, click **Edit** in the menu bar and then click **Undo Clear.** Alternatively, you can press the **Undo** [↺ ▾] button on the Standard toolbar*

3. Click cell **E13,** drag the mouse down through cell **E16,** and release the mouse

4. **Right-click** anywhere within the selected range of cells. A pop-up command list appears (see Figure 1.18)

5. Click **Clear Contents** from the pop-up command list to clear the contents of the selected cell range

6. Click on any cell to deselect the range

7. To save the workbook under a new name, click **File** and then click **Save As**

EXCEL

FIGURE 1.18

Selecting Clear Contents from a
pop-up command list

Clear Contents

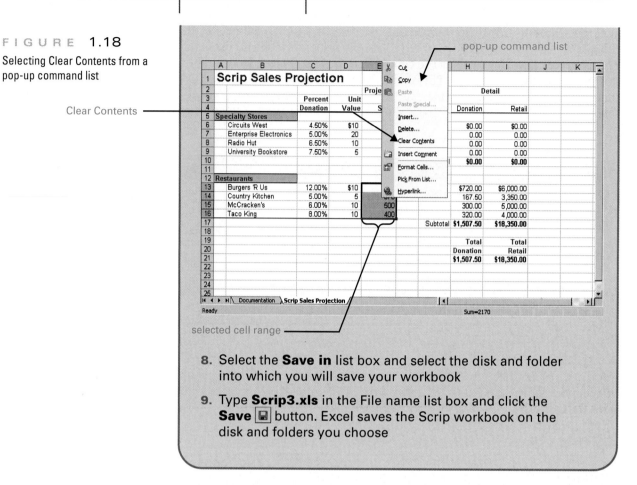

FIGURE 1.18

Selecting Clear Contents from a pop-up command list

8. Select the **Save in** list box and select the disk and folder into which you will save your workbook

9. Type **Scrip3.xls** in the File name list box and click the **Save** 🖫 button. Excel saves the Scrip workbook on the disk and folders you choose

You may be alarmed that the subtotal values and the total values are all zero. Do not be concerned. Cells that reference empty cell ranges often display zero because empty cells are treated mathematically as if they contained zero. The moment anyone types a value into any cell in the Projected Unit Sales column adjacent to one of the merchant rows, all the subtotals and totals will recalculate nonzero values. Looking at the calculated values for different sets of input information is performing what-if analysis. Doing so can reveal how many units a factory needs to produce in order to be profitable, or how many scrip units a rugby team must sell to produce $3,000 in profits. You will do that next.

CONDUCTING WHAT-IF ANALYSIS

The power of a workbook lies in its ability to recalculate the entire workbook quickly whenever you enter new values to see the overall affect of the changes you propose. Using your knowledge of students' preferences and how many students are likely to purchase scrip, you can change the values for some or all of the Projected Unit Sales values for each merchant and observe how much profit each combination of values generates. Cell H21 displays the total donations, or club profit. That value is recalculated whenever you enter new data.

You can examine the effect on Total Donations of selling larger numbers of Burgers 'R Us scrip, which pays the highest percentage of total sales. Similarly, you can determine what would happen if you sold 400 units of every merchant's scrip. Trying different combinations of scrip sales units in the worksheet produces results that help the team decide where it wants to focus its scrip sales efforts. What-if analysis like this may reveal whether or not selling scrip generates enough profit to be worthwhile. For example, if everyone agrees that students won't purchase enough scrip to make a significant dent in the club's expenses, they may choose to pursue other fundraising opportunities.

Stirling wants you to try another set of Projected Unit Sales values to see if you can raise at least $2,500. He e-mails you a note with the scrip sales values he wants you to try along with a request that you print out the resulting worksheet. Stirling wants to see the profit generated if the team could sell 400 units of each merchant's scrip, except for Burgers 'R Us. "Let's plug in 850 units for Burgers 'R Us and see what happens," Stirling's e-mail concludes.

Conducting what-if analysis by changing all unit sales values:

1. With the Scrip Sales Projection worksheet open, click cell **E6** and drag the mouse down through cell **E9** to select the cell range E6:E9. After selecting a range of cells, you can enter data into the range by typing each cell's contents and pressing Enter to move to the next cell. Excel proceeds through the entire list of selected cells, eventually returning to the first cell after you have pressed Enter a sufficient number of times. Using this technique can save time
2. With the cell range E6:E9 highlighted, type **400** and press **Enter.** Cell E7 becomes the active cell and Excel recalculates formulas
3. Type **400** and press **Enter.** Repeat this step two more times to fill each of the four selected cells with the value 400
4. Click cell **E13** and drag the mouse down through cell **E16** to select the cell range E13:E16
5. Type **850** and press **Enter.** The value 850 appears in cell E13
6. Type **400** and press **Enter**
7. Repeat step 6 two more times to enter the remaining two values
8. Click any cell to deselect the block of cells. Your worksheet should resemble the worksheet in Figure 1.19

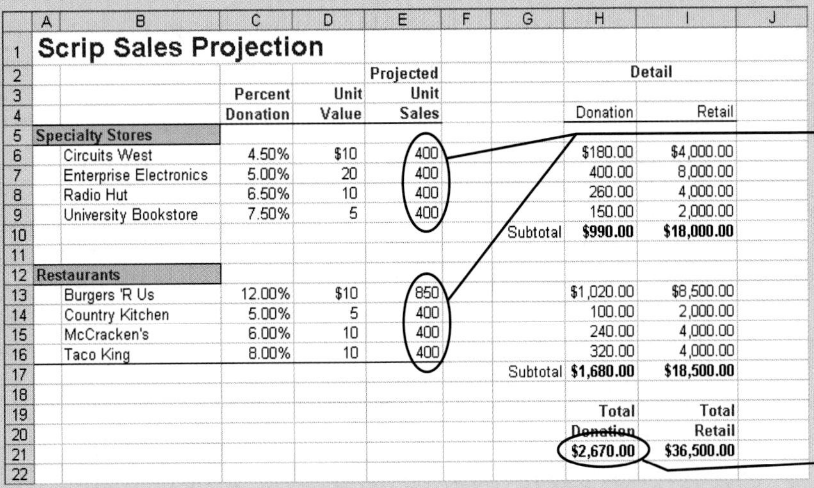

	A / B	C	D	E	F	G	H	I	J
1	Scrip Sales Projection								
2				Projected			Detail		
3		Percent	Unit	Unit					
4		Donation	Value	Sales			Donation	Retail	
5	Specialty Stores								
6	Circuits West	4.50%	$10	400			$180.00	$4,000.00	
7	Enterprise Electronics	5.00%	20	400			400.00	8,000.00	
8	Radio Hut	6.50%	10	400			260.00	4,000.00	
9	University Bookstore	7.50%	5	400			150.00	2,000.00	
10						Subtotal	**$990.00**	**$18,000.00**	
11									
12	Restaurants								
13	Burgers 'R Us	12.00%	$10	850			$1,020.00	$8,500.00	
14	Country Kitchen	5.00%	5	400			100.00	2,000.00	
15	McCracken's	6.00%	10	400			240.00	4,000.00	
16	Taco King	8.00%	10	400			320.00	4,000.00	
17						Subtotal	**$1,680.00**	**$18,500.00**	
18									
19							Total	Total	
20							Donation	Retail	
21							**$2,670.00**	**$36,500.00**	
22									

new unit sales assumptions

rugby team's profit

FIGURE 1.19
What-If analysis example

With the new projected sales units, or sales assumptions, the team will produce a profit of $2,670. That will help a lot to reduce their projected team expenses this season. Naturally, their profit will be more or less if they sell more or fewer units of scrip than shown in the worksheet.

You are ready to show Stirling your work, but you must first print the worksheet so that you can give it to Stirling for review.

PRINTING A WORKSHEET

Printing a worksheet provides you and others with a portable copy that you can peruse, review, and modify with a pen or pencil. When you are ready to try more what-if analysis, take the hand-modified hard copy of the worksheet, enter the changes, save the modified worksheet, and print a copy. You can print an Excel workbook or worksheet using the Print command in the File menu or by clicking the Print button on the Standard toolbar. The toolbar Print button is handy because it is a one-click way to produce output. However, the Print button doesn't offer any printing options. On the other hand, the File menu Print command displays the Print Dialog box allowing you to select a number of values and settings to customize your output. You can adjust a number of important settings such as the number of output copies, which pages to print, whether to print all worksheets in the workbook or just the active sheet or a selected range of cells, and which printer to select. Most importantly, you can click the Print dialog box Preview button to preview your output before you print it—an important way to ensure you don't waste paper when you print the workbook.

First, there are a few preliminary tasks to perform before producing a printed worksheet. One of these important tasks is creating a worksheet header and footer. A *header* contains text that appears automatically at the top of each printed page in the header margin, which is located directly above the worksheet print area on a page. A *footer* contains text that appears automatically at the bottom of each printed page in the footer margin, which is located below the worksheet print area on a page. Though worksheet headers and footers are optional, you will find a well-labeled worksheet is a good way to document and identify your printed worksheets.

Labeling an Output with a Header or Footer

If you are printing your worksheet on a shared printer located in a computer laboratory, several people may be producing the same or similar outputs. To avoid the confusion of determining whose output is whose, you will want to uniquely identify your output so that it is not mistaken for someone else's. The best way to label your output is to either place on the header or footer your first and last names or other identifying information such as your company or student identification number.

There is more than one way to identify your output. You can type your name into one of the worksheet cells, perhaps adding it to a documentation worksheet similar to the Scrip workbook's Documentation worksheet, or you can type your name into the worksheet's header or footer. The advantage of a header or footer is that your identification will appear automatically on *each* output page, not just on the first output page. Having your identification appear on every page, with each page numbered, unequivocally identifies the work as yours. Of course, you want to follow the guidelines your instructor provides for output. Here, you will learn how to create a header and footer prior to printing your worksheet.

task reference
Creating a header or footer

- Click **View** on the menu bar and then click the **Header and Footer** tab
- Click **Custom Header** or **Custom Footer**
- Select the Left section, Center section, or Right section
- Type the header text into any or all of the sections
- Optionally, select text in any section and then click the **Font** button to set font characteristics
- Click **OK** to confirm your header or footer choices
- Click **OK** to close the Page Setup dialog box

Many people use the printer in your laboratory where you are building the Scrip Sales Projection worksheet, so you decide to add a header to identify the worksheet and a footer to display a page number in case the worksheet grows to multiple pages.

An Excel header can appear in three sections: left, center, or right. If you type text in the header's Left section, the text will appear on the top left portion of each page. Text typed into the Center section of the Header dialog box appears in the top center of each page. Text typed into the Right section of the Header dialog box appears in the top right of each page. You decide to place your name on the right side of each page top.

Creating a worksheet header:

1. Ensure that the Scrip Sales Projection worksheet is displayed. Click **View** and then click **Header and Footer.** The Header/Footer tab of the Page Setup dialog box appears
2. Click the **Custom Header** [Custom Header...] button, click in the **Right section** text box, type **Modified by,** and then type your first and last names following "Modified by"
3. Drag the mouse over the text in the Right section to select it, click the **Font** [A] button, click **Bold** under the Font style list, and then click **OK.** The Page Setup dialog box reappears
4. Click the Header dialog box **OK** button to complete the header

Next, you will ensure that your printed worksheet pages contain numbers by placing a page number in the page footer.

Placing a page number in the worksheet footer:

1. With the Page Setup dialog box open, click the **Custom Footer** [Custom Footer...] button, click in the **Center section** text box, and click the **Page Number** [#] button. The

characters &[Page] appear in the Center section. The symbol represents a page number variable that automatically numbers pages in sequence beginning with 1

2. Click the Footer dialog box **OK** button. The Page Setup dialog box reappears. Figure 1.20 shows the Page Setup dialog box. Of course, your page header will be slightly different because you have typed your own name where <u>Stirling Leonard</u> appears in the header preview text box

F I G U R E   **1.20**

Page Setup dialog box with completed header and footer

header appears at the top of each page

page number appears in the footer of each page

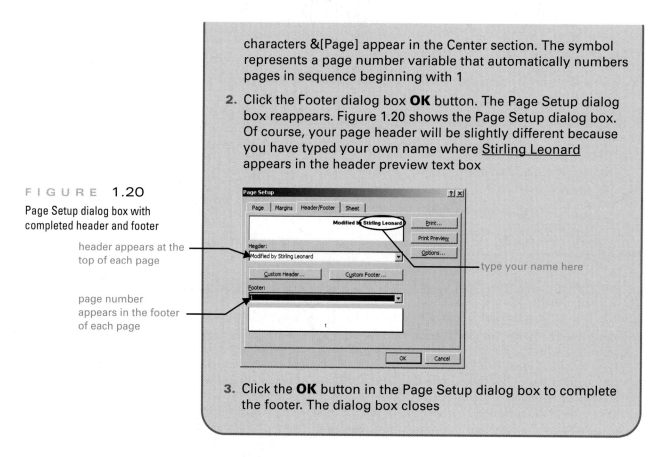

type your name here

3. Click the **OK** button in the Page Setup dialog box to complete the footer. The dialog box closes

Previewing Output

Before you print any worksheet, you should preview the output. Previewing output lets you catch any small errors that might cause more pages to print than you expected. Page margins, font size, and header and footer margins all can affect how many pages you print. Previewing your output gives you a chance to make adjustments so that the worksheet prints correctly and on as few pages as possible.

Previewing output:

1. Click **File** on the menu bar

2. Click **Print Preview** command in the File menu. The first page of output appears on the screen. Although the header and footer are unreadable at the standard magnification, you can zoom in to inspect them

tip: *Preview output quickly by clicking the **Print Preview** [image] button found on the Standard toolbar*

3. Click the **Margins** button, and then move the mouse to the top right portion of the preview page—near the header. The mouse pointer becomes a magnifying glass. Click the mouse to increase the magnification. The enlarged worksheet makes the header easy to read. The dashed lines indicate the page margins. See Figure 1.21

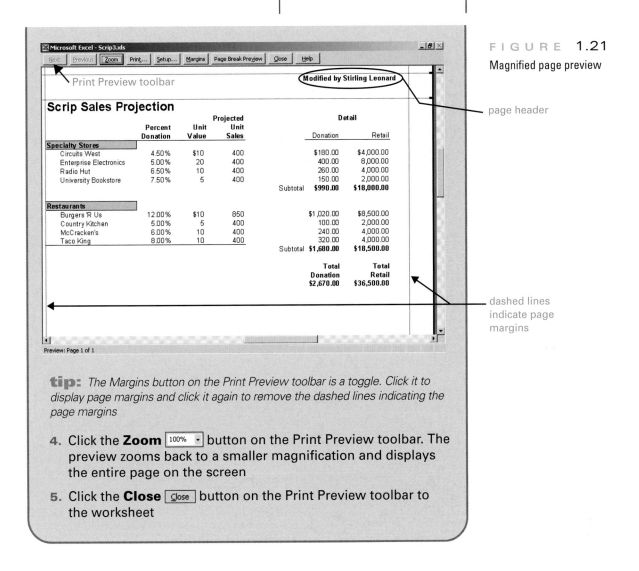

FIGURE 1.21
Magnified page preview

page header

dashed lines
indicate page
margins

tip: *The Margins button on the Print Preview toolbar is a toggle. Click it to display page margins and click it again to remove the dashed lines indicating the page margins*

4. Click the **Zoom** `100%` button on the Print Preview toolbar. The preview zooms back to a smaller magnification and displays the entire page on the screen

5. Click the **Close** `Close` button on the Print Preview toolbar to the worksheet

Printing

The output appears to be fine, and the header and footer are where you expected them to be. You are ready to print the worksheet.

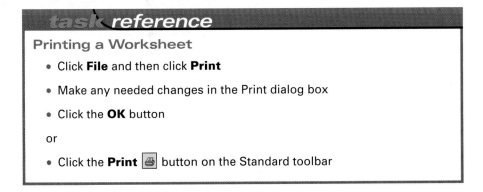

task reference

Printing a Worksheet

- Click **File** and then click **Print**
- Make any needed changes in the Print dialog box
- Click the **OK** button

or

- Click the **Print** button on the Standard toolbar

You are ready to print your worksheet. The print preview revealed that the entire worksheet would fit on one page. You decide that you want to check the print settings before printing, so you select the Print command from the File menu rather than risk using the Print button—at least until you become more comfortable with printing.

One of the important settings you will want to check in the Print dialog box is in the *Print what* section of the Print dialog box. Which of the three option buttons you choose determines how much and which portions of the workbook or worksheet print. You can choose one of *Selection, Active sheet(s),* or *Entire workbook.* Click Selection if you have highlighted a block of cells and want to print only that section of a worksheet. Click Active sheet(s) if you want to print the active worksheet or if you have selected more than one worksheet and want to print the selected worksheets from one workbook. Select Entire workbook if you want to print all of a workbook's worksheets. You will see where these choices appear in the steps that follow.

Checking the print settings and printing the worksheet:

1. If you are using your own printer, make sure it is turned on and contains paper. If you are using a network printer, assume it is turned on and full of paper.

2. Click **File** on the menu bar and then click **Print.** The Print dialog box opens (see Figure 1.22).

FIGURE 1.22

Print dialog box

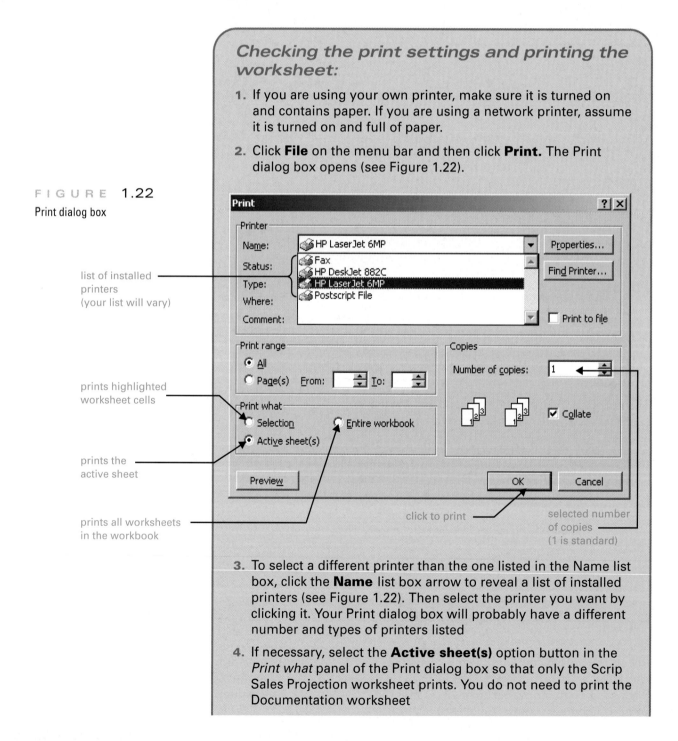

list of installed printers (your list will vary)

prints highlighted worksheet cells

prints the active sheet

prints all worksheets in the workbook

click to print

selected number of copies (1 is standard)

3. To select a different printer than the one listed in the Name list box, click the **Name** list box arrow to reveal a list of installed printers (see Figure 1.22). Then select the printer you want by clicking it. Your Print dialog box will probably have a different number and types of printers listed

4. If necessary, select the **Active sheet(s)** option button in the *Print what* panel of the Print dialog box so that only the Scrip Sales Projection worksheet prints. You do not need to print the Documentation worksheet

5. Click **All** in the Print range section, if necessary

6. Ensure that the Number of copies box displays 1. You need only one copy of the worksheet

7. Click the **OK** button to print the worksheet. Figure 1.23 shows the printed worksheet. Of course, your worksheet will contain your name in the header instead of Stirling Leonard

Modified by Stirling Leonard

Scrip Sales Projection

	Percent Donation	Projected		Detail Donation	Retail
Specialty Stores					
Circuits West	4.50%	$10	400	$180.00	$4,000.00
Enterprise Electronics	5.00%	20	400	400.00	8,000.00
Radio Hut	6.50%	10	400	260.00	4,000.00
University Bookstore	7.50%	5	400	150.00	2,000.00
			Subtotal	$990.00	
Restaurants					
Burgers 'R Us	12.00%	$10	850	$1,020.00	$8,500.00
Country Kitchen	5.00%	5	400	100.00	2,000.00
McCracken's	6.00%	10	400	240.00	4,000.00
Taco King	8.00%	10	400	320.00	4,000.00
			Subtotal	$1,680.00	
			Total Donation	$2,670.00	

1

FIGURE 1.23

Printed Scrip Sales Projection worksheet

Printing Worksheet Formulas

Part of documenting a worksheet and learning how Excel works is printing the worksheet's formulas. Typically, businesses do not require that reports showing Excel worksheet results also show the formulas. However, you may want to refer to both the worksheet output and the formulas that produced that output. Additionally, your instructor may want to view the worksheet formulas so that she or he can see exactly what formulas and functions you used to produce the results. Your instructor may request that you print and turn in worksheet formulas along with the regular worksheet printout. In any case, it is helpful to know exactly how to print worksheet formulas in case Stirling wants to study them and give you suggestions.

---

task **reference**

Printing Worksheet Formulas

- Click **Tools** and then click **Options**

- Click the **View** tab

- Click the **Formulas** check box in the Window options panel to place a checkmark in it

- Click **OK**

- Click **File** and then click **Print**

- Click **OK** to print the worksheet formulas

You ask Stirling if he wants worksheet formulas for documentation. Stirling thinks that is a great idea and thanks you for thinking of it.

Printing worksheet formulas:

1. Click **Tools** on the menu bar and then click **Options.** The Options dialog box opens

2. Click the **View** tab on the Options dialog box

3. Click the **Formulas** check box to check it. The Formulas check box is located in the Window options section of the dialog box. See Figure 1.24

FIGURE **1.24**

Selecting the Formulas check box

Formulas check box checked ————

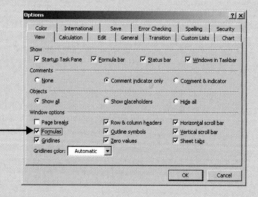

4. Click **OK** to close the Options dialog box

5. Click the Formula Auditing toolbar **close** button, if necessary, to close the toolbar. The Excel worksheet displays its formulas on screen

6. Drag the **horizontal scroll arrow** until columns H and I come into view. See Figure 1.25. With the Formulas option selected, you can print formulas for the entire worksheet or for a selection of cells

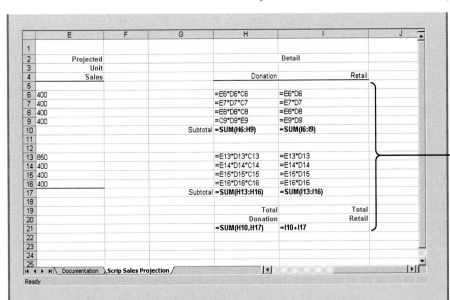

FIGURE 1.25
Excel formulas on screen

formulas that underlie calculated values

7. Click **File** and then click **Print**

8. Click **OK** in the Print dialog box to print the worksheet formulas. Excel prints your worksheet's formulas

tip: *Excel remembers the settings you choose in the Options dialog box. It is best to return those settings to their original values. Once the worksheet starts printing its formulas, revisit the Options dialog box and clear the Formulas check box before continuing work*

9. Click **Tools**, click **Options,** and then click the **View** tab

10. Click **Formulas** check box to clear it and then click **OK.** Excel redisplays values in place of formulas

CLOSING A WORKBOOK

When you finish a worksheet and the workbook containing it and want to move on to another activity, you close the workbook. If you have made changes to the worksheet that you have not saved, Excel will display a dialog box asking if you want to save the altered workbook before closing it. Normally you should affirm saving a changed workbook, even if you cannot remember making any changes to it. That way, the most current version is saved on disk.

---

task reference

Closing a Workbook

- Click **File**
- Click **Close**
- Click **Yes** to save changes

Your work is finished for now and you are ready to close the Scrip workbook.

EXCEL

> ### Closing an Excel workbook:
>
> 1. Click **File** on the menu bar and then click **Close**. A dialog box opens and displays the message "Do you want to save the changes you made to 'Scrip3.xls'?"
>
> **tip:** *You can close the active workbook by clicking the workbook's* **Close Window** `Close` *button. If the workbook window is maximized, the workbook's Close Window button appears on right side of the Excel menu bar. Always be careful to not click the Close Application button, which is located on the Excel Title bar. That will cause Excel to close all loaded workbooks, not just the active workbook*
>
> 2. Click **Yes** to save the changes you made since you last saved the workbook before closing it. (If you click No, Excel does not save the changes before closing the workbook. If you click Cancel, Excel cancels the close operation and redisplays the active worksheet.)

Excel remains available, allowing you to create new workbooks or open existing ones. You can exit Excel because you have finished your work.

EXITING EXCEL

Exiting Excel unloads it from memory and closes any open workbooks. When you are finished using Excel, it is wise to close it so that the internal memory it occupies becomes available to other programs. Follow these steps to close Excel.

> ### Exiting Excel:
>
> 1. Click **File** on the menu bar and then click **Exit**
>
> **tip:** *You can close Excel by clicking the* **Close** *button on Excel's Title bar.*

Stirling has reviewed your work on the Scrip Sales Projection sheet and is pleased with your work. He's also enthusiastic about the projected sales and is holding a team meeting next Saturday to discuss the details about obtaining and selling scrip to Western University students.

*another*word

. . . on Exiting Excel

Wait to remove your floppy disk containing your Excel worksheets until after you have exited Excel. Sometimes Excel does a final bit of housekeeping on the workbook you stored on your floppy disk, such as writing the last little piece of the workbook to the file just before exiting Excel.

SESSION 1.3 SUMMARY

Excel is a spreadsheet program in which you can type text, values, formulas, and functions and conduct what-if analysis by changing worksheet assumptions and viewing the changes. You can edit worksheet entries by selecting a cell, pressing

making *the grade*

1. An Excel worksheet cell can contain text, values, formula, and _____ entries.

2. Indicate which of the following cell entries are text, values, or formulas.
   a. =A1+B2
   b. 11/12/02
   c. 42,350
   d. Sum(A1:B2)
   e. 1st Quarter Sales
   f. 401-555-1212
   g. =11/12/19

3. You could write the formula **=B4+B5+B6+C4+C5+C6** to sum values in the six cells, but the SUM function is a better solution. The SUM function to sum the preceding six cells is _____.

4. You can store an Excel workbook on disk by executing the **File** menu _____ or _____ _____.

5. To empty the contents of a worksheet cell, right-click the cell and then click _____ _____ on the pop-up menu.

6. The ability to type into worksheet cells different values and see their effect on a worksheet is called _____ analysis.

7. A worksheet _____ appears on the top of each printed worksheet page.

8. Modify the Scrip Sales Projection worksheet, saved as **scrip v3.xls,** in the following ways: Type **400, 500, 600,** and **700** in cells E6 through E9. In cell E10, type a function to sum the projected sales units for cells E6 through E9. Similarly, type into cell E17 a function to sum the projected sales units for cells E13 through E16. Print the worksheet and then print the worksheet formulas.

F2, and typing the changes. Completely replace cell contents by selecting a cell and typing the new contents. Save a workbook periodically to preserve its contents on disk. Click File and then click Save to save an existing workbook or Save As to save a workbook under a new file name or for the first time.

Clear cell contents by selecting the cell or cells and then pressing the Delete key. Clearing cells empties their contents; pressing the spacebar does not clear a cell—it places a blank in a cell. Click F1 or click Help on the menu bar to search for help on any Excel topic. Preview a worksheet before printing it to ensure that the correct cells and pages will print. Print a worksheet for review or documentation purposes by clicking File, Print, and selecting print parameters.

When you have completed your Excel work, close the workbook and then close Excel. Excel will prompt you to save any workbooks whose contents have changed since they were last saved. You can choose to save the workbook, not save it, or cancel the Excel exit operation. Be sure to visit the series Web site at www.mhhe.com/i-series for more information.

EXCEL

MOUS OBJECTIVES SUMMARY

- Open a workbook (MOUS) Ex2002-2-1
- Type into worksheet cells text, values, formulas, and functions (MOUS) Ex2002-1-2
- Edit and clear cell entries (MOUS) Ex2002-1-2
- Save a wookbook (MOUS) Ex2002-2-3
- Adding a header and a footer (MOUS) Ex2002-3-6
- Previewing output (MOUS) Ex2002-3-7

task reference round-up

Task	Location	Preferred Method
Workbook, open	EX 1.11	• Click **File**, click **Open**, click workbook's name, click the **Open** button
Formula, entering	EX 1.17	• Select cell, type **=**, type formula, press **Enter**
Sum function, entering	EX 1.20	• Select cell, type **=SUM(**, type cell range, type **)**, and press **Enter**
Editing cell	EX 1.22	• Select cell, click formula bar, make changes, press **Enter**
Workbook, saving	EX 1.24	• Click **File**, click **Save As**, type file name, click **Save** button
Help, obtaining	EX 1.25	Obtaining help
		• Click the **Microsoft Excel Help** command from the **Help** menu (or click the Microsoft Excel **Help** button on the Standard toolbar)
		• Click the **Answer Wizard** tab
		• In the What would you like to do text box, type an English-language question (replacing the words displayed and highlighted in blue) on the topic with which you need help and click the **Search** button
Contents, clearing	EX 1.27	• Click cell, press **Delete** keyboard key
Header/Footer, creating	EX 1.31	• Click **View**, click **Header and Footer**, click **Custom Header** or **Custom Footer**, select section, type header/footer text, click the **OK** button
Worksheet, printing	EX 1.33	• Click **File**, click **Print**, click the **OK** button
Worksheet formulas, printing	EX 1.36	• Click **Tools**, click **Options**, Click the **View** tab, click **Formulas** check box, click **OK**, click **File**, click **Print**, click the **OK** button
Workbook, closing	EX 1.37	• Click **File**, click **Close**, click **Yes** to save

CROSSWORD PUZZLE

ACROSS

1. A single electronic page of a workbook
5. Currently working on this cell, it is the _____ cell
6. A _____ bar contains menus
8. Create a heading with this type of data
9. Prerecorded formulas built into Excel
10. Click to move to another worksheet

DOWN

2. A program used to analyze numeric information
3. The _____ Pane is a dockable dialog window
4. Data representing a quantity, date, or time
7. An expression beginning with an equal sign

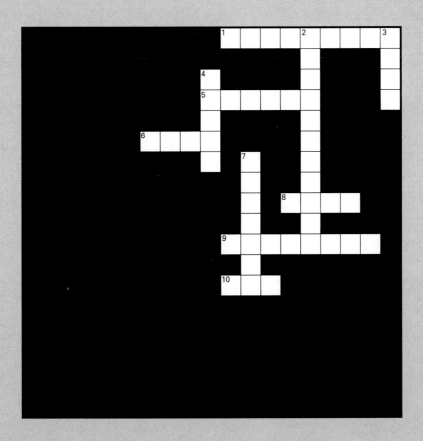

FILL-IN

1. A _____ is the name of the entity that holds a text entry, value, or formula.

2. The first spreadsheet program, called_____, was introduced in 1979.

3. To the left of the formula bar is the _____, which contains the name of the active worksheet cell.

4. Click the _____ to make another worksheet of a workbook active.

5. Suppose you type 333-56-8866 in a cell. Excel interprets the entry as a _____ entry.

6. The address of a cell at the intersection of row 43 and column F is _____.

REVIEW QUESTIONS

1. Suppose cells A3 through A5 contained the values 5, 10, and 15, respectively. Discuss what would happen if you typed **SUM(A3:A5)** in cell B15. Hint: You type only the 10 characters shown. Do not assume anything.

2. What is the most important feature of electronic spreadsheet software that makes them especially attractive when compared to the way people created spreadsheets with pencil and paper? In other words, electronic spreadsheets save time. However, which general feature of electronic spreadsheets do you think saves time?

3. Discuss what happens if a text label is wider than the cell in which you enter it and the adjacent cell contains information.

4. Why should you save a workbook to disk?

CREATE THE QUESTION

For each of the following answers, create an appropriate short question.

ANSWER	QUESTION
1. A built-in formula that is a shortcut for complex calculations	_____
2. It is shorter than writing =A1+A2+A3+A4+A5	_____
3. The F2 function key	_____
4. The Office Assistant appears	_____
5. Although the cell appears empty, it is not. It contains the blank text character, and doing this activity can cause problems later	_____
6. You should do this before printing a worksheet to ensure that you don't print more pages than you expected	_____

1. Creating an Income Statement

Carroll's Fabricating, a machine shop providing custom metal fabricating, is preparing an income statement for its shareholders. Betty Carroll, the company's president, wants to know exactly how much net income the company has earned this year. Although Betty has prepared a preliminary worksheet with labels in place, she wants you to enter the values and a few formulas to compute cost of goods sold, gross profit, selling and advertising expenses, and net income.

1. Open the workbook **ex01Income.xls** in your student disk in the folder Ch01
2. Click **File** and then click **Save As** to save the workbook as **Income2.xls** in the folder Ch01
3. Scan the Income Statement worksheet and type the following values in the listed cells: Cell C5, **987453**; cell B8, **64677**; cell B9, **564778**; cell B10, **-43500**; cell B15, **53223**; cell B16, **23500**; cell B17, **12560**; cell B18, **123466**; cell B19, **87672**
4. In cell C10, write the formula **=SUM(B8:B10)** to sum cost of goods sold
5. In cell C12, type the formula for Gross Profit: **=C5-C10**
6. In cell C19, type the formula to sum selling and advertising expenses: **=SUM(B15:B19)**
7. In cell C21, type the formula **=C122C19** to compute net income (gross profit minus total selling and advertising expenses)
8. In cell A4, type **Prepared by** <your name>
9. Click the Save button on the Standard toolbar to save your modified worksheet
10. Print the worksheet

2. Creating a Timecard Worksheet

You have a part-time job at Harry's Chocolate Shop, an ice cream parlor near the university. You work Tuesdays, Thursdays, and Saturdays. Every Saturday, you fill out a time card indicating the hours you worked the previous week and leave it on your manager's desk. Last week, you worked Tuesday, October 15, from 9:30 A.M. to 12:00 P.M., took a one-hour lunch break, and then worked until 3:00 P.M. Thursday, you worked 8:00 A.M. to 11:00 A.M., and on Saturday, you worked from 8:00 A.M. until 5:00 P.M. with an hour break from noon until 1:00 P.M. Fill out your timecard and write a formula to compute your total work hours for the week.

1. Open the workbook **ex01Timecard.xls** in your student disk in the folder Ch01. Notice that there are no worksheet gridlines. This is an option you will learn about later. Several cells, especially those containing formulas, are protected so that valuable prewritten formulas cannot be disturbed inadvertently
2. Click cell **B11** and try to type **10**. An error message dialog box opens, demonstrating that some cells are protected from change
3. Click **OK** to close the dialog box, click cell **A2,** type your first and last names, and then press **Enter**
4. Click cell **A4** and type **334**; click cell D4 and type **25**; click cell F4 and type **12**; click cell G4 and type **123-45-6789**
5. Click cell **B6,** type **10/14/02,** and press the **right arrow** key to move to cell C6
6. Repeat step 5 a total of six times, typing the remaining dates, in sequence, into cells **C6** through **H6**
7. Click cell **C7** and type **9:30 am** (type a space before "am") and press **Enter.** You notice that cell C11 displays #NUM! Don't be concerned with that error message. It will go away once you enter all your times in and out that day
8. Click cell **C8,** type **12:00 pm** (remember to type a space before "pm"), click cell **C9,** type **1:00 pm**, click cell **C10,** and type **3:00 pm**. Cell C11 should display the value 4.5.

> **tip:** If you see the error message #VALUE! in cell C11, check to make sure you did not type a semicolon instead of a colon in the time entries

9. Type in your hours (see the introductory paragraph before these steps for the hours) for Thursday and Saturday, using step 8 as a guide
10. Click cell **I11** ("eye-eleven") and type a Sum formula to total hours for the cell range C11:H11
11. Print your timecard worksheet
12. Sign and date your timecard on the line above the Employee signature and Date found near the bottom of the timecard

challenge!

1. Creating a Purchase Order

Sheridan's Fresh Flowers is a retail flower store that produces flower arrangements from flowers that the store orders from wholesalers. Allison Sheridan, the owner, did a quick inventory check last night and found that she needed more supplies. Today is the last Friday of the month, and Allison must place her order with her wholesaler for supplies for the next month. By carefully reading her wholesaler's catalog, Allison knows the wholesale price for each of the flower supplies she needs. In addition to the charges for items Allison orders, her wholesaler charges $75 to ship any size order to Sheridan's Fresh Flowers.

Because Sheridan's purchases supplies for resale, it does not pay state sales tax to the wholesaler for its purchases. Allison needs to know how much each item will cost and the total charges, including shipping.

Open a new workbook and create a new worksheet containing the text and values shown in Figure 1.26. In addition, place the title "Sheridan's Fresh Flowers" in the first row of the worksheet. Write formulas to compute each item's total cost and place them in the Item Total Cost column. Write a formula to sum the item costs and place that formula next to the Subtotal label. In the cell to the right of Shipping, place the shipping cost. Finally, write a formula to sum the Subtotal and Shipping values and place it in the cell to the right of the Total label. Place your name in the worksheet header. Print the worksheet and be prepared to turn it in to your instructor.

2. Tracking Inventory with a Worksheet

Thurgood Johnson's Hardware has been offering some new products and wants to see how they are selling. Thurgood Johnson, the store owner, has been keeping track of the number of each item sold. Figure 1.27 shows the number of items Johnson's has sold by month and item.

Open the worksheet **ex01Johnsons.xls**. Modify the worksheet in the following ways. Title the worksheet "Thurgood Johnson's Hardware" by placing that text

in cell A1. Place the label **Products** in the cell above the product names. Write formulas to sum the number of items sold each month, placing each of the six sums in their column in row 10. Type formulas to sum the number of items sold for each item for six months in column H—the column immediately to the right of June. Label the row-totals column **Totals** and place that text next to the "June" text. Finally, in cell H10, write a formula that is the grand total of all the items sold for all six months.

Locate the product that sold the fewest items overall for six months and type the fewest number of items sold to the right of its row sum. Locate the product that sold the largest number of items overall for six months and type largest number of items sold to the right of its row sum. Place your first and last names in one of the unoccupied worksheet cells in row one. Print the worksheet.

FIGURE **1.26**

Sheridan's flower supplies order worksheet

Supplies	Quantity Needed	Unit Cost ($)	Item Total Cost ($)
Baskets	10	15.55	
Bows	20	15.95	
Candles	20	4.25	
Cutter	30	7.75	
Knife	40	7.75	
Leafshine	20	5.25	
Ribbons	10	30.45	
Snapper	20	11.25	
Styrofoam	20	13.56	
		Subtotal:	
		Shipping:	
		Total:	

FIGURE **1.27**

Johnson's hardware supplies worksheet

	A	B	C	D	E	F	G
1							
2		January	February	March	April	May	June
3							
4	Drills	57	58	54	11	25	10
5	Hacksaws	46	21	36	10	42	19
6	Hammers	45	57	29	59	59	22
7	Levels	34	16	61	10	53	60
8	Pliers	66	13	10	45	45	65
9	Saws	33	12	19	32	50	37

1. Tracking Product Sales by Store Location

The Coffee and Tea Merchant has been selling coffee in the same store in the mall for almost 10 years. They have hired a consultant to build a Web site where they can advertise their store and some of their coffees. The Coffee and Tea Merchant is not ready to build an electronic commerce store, but they do want to be competitive with similar online coffee stores. They want to prepare a worksheet comparing the prices of coffee beans from several coffee regions. Go to the Web and look for three online coffee stores. Record in a worksheet the coffee prices per pound from the three online stores to serve as a comparison. The coffees are shown in Figure 1.28.

Create a new workbook whose worksheet is similar to Figure 1.28. Fill in real store names in place of Store 1, Store 2, and Store 3. Fill in coffee prices in the columns below the store names. Use the Web and search engines to locate prices per pound for the listed coffee types. Search for online coffee stores by going to www.hotbot.com. Hotbot has an excellent search engine. In the search box, type **coffee beans** and click the **Search** button. Then click several links that Hotbot returns in search of three representative online coffee stores.

Write formulas to compute the average price of each type of coffee by summing the prices for each and dividing by three. Place your name and other required identification information in a worksheet header. Either print the worksheet or execute Save As, according to the direction of your instructor.

2. Building a Product Feature and Price Comparison Worksheet

You want to purchase a new personal computer, but you aren't sure which manufacturer offers the best deal for the machine you want. You've drawn up a list of features that your computer should have and you want to compare machines from three manufacturers: Dell, Gateway, and IBM. First, load and print the worksheet **ex01Computer.xls** in the folder Ch01. The worksheet lists features in column A and each of the three computer makers' names at the top of a column.

With the preliminary worksheet as your guide, go to the Web and shop for a Dell, Gateway, and IBM desktop computer, noting any additional price for component upgrades listed in the worksheet. Select a PC category called **Home and Home Office** for each manufacturer, and locate and click the **CUSTOMIZE** button when available. The customization process will reveal individual prices for upgraded hardware. When you have jotted down base prices and any additional component costs, load **ex01Computer.xls** and immediately save the worksheet as **Computer2.xls.** Then, enter the values under the manufacturer's column and in the row associated with the machine or component. Write a formula, in the Total row, to compute the total price of each machine. Type your name in cell C1. Print the worksheet.

FIGURE 1.28

Coffee price comparison

The Coffee Merchant					
Coffee Price per Pound Comparison					
					Average
		Store 1	Store 2	Store 3	Price
Ethiopia Sidamo					
Kenya AA					
Kona					
Zimbabwe					

e-business

1. Web Host Price Comparison Worksheet

All About Batteries sells batteries for hundreds of electronic devices ranging from CD players to mobile phones. The business generates most of its revenue through catalog sales. Some customers still prefer to order from the store where they can talk to a salesperson about their needs. Producing and mailing catalogs every three months to thousands of customers and potential customers is costly, and Paul DeMaine, the owner of All About Batteries, wants to open an online store and place the entire catalog online. He knows he must find an online commerce service provider to host his online business. Figure 1.29 shows a list of Web hosting services, their monthly fees for a basic Web hosting package, and the amount of disk storage they provide for their monthly service fees.

Create a workbook that contains this information. Write a formula for each Web host that calculates the cost of the first year of hosting—the setup fee plus 12 times the monthly fee—and place those formulas in the Cost for First Year column. Compute the average monthly cost per megabyte of storage for each listed host, placing that formula in the row corresponding to the Web host name. Place a label next to the Web host that provides the least costly storage per megabyte. Label your output with your name. Execute either Print or Save As, according to your instructor's direction. If you are interested in learning more about Web hosting costs and options, point your Web browser to www.hostcertify.com and read through their pages. Web hosting costs change quickly.

FIGURE 1.29

Web hosts and their fees

Web Hosts					
Company Name	Monthly Service Fee	Disk Storage (MB)	One-time Setup Fee ($)	Cost for First Year	Cost Per Megabyte
HalfPrice Hosting	16.63	100	50		
HostPro	14.95	40	40		
Interland	19.95	150	40		
Webhosting.com	29.95	125	50		
Verio.com	49.95	60	50		

www.mhhe.com/i-series

EX 1.46

1. Comparing Gross National Products of Several Countries

Your economics professor has asked you to look up statistics about the population, surface area, and gross national product (GNP) of eight countries. Furthermore, the economics professor would like you to create a worksheet showing the data and displaying the population density and GNP per capita (a measure of productivity) for each country. Start by loading the worksheet on your student disk called **ex01GNP.xls**, which contains the selected eight countries along with population data and GNP data, and save the worksheet as **GNP2.xls.**

To complete the worksheet, type formulas for population density and GNP per capita for each of the eight countries listed. Population density is the number of people per square kilometer. You calculate that number by dividing the population by the surface area. Remember that the population value is in millions, so you will have to multiply the population in the formula by one million; the surface area of each country is in thousands of square kilometers, so remember to multiply that number in the formula by 1000.

Alternatively, simply divide the population number by the surface area and multiply the entire value by 1000. For example, the per capita GNP is $290.3*1,000,000,000/36*1,000,000. You can divide both the numerator and denominator by 1 million to reduce the value to $290.3*1000/36, or approximately $8,000 per capita. Of course, you will use cell references in place of values in all your formulas. Place your name in the worksheet header and print the worksheet.

running project

Pampered Paws

Pampered Paws is a pet store and provides a sitting service for clients who do not want to board their animals in a kennel. Pampered Paws' pet sitting clients prefer to leave their pets at home—in surroundings that are familiar and comforting to their pets. For a small daily fee, a Pampered Paws' employee will visit a client's pet two or three times per day. During each of the 15-minute visits, the employee plays with the owner's pet and checks the pet's food and water. The employee will walk dogs and, on occasion, cats as part of the service. (They draw the line at turtles, however.) Pampered Pets employs several people on a part-time basis when the service becomes especially busy during the holiday season and summertime. These well-trained part-time employees, known as *walkers,* have varying work schedules that accommodate their other jobs' work requirements. Several of the part-timers have asked for a raise from their current rate of $7.75 per hour to $8.50 per hour. Grace Jackson, the service's owner, wants to compute the total cost of the raise given the typical work schedule of her part-time walkers.

Figure 1.30 shows a worksheet Grace has started. Create a workbook containing a worksheet that looks like Figure 1.30. Fill in the Weekly Current Wage column with formulas that multiply each employee's hours per week times the current hourly rate. Be sure to write the formula to reference the cell containing 7.75 rather than use 7.75 in the formula directly.

Write a similar formula to fill in the Weekly Proposed Wage column, but this time multiply Hours per Week values times the proposed hourly rate cell for each employee. Finally, write formulas in the Wage Difference column to compute the difference between the proposed wage and the current wage for each employee. Sum the Wage Difference column at its foot to see the total effect of the proposed wage increase for the company. Identify your worksheet with your name and print it.

FIGURE 1.30

Employee wage analysis

Pampered Paws Part-time Employees Wage Analysis					
7.75	current hourly rate				
8.50	proposed hourly rate				
			Weekly	Weekly	
First Name	Last Name	Hours per Week	Current Wage	Proposed Wage	Wage Difference
Ellen	Fittswater	12			
Kim	Fong	8			
Ted	Garcia	4			
Randy	Hutto	14			
Luca	Pacioli	9			
Sharon	Stonely	18			

did you know?

the penny is the only coin currently minted in the United States with a profile that faces to the right. All other U.S. coins feature profiles that face to the left.

the world's largest wind generator is on the island of Oahu, Hawaii. The windmill has two blades 400 feet long on the top of a tower, 20 stories high.

the only house in England that the Queen may not enter is the House of Commons, because she is not a commoner. She is also the only person in England who does not need a license plate on her vehicle.

former U.S. Vice President Al Gore and Oscar-winning actor Tommy Lee Jones were roommates at Harvard.

Chapter Objectives

- Plan and document a workbook

- Create formulas containing cell references and mathematical operators (MOUS Ex2002-5-1)

- Write functions including Sum, Average, Max, and Min (MOUS Ex2002-5-2)

- Use Excel's AutoSum feature to automatically write Sum functions

- Learn several ways to copy a formula from one cell to many other cells

- Differentiate between absolute, mixed, and relative cell reference (MOUS Ex2002-5-1)

- Adjust column widths (MOUS Ex2002-3-2)

- Set a print area (MOUS Ex2002-3-7)

- Move text, values, and formulas (MOUS Ex2002-1-1)

- Insert and delete rows and columns (MOUS Ex2002-3-2)

- Format cells (MOUS Ex2002-3-1)

- Create cell comments (MOUS Ex2002-7-3)

chapter case
Intercity Recycling Contest

Each year for 12 years, a group of five California cities has held a recycling contest to see which city does the best job of recycling plastic, glass, and aluminum. Cities participating in this year's contest are Arcata, Los Gatos, Pasadena, San Diego, and Sunnyvale. Mayors of each of the competing cities elect a contest organizer from a slate of candidates. Although the Recycling Contest Chairperson position is unpaid, it is a great honor to be chairperson. Many candidates vie for the chairperson's position. To avoid any conflict of interest, contest rules require that the chairperson not be a resident of any of the competing cities.

This year's contest chairperson is Kelly Allison. She is a member of the Los Angeles Chamber of Commerce and well known in the Los Angeles area for her work with businesses and the Los Angeles city council. Because chairing the recycling contest is more than a part-time job, Kelly has requested a leave of absence for the contest's three-month duration. She will need help from several volunteers to carry out various tasks associated with the contest, to meet with officials from contesting cities, and to periodically monitor recycling.

This year, the contestants want to recycle aluminum cans. To help keep track of each city's recycling, Kelly has designated several recycling collection points in each of the five cities. The number of recycling centers is proportional to each city's population so that no city has to cope with a recycling congestion problem. Because the populations of the participating cities are wide ranging, a large city such as San Diego will probably recycle the largest number of aluminum cans as its population is over 2.8 million people. To make the contest fair for both large and small cities, the winning city will be the one that recycles the largest number of cans per capita—the number of cans recycled by a city divided by the number of residents of that city.

Each city has a recycling supervisor who monitors and records that city's recycling for every month for the contest's duration. The first of each month, the contest supervisors e-mail the recycling numbers to Kelly Allison. Kelly needs your help to compile the numbers in an Excel worksheet and create the formulas to compute the total recycling by city each month, total recycling for all cities each month, and the all-important per capita recycling value that determines the contest winner. In addition, Kelly wants to know a few statistics about the monthly recycling efforts including the minimum, average, and maximum number of cans recycled.

Figure 2.1 shows the completed Aluminum Can Recycling Contest worksheet. You will be developing the worksheet in this chapter.

FIGURE 2.1

Completed Can Recycling
Contest worksheet

	A	B	C	D	E	F	G	H	I	J	K
1	0.02	per can									
2											
3			Aluminum Can Recycling Contest								
4											
5	City	Population	Jan	Feb	Mar	Total	Per Capita				
6	Arcata	15,855	10,505	24,556	12,567	47,628	3.00				
7	Los Gatos	28,951	24,567	21,777	26,719	73,063	2.52				
8	Pasadena	142,547	102,376	105,876	121,987	330,239	2.32				
9	San Diego	2,801,561	2,714,664	2,503,344	1,999,877	7,217,885	2.58				
10	Sunnyvale	1,689,908	1,523,665	1,487,660	1,002,545	4,013,870	2.38				
11	Total	4,678,822	4,375,777	4,143,213	3,163,695	11,682,685	2.56				
12											
13		Minimum	10,505	21,777	12,567						
14		Average	875,155	828,643	632,739						
15		Maximum	2,714,664	2,503,344	1,999,877						
16						Total Revenue					
17	Potential Revenue		$ 87,516	$ 82,864	$ 63,274	$ 233,654					
18											

INTRODUCTION

Chapter 2 covers writing formulas in worksheet cells, using Excel functions, copying and moving cell contents, and formatting. In this chapter you will create a new workbook from scratch. First, you will type text to identify the worksheet's columns of numbers. You will write expressions using the Excel functions SUM, MIN, AVERAGE, and MAX. Using Excel's AutoSum feature, you will build expressions to total columns by selecting cell groups and then clicking the AutoSum to automatically build the SUM function. You will learn to write formulas and then save time by copying them to other cells in the worksheet to create a family of related formulas. Chapter 2 describes the differences between using relative, mixed, and absolute cell references in expressions and the advantages of each form. You will learn how to use spell-checking to reduce the chances of your worksheets containing misspellings and how to save your workbook. Finally, Chapter 2 describes how to adjust a worksheet page's print settings such as print margins and the print area.

SESSION 2.1 WRITING FORMULAS, USING FUNCTIONS, AND COPYING AND MOVING CELL CONTENTS

In this section, you will learn how to build a worksheet; enter text, formulas, and use Excel functions; and copy and paste formulas to create a family of related formulas.

CREATING WORKBOOKS

Workbooks that endure are well planned and organized. Workbooks designed in a haphazard way grow into finished products that are hard to understand and use. The process from designing a workbook to producing the final printed result follows a series of steps that increase the likelihood of a successful finished workbook.

- First, determine the purpose of the workbook and the worksheets it contains and decide on its overall organization.

EX 2.3

EXCEL

- Next, enter text, values, and formulas into the worksheet.
- Then, test the worksheet's robustness by entering various values into it and viewing the results.
- Modify formulas that display incorrect results.
- Create documentation such as a description of the worksheet's purpose, the worksheet author's name, names and dates of any modifications, and which cells contain data—the assumptions—and which are formulas.
- Review and implement appearance changes to render the worksheet's displayed values and text more attractive.
- Save the workbook.
- Print the worksheet and its formulas.

PLANNING A WORKBOOK AND ITS WORKSHEETS

Kelly brainstorms with you about the recycling contest and the structure of the worksheet that will record the recycling values reported by contest supervisors. The worksheet should show in the clearest possible way the following:

- What is the overall purpose of the worksheet?
- What are the important results to display in the worksheet?
- What types of data must the supervisors collect and report back to Kelly in order to compute the results?
- What formulas and functions create the answers? The answer to this question specifies the formulas the worksheet designer must write.

With the preceding questions in mind, Kelly creates a list answering the questions. Purposefully general, the answers will guide her in designing the worksheet or directing someone else to do so. The following is a list of specific answers to the preceding worksheet design questions. See Figure 2.2.

FIGURE 2.2

Recycling contest worksheet planning guide

Objective:

Produce a worksheet comparing per-capita recycling among cities

Input Data:

1. City names
2. City populations
3. Recycling amounts by city for each of the three months

Calculated Results (formulas):

- Per capita recycling for each city
- Total recycling per month for all cities
- Smallest recycling amount for each month
- Average recycling amount for each month
- Maximum recycling amount for each month
- Three-month recycling total for each city
- Grand total recycling for all cities for the entire contest period
- Total revenue generated for all recycled cans

With the list of input data values and formulas that Kelly wants to appear in the worksheet, she draws a rough sketch. This helps her decide where totals, labels, and input values look best and allows her to visualize the worksheet's design. Figure 2.3 shows her sketch of the finished worksheet with x representing values or calculated results.

BUILDING A WORKSHEET

Using Kelly's worksheet planning guide (Figure 2.2) and her hand-drawn sketch of the layout (Figure 2.3), you proceed to create the worksheet.

Starting Microsoft Excel:

1. Start Excel by clicking **Start,** pointing to **Programs,** and clicking **Microsoft Excel**

2. Place your floppy disk in the floppy disk drive so that you can save the worksheet later

3. Ensure that both Excel and the empty worksheet are maximized

Entering Text

Frequently, people begin building a worksheet by entering most or all of the text (labels). With labels in place, the worksheet has a guide indicating where to place values and formulas. It is a good idea to enter row and column labels first. Leave room for spreadsheet titles above the data and text labels. If you forget to leave space, you can always insert rows and columns where needed. You recall from Chapter 1 that when you enter a label that is wider than its cell, the label spills over into one or more cells to its right. Whenever the adjacent cell is not empty, Excel displays only as much of the label as fits in the cell. Though the entire label may not be visible, it is all stored in a single cell. Begin by entering the worksheet title and column labels.

FIGURE 2.3
Worksheet sketch

revenue per recycled can: 0.02

Aluminum Can Recycling Contest

City	Population	Jan	Feb	Mar	Total	Per Capita
Arcata	xxxxxx	xxxxxx	xxxxxx	xxxxxx	xxxxxx	x.xxxx
Los Gatos	xxxxxx	xxxxxx	xxxxxx	xxxxxx	xxxxxx	x.xxxx
Pasadena	xxxxxx	xxxxxx	xxxxxx	xxxxxx	xxxxxx	x.xxxx
San Diego	xxxxxx	xxxxxx	xxxxxx	xxxxxx	xxxxxx	x.xxxx
Sunnyvale	xxxxxx	xxxxxx	xxxxxx	xxxxxx	xxxxxx	x.xxxx
Total # Cans	xxxxxxxx	xxxxxxxx	xxxxxxxx	xxxxxxxx		
Minimum	xxxxxx	xxxxxx	xxxxxx			
Average	xxxxxx	xxxxxx	xxxxxx			
Maximum	xxxxxx	xxxxxx	xxxxxx			
Revenue	xxxxx.xx	xxxxx.xx	xxxxx.xx	xxxxx.xx		

EXCEL

Typing a worksheet title and column labels:

1. Click cell **A1**, type **Aluminum Can Recycling Contest**, and press **Enter**

    Notice that the title spills over into adjacent cells B1 through C1

2. Click cell **A3** and type **City**

3. Click cell **B3** and type **Population**

4. Enter the remaining column heads as indicated below

tip: *When you are entering data in a row, press the **right arrow** key after typing a cell's entry to finalize the contents and move right one cell in the row. That saves time.*

Cell C3: **Jan**

Cell D3: **Feb**

Cell E3: **Mar**

Cell F3: **Total**

Cell G3: **Per Capita**

See Figure 2.4.

FIGURE 2.4

Worksheet with title and column headings in place

worksheet title

column labels

tip: *If you make a mistake typing any cell's text, select that cell and simply retype it. For short labels, it is usually faster to retype the text than to edit and correct mistakes.*

This year, five cities are entered in the recycling contest. Kelly wants you to enter the city names in alphabetical order in a single column. Enter the city names next.

Entering the names of participating cities:

1. Click cell **A4**, type **Arcata,** and press the **down arrow** keyboard key to move to cell A5

2. Type **Los Gatos** and press the **down arrow** keyboard key to move to cell A6

3. Enter the remaining city names as follows:

    Cell A6: **Pasadena**

    Cell A7: **San Diego**

    Cell A8: **Sunnyvale**

Next, enter summary statistics labels. They identify the values that will appear to their right to indicate the sum, smallest, average, and largest recycling value for each month from the five cities.

Entering summary labels:

1. Click cell **A9,** and type **Total**

2. Click cell **A10** and type **Minimum**

3. Click cell **A11** and type **Average**

4. Click cell **A12,** type **Maximum**, and press **Enter**

Figure 2.5 shows the worksheet containing the labels you just typed.

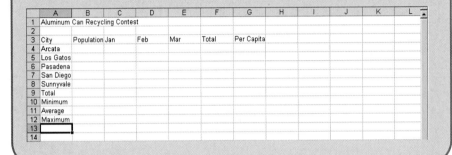

FIGURE 2.5
Worksheet with all labels entered

Entering Values

With a little Web research, Kelly has gotten accurate population data for each of the cities entered in the recycling contest. In addition, the recycling data arrived in Kelly's office and she wants you to enter both the population data and three month's recycling values into the worksheet. Throughout the data entry process, be sure to type the number zero and the number 1 and *not* the letter o ("oh") or the letter l ("ell").

Entering population and recycling values:

1. Click cell **B4** and type **15855**

2. Click cell **B5,** type **28951,** and press **Enter**

3. Enter the remaining population values as follows, pressing Enter after each entry:

   Cell B6: **142547**

   Cell B7: **2801561**

   Cell B8: **1689908**

4. Click cell **C4,** type **10505,** which is the number of cans that Arcata recycled in January, and press the **down arrow** keyboard key

5. Continue entering the recycling values as follows. (Press Enter or the down arrow key to move down the column to the next cell after typing each entry)

   Cell C5: **24567**

   Cell C6: **102376**

   Cell C7: **2714664**

   Cell C8: **1523665**

6. Click cell **D4,** type **24556,** and press **Enter**

7. Continue entering the recycling values for February as follows (press **Enter** after typing each value):

   Cell D5: **21777**

   Cell D6: **105876**

   Cell D7: **2503344**

   Cell D8: **1487660**

8. Click cell **E4,** type **12567,** press **Enter,** and then continue entering the recycling values for March as follows (press Enter after typing each value):

   Cell E5: **26719**

   Cell E6: **121987**

   Cell E7: **1999877**

   Cell E8: **1002545**

Figure 2.6 shows the worksheet with the Population and three months' recycling values entered.

FIGURE 2.6

Worksheet with completed population and recycling values

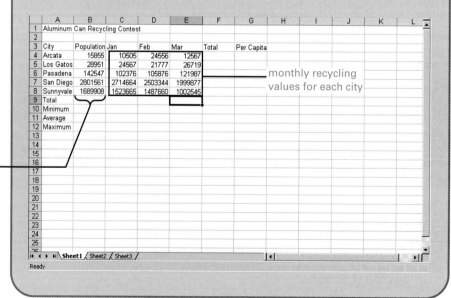

city population values

monthly recycling values for each city

Saving Your Worksheet

Once you have invested more than 30 minutes or so developing a worksheet, especially a new one, you should save it—even if you haven't completed it. More times than you can believe, nearly completed worksheets are lost due to power failures, computer glitches, or other mistakes. Because you created the worksheet from scratch, you do not have a back-up copy stored safely on disk. Now is a good time to save it.

Saving your worksheet:

1. Click **File,** and then click **Save As.** The Save As dialog box appears

2. Using the Save in list box at the top of the Save As dialog box, navigate to the disk drive and folder where you want to store your workbook

3. Type **Recycle** in the File name text box to change the work-book's name

4. Click the Save As dialog box **Save** button to save the file. The new name appears in the Excel Title bar

---

Now you have a backup copy safely stored on your floppy disk. If something would happen to reset the computer on which you are working, then you can use the **Recycle.xls** worksheet you stored on disk as the starting point to rebuild any lost work.

WRITING FORMULAS

Now you have the fundamental recycling data on which you can base formulas that compute the results. Among the first results that Kelly wants you to create are the formulas that display each month's minimum, average, and maximum recycling values. The first formula Kelly would like you to write is one to total each month's recycling values.

Creating Excel Sums Automatically

The most frequently used Excel function is SUM. It totals one or more cells. Because the SUM function is so popular, Excel provides the AutoSum button on the Standard toolbar. When you click the AutoSum button, Excel creates a SUM function, complete with a proposed range of cells to be totaled. Excel makes assumptions about which group of contiguous cells you want to total and creates a SUM function based on cells adjacent to the current active cell. You accept Excel's proposed cell range by pressing Enter, or you can select a different range of cells by using arrow keys or the mouse.

---

task reference

Writing Formulas

- Select the cell to contain a formula

- Type **=**

- Type the remainder of the formula

- Press **Enter** or press an arrow key to complete the entry and move to another cell

---

Next, you will use the AutoSum button to create a SUM function to total the recycling values for January.

Calculating the number of cans recycled in January:

1. Click cell **C9,** the cell to contain the total cans recycled in January

2. Click the **AutoSum** Σ - button on the Standard toolbar. Excel creates a SUM function in cell C9 and suggests a cell range to sum by placing a dashed line around the cell range C4:C8 (see Figure 2.7). That is the correct cell range. Figures 2.6 and 2.7 show the worksheet with the Population and three months' recycling values entered.

FIGURE 2.7

Using AutoSum to build a SUM formula

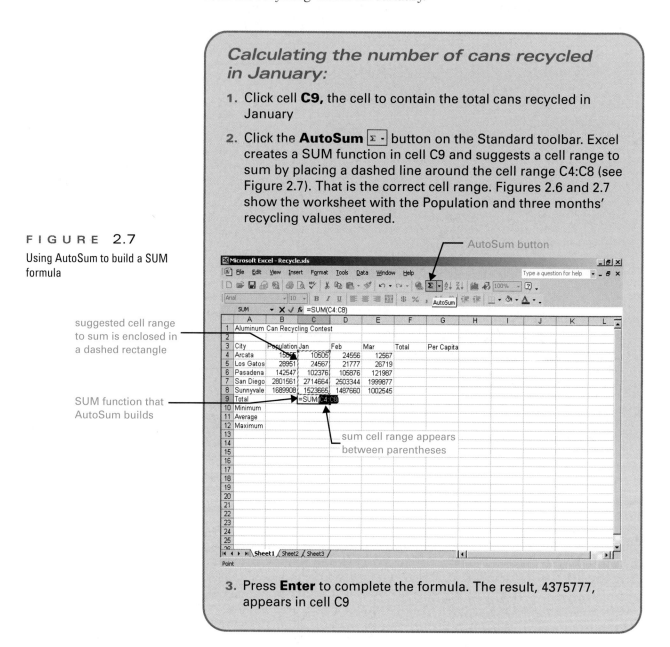

suggested cell range to sum is enclosed in a dashed rectangle

SUM function that AutoSum builds

AutoSum button

sum cell range appears between parentheses

3. Press **Enter** to complete the formula. The result, 4375777, appears in cell C9

Using the same approach, create the remaining two sums. Notice that Kelly did not ask you to total population for the five cities because the total population is not a meaningful value in this application.

Entering formulas to calculate the number of cans recycled in February and March:

1. Click cell **D9,** the cell to contain the total cans recycled in February

2. Click the **AutoSum** $\Sigma \cdot$ button on the Standard toolbar. Excel creates the appropriate SUM function in cell D9

3. Press **Enter** to complete the formula. The result, 4143213, appears in cell D9

tip: *If the sum your worksheet displays for column D does not match the preceding value, be sure to check the values in cells D4 through D8 to make sure they match the values shown in Figure 2.7*

4. Click cell **E9,** the cell to contain the total cans recycled in March

5. Click the **AutoSum** button. Excel creates the appropriate SUM function in cell E9

6. Press **Enter** to complete the formula. The result, 3163695, appears in cell E9

*another*word

. . . on quickly viewing the sum of a selected cell range

If you select a range of cells, their sum appears in the status bar located at the bottom of the worksheet. Selecting a range provides you a quick view of the sum without writing a SUM function in the worksheet.

Modifying AutoSum-Suggested Cell Ranges

Each city's total three-month recycling number is crucial to calculating which city wins the contest. Kelly asks you to enter formulas to total each city's recycling and to create a grand total that is the number of total cans recycled by all cities for three months. Each city's total and the grand total recycling numbers will appear in column F, headed by the column label Total.

*task*reference

Modifying an AutoSum Cell Range by Pointing

- With the AutoSum cell range outlined, press an arrow key repeatedly to outline the leftmost or topmost cell in the range through to the desired starting cell of the range
- Press and hold the **Shift** key
- Press the **right** or **down arrow** key repeatedly to move right or down until reaching the last cell in the cell range
- Release the **Shift** key
- Press **Enter** to complete the AutoSum formula

Create the row totals for each city next.

EXCEL

FIGURE 2.8

Changing the beginning cell in an
AutoSum cell range

Creating a row total for each city with AutoSum and changing the summed cell range:

1. Click cell **F4,** the cell to contain the total cans recycled by Arcata

2. Click the **AutoSum** button. Excel suggests summing the cell range B4:E4. Because cell B4 is Arcata's population, you will exclude it from the sum in the next steps

3. Press the **right arrow** key to move the outline to cell C4 (see Figure 2.8)

outline indicates cell selected by pointing

	A	B	C	D	E	F	G	H	I	J	K	L
1	Aluminum Can Recycling Contest											
2												
3	City	Population	Jan	Feb	Mar	Total	Per Capita					
4	Arcata	15855	10505	24556	12567	=SUM(C4)						
5	Los Gatos	28951	24567	21777	26719							
6	Pasadena	142547	102376	105876	121987							
7	San Diego	2801561	2714664	2503344	1999877							
8	Sunnyvale	1689908	1523665	1487660	1002545							
9	Total		4375777	4143213	3163695							
10	Minimum											
11	Average											
12	Maximum											
13												

partially complete SUM formula

4. Press and hold the **Shift** key

5. Press the **right arrow** key twice to outline the cell range C4:E4

6. Release the **Shift** key

7. Press **Enter** to finalize the formula. The value 47628 appears in cell F4, along with a cell error Smart Tag symbol that appears in the upper-left corner of the cell. The Smart Tag warns that the sum range has omitted a value adjacent to it. That's okay

You can ask Excel to create more than one SUM function at a time by selecting rows or columns of values with an empty adjacent column or row (respectively) in the range of cells. Then you click the AutoSum button to have Excel build multiple sum functions in one operation.

Creating multiple sum functions at once:

1. Click cell **C5** and drag the mouse through cell **F8** to select the cell range C5:F8

2. Click the **AutoSum** button. Excel automatically creates sum functions in the cell range F5:F8. Additional cell error Smart Tags appear in the cell range F5:F8

3. View a Smart Tag by clicking cell **F5** and then hovering the mouse over the Smart Tag icon. A warning message appears stating "The formula in this cell refers to a range that has additional numbers adjacent to it." (see Figure 2.9)

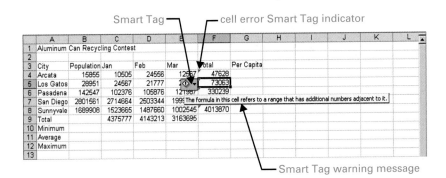

FIGURE 2.9
Smart Tag and warning message

another word

. . . about Smart Tags

Microsoft Office Smart Tags are a set of buttons that are shared across the Office applications. The buttons appear when needed, such as when Excel detects you may have made an error in an Excel formula, and gives the user appropriate options to change the given action or error.

Finally, Kelly asks you to write a formula for the grand total—the total number of cans the five cities recycled during the three-month contest. You do that next.

Creating a grand total formula:

1. Select cell **F9,** and then click the **AutoSum** button. Excel suggests the sum range F4:F8

2. Press **Enter** to accept the suggested cell range and complete the SUM formula. The grand total value 11682685 appears in cell F9. This means that the cities involved have recycled nearly 12 million cans (see Figure 2.10)

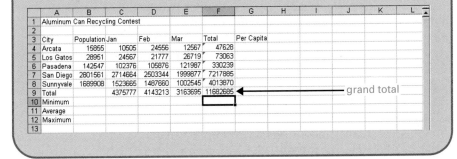

FIGURE 2.10
Worksheet with row totals and grand total

The cell error indicators in cells F4 through F8 are distracting to Kelly and she asks you to remove them.

> **Removing cell error indicators from cells:**
>
> 1. Select the cell range **F4:F8**
>
> 2. Hover the mouse over the Smart Tag, then click the **Smart Tag list arrow** to open the list of choices
>
> 3. Click **Ignore Error** in the list of choices displayed in the Smart Tag list. Excel removes the cell error indicators from all selected cells
>
> 4. Click any cell to deselect the cell range

Using Mathematical Operators

Excel formulas begin with an equal sign (=) and are followed by a mixture of cell references, Excel functions, and values mathematically combined into a meaningful expression. When you type an equal sign, you are signaling to Excel that you are writing a formula, not a label or a value. For example, you recall that Excel recognizes 11/22/02 as a value—the date November 22, 2002. However, if you type =11/22/02, Excel knows you are entering a formula that instructs Excel to divide 11 by 22 and divide that result by 02. Excel computes and displays the result, 0.25.

The divide sign (/) is one of several mathematical operators. A *mathematical operator* is a symbol that represents an arithmetic operation. When several mathematical operators occur in a formula, Excel employs the widely recognized *precedence order* to determine the order in which to calculate each part of the formula—which mathematical operators to evaluate first, which to evaluate second, and so on. If a formula contains more than one operator, the order of precedence determines which operations to perform first. For example, Excel evaluates the formula =A1/(B1+B2)*C1^D1 following the precedence order rules. First, Excel computes the value of B1+B2, because that expression is inside parentheses and saves the result temporarily. Then, Excel computes C1^D1, which is the value in cell C1 raised to the power in cell D1 power, and temporarily saves that partial result. When the remaining operators are all of equal precedence, Excel evaluates an expression left to right. Therefore, Excel divides A1 by the value derived earlier for B1+B2. Finally, Excel multiplies the previous partial result, A1/(B1+B2), by the temporarily saved value of C1^D1. For example, the result of the formula =20+2*5−15/3 is 25. Because multiplication and division have precedence over either subtraction or addition, Excel computes 2*5 first, which is 10. Then, Excel computes the value of 15/3—the value is 5. The final expression, with the preceding partial results plugged in, is =20+10−5—the value is 25.

Whenever Excel encounters an expression in which all operators are of equal precedence, it evaluates the expression left to right. For instance, Excel proceeds left to right forming the value of the expression =10*5/2*4, whose evaluation yields 100. Similarly, Excel evaluates the formula =89+A4−B6+B4 left to right, because the addition and subtraction operators are of the same precedence, or importance. How would Excel evaluate the expression =9+12/3? Because division is higher precedence than addition, Excel first divides 12 by 3 and then adds that result to 9. The expression's value is 13, not 7.

On the other hand, if you wanted Excel to first add 9 and 12 before dividing the result by 3, you must rewrite the formula as =(9+12)/3. Excel evaluates expressions enclosed in parentheses first. Thus, Excel divides the sum of 9 and 12 by 3 to yield the answer 7 in the reformulated expression. Figure 2.11 shows the Excel mathematical operators in precedence order, first to last.

Although you may not consider parentheses a mathematical operator, they alter the normal order of precedence wherever they appear in a formula. Therefore, parentheses have highest precedence—they precede all other mathematical operators when Excel evaluates a formula. Figure 2.12 shows other examples of formulas, precedence rules, and computed results. You will write formulas using mathematical operators throughout the book.

Whichever city recycles the largest number of cans during a given period is certainly important, but using that measure to determine the recycling winner would always favor larger cities over smaller ones. You recall that the winner of the recycling contest is the city that has the highest per capita recycling. Per capita (per citizen) recycling is simply the total recycling

FIGURE 2.11

Precedence order of mathematical operators

Precedence	Operator	Description
1	( )	Parentheses. Alters the order of evaluation. Expressions inside parentheses are evaluated first
2	^	Exponentiation. Raises to a power
3	/ or *	Division or multiplication
4	- or +	Subtraction or addition

FIGURE 2.12

Examples of expressions and precedence rules

Formula	Result	Precedence Rule
A1 = 30	A2 = 20	A3 = 10
=A3+A2*A1	610.00	Multiplication first followed by addition
=(A3+A2)*A1	900.00	Parentheses force addition to occur first followed by multiplication
=A3*A2/A1	6.67	Equal precedence among the two operators; proceed left to right
=A1/A2+A3	11.50	Division higher precedence than addition
=A1/(A2+A3)	1.00	Parentheses force addition to occur before division
=A3/A2*A1	15.00	Equal precedence among the two operators; proceed left to right
=A1+A2-A3	40.00	Equal precedence among the two operators; proceed left to right

EXCEL

divided by the city's population. In this contest, the judges compute that number for each city by dividing the city's number of cans recycled in three months by their population. You build that formula next.

> **Writing Arcata's per capita recycling formula:**
>
> 1. Select cell **G4** to make it the active cell
>
> 2. Type **=F4/B4** and then press **Enter** to complete the formula. The value 3.003974 appears in cell G4. In other words, Arcata's recycling amounted to slightly over three cans per person for every person living in the city

While it seems natural to write the remaining Per Capita formulas for the remaining cities, you have a feeling that there may be a better way. You've heard Kelly mention that you can copy formulas that belong to a family of similar formulas, so you wait until you have a chance to talk to her before writing the rest of the per capita recycling formulas in column G.

USING EXCEL FUNCTIONS

Based on Kelly's Recycling Contest Worksheet Planning Guide (Figure 2.2), you need to write formulas to produce statistics for each month. To enter these statistics, you will use three of the Excel functions that are in the same group of functions as the SUM function. The group, called statistical functions, contains several functions including AVERAGE, MAX, and MIN.

An Excel function, you recall from Chapter 1, is a built-in or prerecorded formula that provides a shortcut for complex calculations. Excel functions compute answers, such as the average or maximum, using software instructions that are hidden from view and, frankly, of little interest. Excel has hundreds of functions ranging from a function to generate a random number to a function to compute the monthly payment for a particular loan amount. Excel functions are organized in categories containing related functions. The categories include Database, Date & Time, Engineering, Financial, Information, Logical, Lookup & Reference, Math & Trig, Statistical, and Text.

Functions are written in a particular way. Rules governing the way you write Excel functions are called the function's *syntax.* Syntax rules include properly spelling the function's name, whether or not the function has arguments, and the order in which you list the function's arguments. A function's *argument list* is data that a function requires to compute an answer, and individual list entries are separated by commas. The entire argument list is enclosed in parentheses and follows the function name with no intervening space.

For example, the function SUM(A1, C8:C20, 43.8) contains three arguments in the argument list: a cell reference (A1), a cell range (C8:C20), and a value (43.8). You can write the function name in uppercase, lowercase, or a mixture. Excel converts the function name to uppercase after you enter the complete formula and move to another cell. The general form of an Excel function is this:

Function name(argument$_1$, argument$_2$, . . . , argument$_n$)

A function's name describes what action the function takes. AVER-AGE, for example, computes the mean of all arguments in its argument list. The function's *arguments,* which specify the values that the function uses to compute an answer, can be values, cell references, expressions, functions, or an arbitrarily complex combination of the preceding that results in a value.

You can enter functions into a cell alone or enter functions as part of a larger expression either by typing the function or by using the Paste Function button located on the Standard toolbar. The Paste Function button opens a dialog box in which you can simply point to the arguments to include in the function, click OK, and let Excel build the complete, syntactically correct function complete with argument list.

MIN Function

MIN is a statistical function that determines the minimum, or smallest value, of all the cells and values in its argument list. It is useful for determining, for example, the lowest temperature from a long list of temperatures or finding the lowest golf score from 800 players' scores. The function is written this way:

$MIN(argument_1, argument_2, \ldots, argument_n)$

Often workbook creators write MIN functions with only one argument—a cell range that Excel examines to determine the smallest value. You must specify multiple arguments when you cannot specify the cells in one cell range. For example, to find the smallest value of those in cells A1, A2, A3, B4, B5, C4, and C5, you must write two arguments, one for each cell range:

MIN(A1:A3, B4:C6)

Like other statistical functions, MIN ignores empty cells and cells containing text when computing its answer.

---

task reference

Writing a Function Using the Paste Function Button

- Click the cell to contain the function
- Click the Standard toolbar **Paste Function** button to open the Paste Function dialog box
- Click the Function category of the function type you want
- Scroll the Function name list, if necessary, to locate the function you want
- Click the function you want in the Function name list box
- Click **OK** to open another dialog box
- Enter information in the edit boxes for each argument
- Click **OK** to close the dialog box and complete building the function in the selected cell

---

Kelly wants you to write the MIN function to produce the smallest recycling value for January.

EXCEL

Building a MIN function using the Paste Function button:

1. Ensure that Excel is running and that the Recycle workbook is loaded

2. Select cell **C10,** the cell in which you want the MIN function built

3. Click **Insert** on the menu bar, click **Function,** and then click the **Or select a category list arrow.** A list of available function categories appears

4. Click **Statistical** in the *Or select a category* list to choose the category containing the MIN function

5. Drag the **Select a function scroll box** until you locate MIN in the alphabetically sorted list of statistical functions

6. Click **MIN** in the Select a function list. Figure 2.13 shows the MIN function syntax in the Insert Function dialog box. A brief description appears there also

F I G U R E   2.13

Insert Function dialog box

list of function categories available in the list box

some of the statistical functions

MIN function syntax

Select a function list scroll box

MIN function description

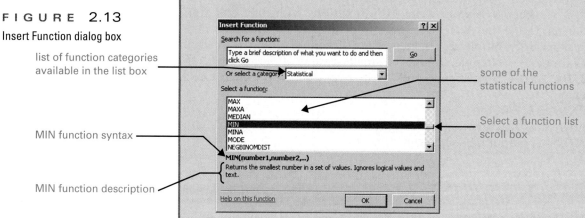

7. Click the **OK** button to open the Function Arguments dialog box. Two text boxes appear, one for each of two arguments. The dialog box also displays a description of the function, a description of the argument list, the current values of the arguments, the current results of the function, and a model of the entire formula. Notice that Excel suggests the cell range C4:C9 for Argument1. That is not the correct cell range, so you will correct it next (see Figure 2.14)

F I G U R E   2.14

The Function Arguments dialog box

description of the function and its arguments

current value of the formula containing the function

collapse/expand dialog box button

partial list of function arguments

function's current value

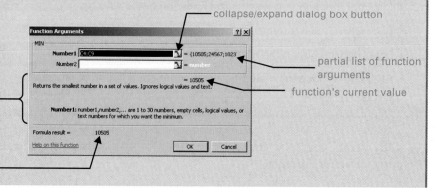

8. Click the **Collapse Dialog Box** ⊞ button appearing to the right of the Number1 text box. The Function Arguments dialog box collapses to its title bar, making it easier for you to locate and point to the correct cell range

9. Click the **Function Arguments dialog box title bar** and drag it to the right so that you can see cells C3 through C9

10. Click and drag the cell range C4:C8. Notice that as you are dragging the cell range, the ScreenTip 5R x 1C appears, indicating you have selected five rows and one column

11. Click the **Expand Dialog Box** button to restore the collapsed dialog box. Notice that the correct range, C4:C8, appears in the Number1 text box, and the minimum value 10505 appears near the bottom of the dialog box next to the text "Formula result ="

12. Click the **OK** button to accept the MIN formula that Excel built for you and return to the worksheet. The minimum value of the selected range, 10505, appears in cell C10

Based on Kelly's plan, you need to enter two more functions to complete January's statistical information. Those functions yet to be added to the worksheet are AVERAGE and MAX.

AVERAGE Function

AVERAGE is a statistical function that determines the average (arithmetic mean) of all the cells and values in its argument list. It is useful for determining, for example, the average grade of all students taking a test (empty cells or cells with labels are ignored), determining the average price of a stock from a list of weekly closing prices, or computing the average rainfall for the year. The function is written this way:

AVERAGE(argument$_1$, argument$_2$, . . . ,argument$_n$)

It is common to see an AVERAGE function with one argument—a cell range—that Excel examines to calculate the average value of the range of values. Similar to other statistical functions, AVERAGE can have up to 30 arguments separated by commas in its argument list.

Kelly wants you to use the AVERAGE function to compute and display the average number of cans recycled each month. You begin by writing an AVERAGE function to determine the average number of cans recycled in January.

Writing an AVERAGE function:

1. Click cell **C11**, if necessary, to make it the active cell

2. Type **=AVERAGE(C4:C8)** and then press **Enter.** Cell C10 displays 875155.4, the average number of cans recycled in January by all five cities

The last statistical value you need is the maximum number of cans recycled in January. For that formula, you will use the MAX function.

MAX Function

MAX is a statistical function that determines the largest number. MAX can seek out, for example, the highest-priced real estate from a list of sale prices, the highest examination score, or the largest stock price gain over a time period. The function is written this way:

MAX($argument_1$, $argument_2$, . . . ,$argument_n$)

MAX, like the other statistical functions, can have up to 30 arguments separated by commas. Arguments can be values, cell references, cell ranges, or arbitrarily complex formulas that calculate a numeric value.

Kelly wants you to write a MAX function to compute and display the value for the largest number of cans recycled in January.

Writing a MAX function by pointing to designate cell ranges:

1. Click cell **C12,** if necessary, to make it the active cell, because that cell will contain the formula displaying the maximum number of cans recycled in January
2. Type **=MAX(** to start the formula
3. Move the mouse pointer to cell **C4,** and then click and drag the mouse to select cells **C4** through **C8.** A dashed line indicates the cells you have selected as you drag the mouse
4. Release the left mouse button and press **Enter.** Excel completes the formula and displays the value 2714664, the largest value in the specified cell range. Notice that Excel automatically adds the terminating right parenthesis when you press Enter. Figure 2.15 shows the worksheet with the three statistical functions displaying January's recycling results

FIGURE 2.15
January's statistical functions

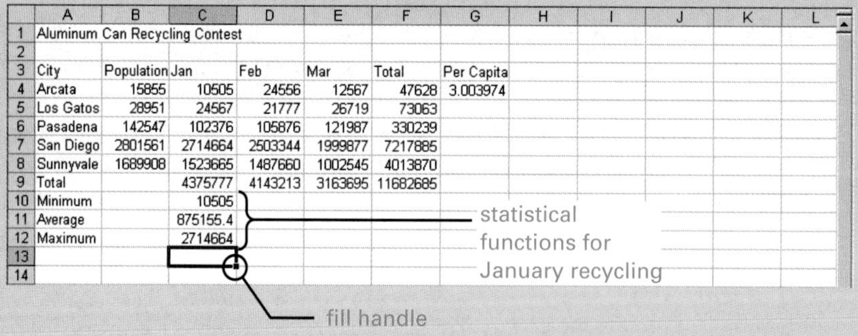

	A	B	C	D	E	F	G	H	I	J	K	L
1	Aluminum Can Recycling Contest											
2												
3	City	Population	Jan	Feb	Mar	Total	Per Capita					
4	Arcata	15855	10505	24556	12567	47628	3.003974					
5	Los Gatos	28951	24567	21777	26719	73063						
6	Pasadena	142547	102376	105876	121987	330239						
7	San Diego	2801561	2714664	2503344	1999877	7217885						
8	Sunnyvale	1689908	1523665	1487660	1002545	4013870						
9	Total		4375777	4143213	3163695	11682685						
10	Minimum		10505									
11	Average		875155.4									
12	Maximum		2714664									
13												
14												

COPYING FORMULAS TO SAVE TIME

Worksheets often contain expressions that are repeated across a row, down a column, or both. Although such expressions may consist of the same mathematical operators and functions, any cell references within formulas are slightly different. Whenever you identify families of expressions—formulas that are identical with the exception of their cell references—avoid creating each expression individually. That approach is time consuming and unnecessary. Instead, take advantage of Excel's ability to create copies of formulas. Examples of functions that you can clone to save time are the MIN, AVERAGE, and MAX. While you could recreate these three formulas manually for the February and March, Excel can do the same job much more quickly.

The key to when you can copy existing formulas is to create a series of formulas. Similarly, you can create four more per capita formulas, or you can copy the existing per capita recycling formula you created for Arcata to the other cities. Unlike a copy operation that Word carries out, Excel copies formulas and then *adjusts* all cell references in the copied formulas. You can choose to copy one cell's contents (a formula, value, or text) to another cell, you can copy one cell's contents to many cells, or you can copy many cells' contents to an equal-sized many-cell group. The copied cell(s) are called the **source cell(s),** and the cell or cells to which the contents are copied are known as **target cell(s).**

There are several equally convenient ways to copy a cell's contents to other cells. You can copy a cell's contents using Excel menu commands, a cell's fill handle, or toolbar buttons. A cell's fill handle is the small black square in the lower-right corner of the active cell (see Figure 2.15).

Copying Formulas Using Copy/Paste

You can copy the contents of one or more cells by copying the cell or cell range to the Clipboard and then pasting the copy into one or more cells in the same worksheet or in a different worksheet. When you copy one or more cells, Excel surrounds the copied cell or cells with a dashed line, or marquee, to indicate the Clipboard's contents. Pressing the Escape key empties the clipboard and removes the dashed line surrounding the copied cells.

The worksheet's plan calls for the cell formula =F5/B5 in cell G5 representing Los Gatos' recycling, =F6/B6 for Pasadena, =F7/B7 for San Diego, and =F8/B8 for Sunnyvale. Rather than create each of those per capita recycling formulas, you can copy the formula in cell G4 to cells G5 through G8. Excel will create a copy of the source cell's contents in each of the target cells and make slight changes to the cell references in the new copied formulas.

---

task reference

Copying and Pasting a Cell or Range of Cells

- Select the cell or cells to copy

- Click the **Edit** menu **Copy** command

- Select the target cell range into which you want to copy the source cell's contents

- Click the **Edit** menu **Paste** command

EXCEL

Copying a formula from one cell to many cells:

1. Click cell **G4** to make it the active cell. The cell's formula, =F4/B4, appears in the formula bar

2. Click **Edit** on the menu bar and then click **Copy** to copy the cell's contents to the Clipboard. Notice that a dashed line encloses the cell whose contents are on the Clipboard

tip: *You can press **Ctrl+C** instead of using the Copy command. Those of you who keep your hands on the keyboard may favor this keyboard shortcut.*

3. Click and drag cells **G5** through **G8** to select them. They are the target range into which you will paste the cell G4's contents

4. Click **Edit** on the menu bar and then click **Paste.** Excel copies the Clipboard's contents into each of the cells in the selected range and then adjusts each cell's formula to correspond to its new location. Notice that the Paste Options Smart Tag appears below and to the right of cell G8 (see Figure 2.16). The Paste Options Smart Tag provides several formatting and copying options in its list. You can access the options by clicking the Smart Tag list arrow

FIGURE 2.16

Copied formulas' results

	A	B	C	D	E	F	G	H
1	Aluminum Can Recycling Contest							
2								
3	City	Population	Jan	Feb	Mar	Total	Per Capita	
4	Arcata	15855	10505	24556	12567	47628	3.003974	
5	Los Gatos	28951	24567	21777	26719	73063	2.523678	
6	Pasadena	142547	102376	105876	121987	330239	2.316703	copied
7	San Diego	2801561	2714664	2503344	1999877	7217885	2.57638	cells
8	Sunnyvale	1689908	1523665	1487660	1002545	4013870	2.3752	
9	Total		4375777	4143213	3163695	11682685		
10	Minimum		10505					
11	Average		875155.4					
12	Maximum		2714664					
13								
14								

Paste Options Smart Tag

tip: *You can press **Ctrl+V** instead of using the Edit menu Paste command to paste the Clipboard's contents. This may be a faster alternative.*

5. Press **Escape** to clear the Clipboard and remove the dashed line from the source cell. Click any cell to deselect the range and view the formulas' results

If you click any cell in the range of cells you just copied, you will see that Excel has made changes to the copied formula. Cell G6 contains the formula =F6/B6. Similarly, Cell G8 contains =F8/B8. The changed cell reference reflects each copied formula's new location compared to the original source cell. For example, cell G8's formula is exactly four rows higher than the source in cell G4. Excel adds four to the row portion of each cell reference to account for its new location four rows higher than the original.

Cell reference such as the preceding ones are called relative cell references. ***Relative cell references*** in formulas always change when Excel copies them to another location. When you copy a function or formula horizontally, Excel changes the column letters automatically while leaving the row number unchanged. When you copy a formula or function vertically, the column letters will stay the same, but Excel changes the row numbers automatically. If this did not happen, then copying worksheet cells would merely clone the same values throughout the target range, an activity that would not save you any time.

Copying Formulas Using the Fill Handle

Sometimes you may find it more convenient and quicker to copy a cell's contents by dragging its fill handle. When target cells are adjacent to the source cell, using the fill handle saves time because you do not have to click menus and commands to accomplish the copy and paste operations.

---

task reference

Copying Cell Contents Using a Cell's Fill Handle

- Select the cell whose contents—value, formula, or text—you want to copy. If you want to copy a group of cells, select the cell range you want to copy

- Create an outline of the target cells by clicking and dragging the fill handle of the source cells to the target cells where you want the copied contents to appear

- Release the mouse button

You want to make a copy of the three statistical formulas summarizing January recycling to the other two months, creating six new formulas.

Copying several formulas at once:

1. Click cell **C10** and drag through cell **C12** and release the mouse to select the three cells containing statistical formulas for January

2. Move the mouse pointer over the fill handle in the lower-right corner of cell C12 until the pointer changes to a thin plus sign

3. Click and drag the mouse to the right to outline cells **D10** through **E12.** See Figure 2.17

4. Release the mouse button to complete the copy operation. Excel copies the three formulas from cells C10 through C12 (noted as C10:C12) to cells D10 through E12 and displays the AutoFill Options Smart Tag

5. Click any cell to deselect the range. Figure 2.18 shows the results after copying the statistical functions

EXCEL

FIGURE 2.17

Dragging the fill handle to copy cells

	A	B	C	D	E	F	G	H
1	Aluminum Can Recycling Contest							
2								
3	City	Population	Jan	Feb	Mar	Total	Per Capita	
4	Arcata	15855	10505	24556	12567	47628	3.003974	
5	Los Gatos	28951	24567	21777	26719	73063	2.523678	
6	Pasadena	142547	102376	105876	121987	330239	2.316703	
7	San Diego	2801561	2714664	2503344	1999877	7217885	2.57638	
8	Sunnyvale	1689908	1523665	1487660	1002545	4013870	2.3752	
9	Total		4375777	4143213	3163695	11682685		
10	Minimum		10505					
11	Average		875155.4					
12	Maximum		2714664					
13								
14								

cell contents being copied ——

target cells receiving copy ——

FIGURE 2.18

Worksheet after copy operation

	A	B	C	D	E	F	G	H
1	Aluminum Can Recycling Contest							
2								
3	City	Population	Jan	Feb	Mar	Total	Per Capita	
4	Arcata	15855	10505	24556	12567	47628	3.003974	
5	Los Gatos	28951	24567	21777	26719	73063	2.523678	
6	Pasadena	142547	102376	105876	121987	330239	2.316703	
7	San Diego	2801561	2714664	2503344	1999877	7217885	2.57638	
8	Sunnyvale	1689908	1523665	1487660	1002545	4013870	2.3752	
9	Total		4375777	4143213	3163695	11682685		
10	Minimum		10505	21777	12567			
11	Average		875155.4	828642.6	632739			
12	Maximum		2714664	2503344	1999877			
13							Copy Options	
14							Smart Tag	

Creating and Copying a Revenue Formula

Kelly wants an estimate of the total value of the aluminum cans recycled during the contest. Although prices paid at recycling centers vary by city, the average is two cents per can. So, Kelly would like you to add a formula to calculate the total value of the recycled cans for each month, placing those formulas below the maximum statistic for each month. Next, you will create a label to identify the row displaying the approximate value of the recycled cans and a label to identify the value per can.

Adding text and a value for the approximate value of each recycled can:

1. Click cell **A14**, type **Potential Revenue,** and press **Enter**

2. Click cell **H1,** type **0.02,** and press the **right arrow** key to make cell I1 the active cell. The value 0.02 (two cents) is the assumed average value per recycled can

3. In cell I1, type **per can** and then press **Enter.** The text you enter identifies the value to its left. The two cells form the phrase "0.02 per can," which is self-explanatory

Kelly wants you to write a formula for the potential revenue for January for all cans recycled by the five cities.

Writing the recycling revenue formula:

1. Click cell **C14** to make it the active cell

2. Type **=C9*H1** and press **Enter.** The expression is the product of the total number of cans recycled in January and the assumed amount per can, 2 cents. Cell C14 displays the result 87515.54. That is, January's recycling efforts by the five cities have yielded an approximate value of almost $88,000

You ask Kelly why she wants the value .02 in cell H1. Instead, why not write the formula =C9*0.02 for January's potential revenue? She responds that the value per can is an *assumption* that she may want to change later to see the effect on the potential value of the recycled cans. If that assumption were written directly into each formula, what-if analysis would require editing the revenue formulas, an unnecessary activity if the assumption is stored in a separate cell.

Next, you will copy the January revenue formula to the right to fill in formulas for February and March. Then, you will copy a formula to two other cells and cause errors to occur. By performing this operation, you will learn how to avoid the problem in other worksheets.

Copying January's revenue formula using copy and paste:

1. Click cell **C14** to make it the active cell

2. Press **Ctrl+C** to copy the selected cell's contents to the Clipboard

3. Click and drag the cell range **D14:E14** and then release the mouse

4. Press **Ctrl+V** to paste the formula into the target cell range, cells D14 through E14. Figure 2.19 shows the results of the copy operation

	A	B	C	D	E	F	G	H	I
1	Aluminum Can Recycling Contest							0.02	per can
2									
3	City	Population	Jan	Feb	Mar	Total	Per Capita		
4	Arcata	15855	10505	24556	12567	47628	3.003974		
5	Los Gatos	28951	24567	21777	26719	73063	2.523678		
6	Pasadena	142547	102376	105876	121987	330239	2.316703		
7	San Diego	2801561	2714664	2503344	1999877	7217885	2.57638		
8	Sunnyvale	1689908	1523665	1487660	1002545	4013870	2.3752		
9	Total		4375777	4143213	3163695	11682685			
10	Minimum		10505	21777	12567				
11	Average		875155.4	828642.6	632739				
12	Maximum		2714664	2503344	1999877				
13									
14	Potential Revenue		875⬦54	#VALUE!	0				
15									
16									
17									

indicates an error may have occurred

copied formulas containing errors

FIGURE 2.19

Worksheet containing errors in copied formulas

EXCEL

5. Press **Escape** to empty the Clipboard and remove the outline from cell C14

6. Click any cell to deselect the cell range

That did not go as expected. Excel displays an error Smart Tag indicating it has detected an error. Cell D14 displays "#VALUE!" This is a special Excel constant called an ***error value.*** The constant indicates that something is wrong with the formula or one of its components. Cell E14 displays "0," which is not correct either. Whenever you encounter unexpected results from a formula, the best action is to examine the cell's formula carefully to determine the error. You do that next.

Viewing a cell's contents:

1. Click cell **D14** to make it the active cell

2. Press the **F2** function key to display the cell's contents within the worksheet grid. F2 is called the Edit function key because you can edit a cell's contents by first pressing that key and then changing the cell's contents. Excel color-keys both the formula and the cells to which the formula refers so that you can easily see which cells depend on which other cells. Notice that cell D14 contains the formula =D9/I1. The first cell reference, D9, is correct because that is February's recycling total. The second cell reference, I1, is incorrect. It should be H1 instead

3. Click cell **E14** to examine its contents in the formula bar

4. Press the **F2** function key to observe how Excel adjusted the cell references in that formula

5. Press the **Escape** key to end the Edit operation on cell E14

The formula errors occur because Excel adjusts all cell references in copied formulas based on their new position relative to the original cell formula. Occasionally, you alter cell references to avoid the kinds of problems that have occurred here. The answer to avoiding these problems lies in understanding three types of cell references: relative, mixed, and absolute.

Relative, Mixed, and Absolute Cell References

Sometimes, you do not want Excel to adjust all the cell references in a formula that you copy. (Any cell reference you have used so far in this text is a relative cell reference.) Excel automatically adjusts relative cell references to reflect the new location of the copied formulas containing the relative cell references. That is what Excel did to the revenue formula.

When you want a cell reference to remain unchanged no matter where the formula containing it is copied, you use an ***absolute cell reference.*** You indicate that a cell reference is absolute by placing a dollar sign ($) before both the column and row portions of the cell reference. For example, in the formula =C14/H1, you can make the cell reference to cell H1 absolute by rewriting the formula as =C14/$H$1. No matter where you copy that formula, Excel will not adjust the $H$1 reference—it remains anchored to cell H1.

A third type of cell reference allows you to specify that one portion of a cell reference remains fixed while the other can be adjusted. A *mixed cell reference* is a cell reference in which either the column or the row is never adjusted if the formula containing it is copied to another location. For example, if you did not want the row to change in the preceding reference to cell H1, then rewrite the formula to =C14/H$1. An easy way to remember this notation is to substitute the word "freeze" for $. Then a cell reference such as H$1 reads "H freeze 1" and helps remind you that the row is unchanging when copying the formula containing the cell reference. The other form of mixed cell reference is to hold the column portion unchanged, for example, $H1.

To include a dollar sign in a cell reference as you create a formula, type a dollar sign as you type the cell reference. Alternatively, you can press the F4 function key when you edit a cell's contents to cycle through the four combinations of references for a cell. Figure 2.20 shows examples of relative, mixed, and absolute cell references.

FIGURE 2.20

Relative, mixed, and absolute cell references

Formula	Cell reference type
=A43	Relative
=$A43	Mixed
=A$43	Mixed
=$A$43	Absolute

task reference

Changing Relative References to Absolute or Mixed References

- Double-click the cell containing the formula that you want to edit or click the cell and then press **F2**
- Move the insertion point, a vertical bar, to the left of the cell reference you want to alter
- Press function key **F4** repeatedly until the absolute or mixed reference you want appears
- Press **Enter** to complete the cell edit procedure

To correct the problem that showed up in the revenue formulas, the best course of action is to correct the original source cell and then re-execute the copy operation. Then both the source cell and the target cells will have a corrected copy of the formula. You want to change the original relative-reference revenue formula in cell C14 from =C9/H1 to the formula =C9/$H1 so that Excel does not adjust the column portion of the reference to the per can recycling cell, H1, when you copy the formula to cells to the right of the existing cell.

Altering a relative cell reference to a mixed reference:

1. Click cell **C14** to make it the active cell

2. Press the **F2** function key to edit the formula in place. Notice that each cell reference in the formula is color coded to an outline surrounding the referenced cell in the worksheet. Called

EXCEL

FIGURE 2.21

Insertion point while editing a cell reference

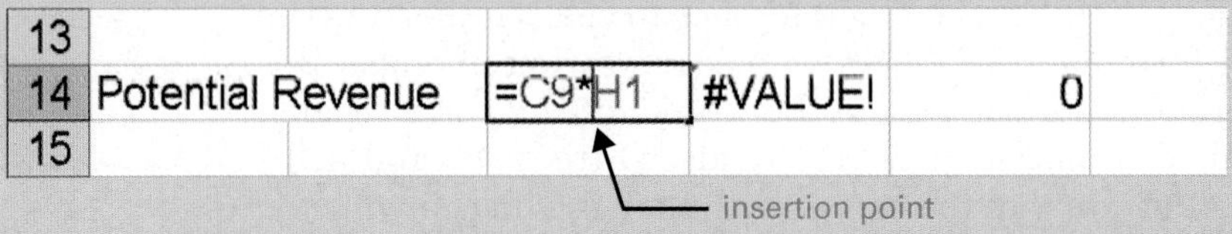

the **Range Finder** feature, it helps you locate cells that the formula references. A cell upon which a formula depends is called a **precedent cell**

3. Ensure that the cell insertion point is to the right of the multiplication operator and next to or within the cell reference H1 by clicking the mouse or using the keyboard arrow keys (see Figure 2.21)

13					
14	Potential Revenue	=C9*H1	#VALUE!	0	
15					

— insertion point

4. Press the **F4** function key three times to change the cell reference to $H1

tip: *If you press F4 too few or too many times, continue pressing it slowly until the desired reference, $H1, appears*

5. Press **Enter** to complete the formula alteration

Now you can recopy the corrected January recycling revenue cell to cells D14 and E14, corresponding to February and March.

Copying January's corrected revenue formula using copy and paste:

1. Click cell **C14** to make it the active cell
2. Press **Ctrl+C** to copy the selected cell's contents to the Clipboard
3. Click and drag the cell range **D14:E14** and then release the mouse
4. Press **Ctrl+V** to paste the formula into the target cell range, cells D14 through E14
5. Press **Escape** to empty the Clipboard and remove the outline from cell C14
6. Click any cell to deselect the cell range. Figure 2.22 displays the corrected revenue results

MOVING TEXT, VALUES, AND FORMULAS

When you modify a worksheet, you may want to rearrange some blocks of cells containing text, values, or formulas so that they appear in other locations. For example, you might decide that key values should be grouped together so that they appear in the top of the worksheet. Whatever the reason, you can move information from place to place with little effort. When

	A	B	C	D	E	F	G	H	I
1	Aluminum Can Recycling Contest							0.02	per can
2									
3	City	Population	Jan	Feb	Mar	Total	Per Capita		
4	Arcata	15855	10505	24556	12567	47628	3.003974		
5	Los Gatos	28951	24567	21777	26719	73063	2.523678		
6	Pasadena	142547	102376	105876	121987	330239	2.316703		
7	San Diego	2801561	2714664	2503344	1999877	7217885	2.57638		
8	Sunnyvale	1689908	1523665	1487660	1002545	4013870	2.3752		
9	Total		4375777	4143213	3163695	11682685			
10	Minimum		10505	21777	12567				
11	Average		875155.4	828642.6	632739				
12	Maximum		2714664	2503344	1999877				
13									
14	Potential Revenue		87515.54	82864.26	63273.9				
15									

corrected revenue cells

FIGURE 2.22

Worksheet with corrected revenue formulas

you move one or more cells, both the contents and the formatting move to the new location. Unlike copying cells, moving cells involves taking a cell's contents and formatting away from its current location and placing them in a new location.

Formulas are not changed when they are moved. Of course, moving text or labels does not change their value either. For example, suppose you moved the formula stored in cell C14 to compute potential revenue for January, =C9*$H1, to cell C2. After the move operation, cell C14 would be empty and the formula =C9*$H1 would occupy cell C2. In other words, Excel does not adjust cell references in the formula that moves. However, all cells that referenced a moved formula are adjusted. For example, if you were to move cell H1 containing the value of a single can to H5, any formulas that referenced cell H1 are adjusted to reference cell H5 automatically. That is, moving a cell's contents causes all dependent cells to adjust their references to the new location of the moved formula.

There are several ways to move cell contents from one cell to another. You can use the mouse to drag and drop the contents of a cell or block of cells, you can cut and paste one or more cells, or you can insert or delete rows or columns in a worksheet and thus change a cell's position. (How to insert and delete rows or columns is described in the next session.)

task reference

Moving Cells' Contents

- Select the cell or cell range that you want to move

- Move the mouse pointer to an edge of the selected range

- When the mouse pointer changes to an arrow, click the edge of the selected cell or cell range and drag the outline to the destination location

- Release the mouse

Kelly would like you to move the four labels in cells A9 through A12 to the right so that they are closer to the values they identify.

FIGURE 2.23

Moving cells' contents

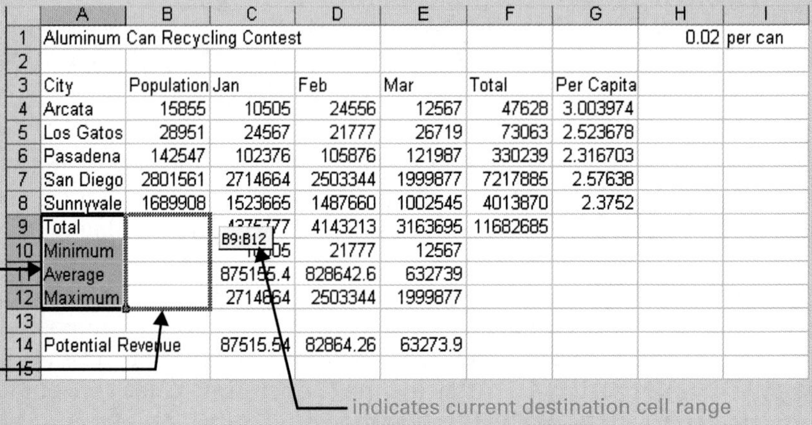

> ### Moving four labels:
>
> 1. Click and drag the mouse through the cell range **A9:A12**
>
> 2. Release the mouse
>
> 3. Move the mouse pointer toward an edge of the selected cell range until the mouse pointer changes from a large plus sign to a four-headed arrow.
>
> 4. Click any edge of the selected cells and drag the outline to the right so that it surrounds cells B9 through B12 (see Figure 2.23)

	A	B	C	D	E	F	G	H	I
1	Aluminum Can Recycling Contest							0.02	per can
2									
3	City	Population	Jan	Feb	Mar	Total	Per Capita		
4	Arcata	15855	10505	24556	12567	47628	3.003974		
5	Los Gatos	28951	24567	21777	26719	73063	2.523678		
6	Pasadena	142547	102376	105876	121987	330239	2.316703		
7	San Diego	2801561	2714664	2503344	1999877	7217885	2.57638		
8	Sunnyvale	1689908	1523665	1487660	1002545	4013870	2.3752		
9	Total		4275777	4143213	3163695	11682685			
10	Minimum		10505	21777	12567				
11	Average		875195.4	828642.6	632739				
12	Maximum		2714664	2503344	1999877				
13									
14	Potential Revenue		87515.54	82864.26	63273.9				
15									

selected cells being moved

outline indicates cell block destination

B9:B12 — indicates current destination cell range

> 5. Release the mouse. Excel moves the cells to their new target location
>
> 6. Click any cell to deselect the cell range

another**way**

. . . to move cells' contents

Drag the mouse across the source cell or cell range you want to move

Click the **Cut** command in the Edit menu

Drag the mouse across the target cell or cell range to which the contents will move

Click the **Paste** command in the Edit menu

Moving a cell's contents to another location is a cut action followed by a paste action. Cutting removes the cell's contents from its current location and places it on the Clipboard temporarily. Pasting moves the Clipboard contents to the new location. Of course, you can move any block of cells in one operation, regardless of its size. If the destination cell or cell range already contains information, Excel issues a warning and asks you if it is okay to overwrite existing contents. Clicking OK approves overwriting cell contents, while clicking the Cancel button calls off the attempted move operation.

RENAMING A WORKSHEET

A handy way to add documentation to a worksheet is to name the sheet in a meaningful way to reflect its contents. Examine the leftmost sheet tab in the recycling workbook you created. Notice the sheet tab is labeled Sheet1, which is the name Excel automatically assigns to the first sheet in a workbook. If your workbook has other worksheets, they are named Sheet2, Sheet3, and so on. (The number of worksheets Excel creates when creating a new workbook depends on how Excel is set up on your computer.) Because your worksheet is nearly complete, you will give it a name that reflects its contents.

Renaming a worksheet:

1. Double-click the **Sheet1** sheet tab to select it

2. Type **Recycling Contest** to replace the current name, Sheet1

3. Press Enter to complete the worksheet renaming operation. The sheet tab displays the name "Recycling Contest"

SPELL-CHECKING A WORKSHEET

Excel contains a spell-check feature that helps you locate spelling mistakes and suggests corrections. Comparing words in Excel's dictionary to the words in your worksheet, Excel finds words that appear to be misspelled and suggests one or more corrections. You can choose to leave unchanged each word Excel locates, or you can select an alternative spelling. You should always spell-check your worksheet before presenting it to others. It is easy to overlook misspelled words in any document, and this is especially true for worksheets.

task reference

Spell-Checking a Worksheet

- Click cell **A1** to begin spell-checking from the top of a worksheet

- Click the **Spelling** command in the Tools menu or click the **Spelling** button on the Standard toolbar

- Choose to correct misspelled words that the spell-checker identifies

- Click **OK** to close the dialog box

Kelly knows that a lot of people will see the recycling contest worksheet. She wants to make sure that any misspellings in the worksheet are corrected. She asks you to check the worksheet for spelling mistakes.

Checking a worksheet's spelling:

1. Click cell **A1** to begin-spell checking at the top of the worksheet

2. Click **Tools** on the menu bar and then click **Spelling** to start the spell-check operation

tip: *you can click the **Spelling** button on the Standard toolbar to check spelling*

3. Correct any misspellings. A message box opens when all spelling is correct

4. Click **OK** to close the message box

EXCEL

SAVING YOUR MODIFIED WORKBOOK

You have made many changes to your worksheet. It is time to save your work permanently on your disk so that you have a portable copy and to preserve it for future use.

> ### Saving your worksheet under its current name:
>
> 1. Click **File**
> 2. Click **Save.** Excel saves the worksheet to your disk

SESSION 2.1

making the grade

1. Explain how AutoSum works and what it does.

2. Suppose you select cell A14 and type D5+F5. What is stored in cell A14: text, a value, or a formula?

3. You can drag the _____, which is a small black square in the lower-right corner of the active cell, to copy the cell's contents.

4. Evaluation of a formula such as =D4+D5*D6 is governed by order of precedence. Explain what that means in general and then indicate the order in which Excel calculates the preceding expression.

5. Suppose Excel did not provide an AVERAGE function. Show an alternative way to compute the average of cell range A1:B25 using the other Excel statistical functions.

SESSION 2.2 FORMATTING CELLS, PRINT SETUP, AND PRINTING

In this session, you will complete the worksheet by formatting it to apply a more professional look, increase the width of a column to accommodate longer text entries, insert rows and columns to provide visual boundaries between worksheet sections, undo worksheet changes, and format groups of cells with Excel's AutoFormat command. You will explore how to establish worksheet headers and footers, set page margins, establish a worksheet's print area, and add cell-level documentation and worksheet-wide documentation.

STRESS TESTING A WORKSHEET

Using an electronic worksheet to produce results sometimes gives the worksheet designer a sense that the formulas and results are correct because the product is, after all, an electronic worksheet. Therefore, the results must be correct. This is not always the case, and mistakes can creep in and linger, undetected, for days or months if you don't examine the results carefully and test the worksheet to prove its validity. Testing need not be a long or complicated procedure. You can choose from several test methods to validate the worksheet's formulas and results.

One way to test a worksheet is to enter valid, small numbers in the input cells and observe the formulas' computed results. For example, you can enter 10 into each city's recycling cells for all three months and then change each city's population to 10. If your worksheets' formulas are correct the recycling per capita will be 3 across all cities—a result you know is correct—and the three-month totals display 30 for all cities. Similarly, the recycling statistical values will all be the same—the minimum, average, and maximum should display 10.

Entering extreme or limit values into a worksheet's non-formula cells is another way to test your worksheet's formulas. For example, if you enter zero into the recycling cells for all cities and all months, then all formulas—totals, per capita recycling, and statistics by month—should all display zero.

Finally, you can try out a few test calculations with your calculator and compare the results with the same values in your worksheet. If the results jibe, your worksheet formulas are correct.

MODIFYING A WORKSHEET'S APPEARANCE

After testing the worksheet, you and Kelly are satisfied that the worksheet is correct. However, Kelly wants to modify the worksheet so that it looks more professional. Cosmetic changes to a worksheet—changes that make the text and numbers *appear* different—occur when you ***format*** a worksheet. While formatting changes the appearance of the results displayed by text, values, and formulas, formatting never changes a cell's contents.

Kelly has identified a few formatting changes that will render the worksheet more professional and easy to read. She wants you to widen the column containing city names so that they have a bit more space between them and the population column to the right. Additionally, she wants you to insert two rows above the Aluminum Can Recycling Contest title and to insert a blank row between the recycling total row and the row containing the Minimum recycling values for each month. She also asks you to insert a blank row between the Maximum values row and the Potential Revenue row, to make the recycling statistics values display their values with commas and no decimal places, and to display the potential revenue values with currency symbols and commas. Finally, Kelly wants you to move the revenue per can value and its label to cells A1 and B1 so that what-if assumption value is near the top of the worksheet.

Inserting and Deleting Rows

You cannot always anticipate where you will need more columns or rows in order to make room for omitted cells or to add a blank row for aesthetic reasons. Fortunately, Excel allows you to add rows or columns at any point and accommodates existing work by moving existing rows to accommodate inserted or deleted rows. Likewise, if you insert or delete columns, Excel automatically moves columns to accommodate them. Inserting rows or columns follows the same procedure: You select the number of rows or columns you want to insert and then click the Insert command. After Excel repositions existing rows or columns to accommodate the insertion operation, it adjusts all cell references in formulas to reflect the new locations of cells referenced by the formulas.

Kelly wants you to insert two rows above the worksheet title currently in row 1.

task reference

Inserting Rows

- Click any cell above which you want to insert a row or select a range of cells in several rows above which you want to insert several rows

- Click **Insert** and then click **Rows.** Excel inserts one row for each row you selected

Inserting Columns

- Click one or more cells in columns to the left of which you want to insert one or more new columns

- Click **Insert** and then click **Columns.** Excel inserts as many new columns as there are in the range you selected

Inserting rows into a worksheet:

1. Click cell **A1** and drag the mouse through cell **A2** to indicate the row above which you want Excel to insert two additional rows

2. Click **Insert** on the menu bar and then click **Rows.** Excel inserts two rows at the top of the worksheet and moves existing rows down

3. Click cell **A11** to prepare to insert a blank row between the Total row, containing monthly recycling totals, and the Minimum row

4. Click **Insert** and then click **Rows.** Excel inserts the new row 11 (see Figure 2.24)

FIGURE 2.24

Inserting three new rows into a worksheet

click the Undo button to cancel last operation

row inserted in the wrong location

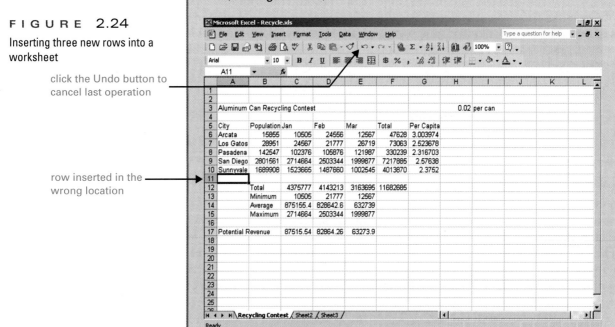

Correcting Mistakes with Edit Undo

The last row you inserted is not where you want it to be. To correct that error, you can delete the newly inserted row or you can click the Undo button to cancel the last operation. You can click the row label to the left of column A to select the entire row. Then, click Delete in the Edit menu to delete the row. You will find the Undo method helpful in so many other situations that you decide to use it to cancel the insert row action. Whenever possible, use the Undo method immediately after you realize that you want to reverse one or more actions.

Canceling the previous row insertion action:

1. Click the **Undo** 🔄 button on the Standard toolbar (see Figure 2.24). Excel deletes the row you previously inserted

---

Now you are ready to insert a new row in the correct position—between the Total and Minimum rows.

Inserting a row into a worksheet:

1. Click cell **A12** to prepare to insert a blank row between the Total row, containing monthly recycling totals, and the Minimum row

2. Click **Insert** and then click **Rows**. Excel inserts the new row—row 12—and moves all other rows below it down one row

---

Because it is convenient to place cells in a convenient location when they are used in what-if analysis, you move the recycling value per can assumption and its label to cells A1 and A2. That way, anyone who wants to see the effect of changing the value per can to three cents can locate the cell quickly and change it easily.

Moving cells to another location in a worksheet:

1. With the mouse, select the cell range **H3:I3,** which contains the value and label you want to move

2. Hover the mouse over cell **H3** and slowly move the mouse toward one of the selected cell range's edges until the mouse pointer changes to a four-headed arrow

3. Click the mouse button and hold it down as you drag the outline to cells **A1** through **B1** (see Figure 2.25)

4. Release the mouse button to complete the move operation. The value *0.02* and label *per can* now occupy cells A1 and B1, respectively

---

EXCEL

FIGURE 2.25
Moving cells' contents

drop cell range
address displayed

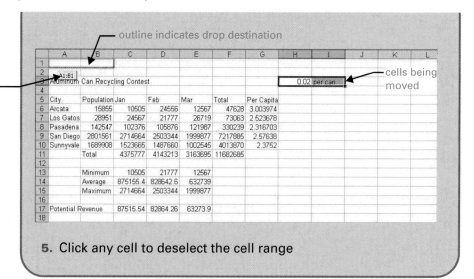

5. Click any cell to deselect the cell range

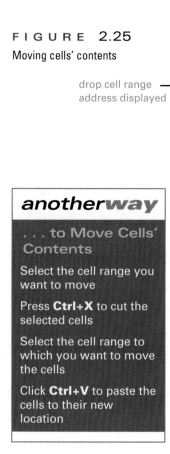

anotherway

**. . . to Move Cells'
Contents**

Select the cell range you
want to move

Press **Ctrl+X** to cut the
selected cells

Select the cell range to
which you want to move
the cells

Click **Ctrl+V** to paste the
cells to their new
location

Using AutoFormat

Excel's AutoFormat feature provides you with a wide selection of predefined formats from which you can select to alter the appearance of your
worksheet. Each of the AutoFormat selections in the portfolio of formats
includes a variety of formatting selections including color, fonts, shading,
and lines. AutoFormat automatically adjusts column widths and heights
and selects cell alignment characteristics that yield the most attractive
presentation. Formatting changes to your worksheet such as those
AutoFormat supplies should be one of the last operations you apply to
your worksheet. If you format cells or cell ranges with AutoFormat or do
so manually before you have built a complete worksheet, you frequently
have to reapply formatting to accommodate larger than expected numeric
values requiring cell width or font size adjustments.

task reference

Applying AutoFormat to Cells

- Click the cell range you want to format

- Click **Format** and then click **AutoFormat**

- Select the format style from the portfolio of styles in the Table Format
  list

- Click **OK** to select and apply the format you choose

Experiment with AutoFormat by formatting rows 3 through 11 of the
recycling worksheet.

Formatting cells with AutoFormat:

1. Select the cell range **A3** through **G11**

2. Click **Format** on the menu bar and then click **AutoFormat.**
   The AutoFormat dialog box opens and displays the first of

several AutoFormat styles (see Figure 2.26). A dark outline appears around the Simple format, because it is the currently selected format

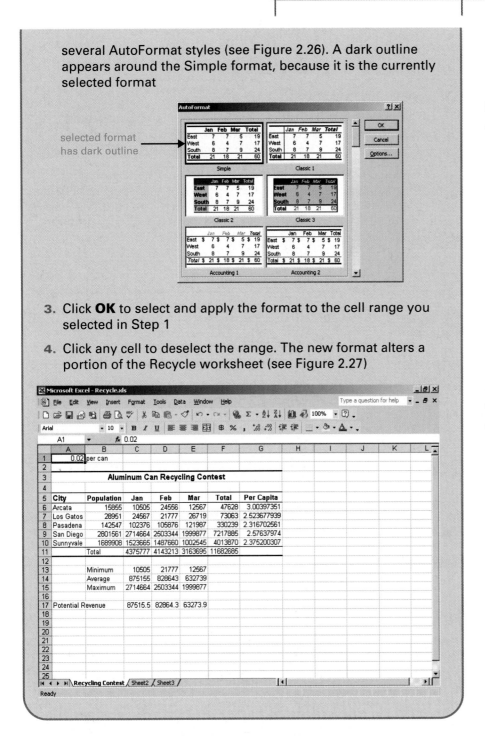

FIGURE 2.26
AutoFormat dialog box

3. Click **OK** to select and apply the format to the cell range you selected in Step 1

4. Click any cell to deselect the range. The new format alters a portion of the Recycle worksheet (see Figure 2.27)

FIGURE 2.27
Worksheet after applying AutoFormat

Formatting Cells Manually

Kelly reviewed your work so far and is pleased. She would like the numeric values to contain commas to make their values easier to read. Kelly would also like you to format the Per Capita column so that the values all contain two decimal places. The Per Capita values are also difficult to read because the decimal points aren't aligned. Finally, Kelly wants the Potential Revenue row values to include currency symbols so that worksheet viewers clearly understand the row contains revenue and not recycling units. You begin by formatting a portion of the worksheet so that numeric values include commas and no decimal places—whole numbers.

Formatting numeric entries to display commas and no decimal places:

1. Select the cell range **B6** through **F15**

2. Click the **Comma Style** ⊡ button on the Formatting toolbar. Several cell entries display ######, which indicates the formatted value is too wide to display the entire value

3. Click the **Decrease Decimal** ⊡ button *twice* (located on the Formatting toolbar) to reduce the number of displayed decimal places to zero. Several cells display values with commas, but some still display the pound sign (#). You will fix that problem soon. Ignore it for now

4. Click any cell to deselect the range

Next, reduce the number of decimal places displayed in the Per Capita column to two.

Formatting numeric entries to display commas and two decimal places:

1. Select the cell range **G6** through **G11**

2. Click the **Comma Style** button on the Formatting toolbar. All values in the Per Capita column display numbers rounded to two decimal places

3. Click any cell to deselect the range

Finally, format the Potential Revenue column so that the currency symbol, $, displays and reduce the number of decimal places to zero.

Formatting numeric entries to display the currency symbol and no decimal places:

1. Select the cell range **C17** through **E17,** which displays the potential revenue for January through March

2. Click the **Currency Style** ⊡ button on the Formatting toolbar

3. Click the **Decrease Decimal** ⊡ button *twice* (see Figure 2.28). The revenue values display a series of # symbols, indicating the column is too narrow to display the value

---

Though it is not yet apparent, the revenue values you just formatted will display dollar signs and no decimal places. To see the several values in cells that are currently displaying pound signs, you will have to widen the columns to accommodate their increased width. You do that next.

	A	B	C	D	E	F	G	H	I	J	K
1	0.02	per can									
2											
3			Aluminum Can Recycling Contest								
4											
5	City	Population	Jan	Feb	Mar	Total	Per Capita				
6	Arcata	15,855	10,505	24,556	12,567	47,628	3.00				
7	Los Gatos	28,951	24,567	21,777	26,719	73,063	2.52				
8	Pasadena	142,547	#####	#####	#####	330,239	2.32				
9	San Diego	2,801,561	#####	#####	#####	#######	2.58				
10	Sunnyvale	1,689,908	#####	#####	#####	########	2.38				
11		Total	#####	#####	#####	#######					
12											
13		Minimum	10,505	21,777	12,567						
14		Average	#####	#####	#####						
15		Maximum	#####	#####	#####						
16											
17	Potential Revenue		#####	#####	#######						
18											

FIGURE 2.28
Worksheet after applying numeric formats

the repeating symbol # indicates the cell is too narrow to display the results

Adjusting Column Width

One way to enhance the appearance of a worksheet is to widen columns. Widening a column to leave some vertical white space between it and its neighbor adds to the worksheet's readability. Several columns in the Recycling worksheet must be widened in order to view the values. The column containing city names is a little narrow also.

There are several ways to alter a column's width. You begin by clicking the column heading—the letter at the top of a column—or drag the pointer to select a series of contiguous columns and then use the Width command in the Format menu to select a width. Alternatively, you can move the mouse to the dividing line on the right side of any selected column header. When the pointer changes to a resize arrow (a double-headed arrow), you can drag the dividing line to the right to increase the column's width or drag it to the left to decrease the column's width. Moving the mouse pointer to the column heading dividing line, you can double-click the right-side dividing line to make the entire column as wide as the widest entry plus one character.

task reference

Modifying a Column's Width

- Select the column heading(s) of all columns whose width you want to change

- Click **Format**, point to **Column**, and click **Width**

- Enter the new column width in the **Column Width** text box and click **OK**, or click **AutoFit Selection** to make the column(s), optimal width as wide as the widest entry in the column

  or

- Double-click the right edge of the column heading line to make the column(s) optimal width(s) as wide as the longest entry in the column(s)

  or

- Drag the column heading dividing line of any one of the selected columns to the left to decrease the column width or to the right to increase the column width

EXCEL

Kelly wants you to increase the column widths of columns A through F to display the city names and values completely.

Increasing the width of column A:

1. Move the mouse pointer to the A column header and move it slowly to the right edge of the column heading dividing line. The pointer changes to a resize arrow ⬌

2. Click and drag the **column heading A dividing line** to the right until the pop-up ScreenTip indicates the width is 11 characters or more

3. Release the mouse button

Next, you will increase the width of columns B through F in one operation. You want the columns to be wide enough to accommodate the widest numeric value so that the repeated pound signs disappear and the computed recycling and statistical values appear in their place.

Optimizing the width of several columns at once:

1. Click **column heading B** and drag the mouse through **column heading F** and release the mouse. This selects the five columns whose width you want to alter

2. Move the mouse pointer to the heading dividing line between any two selected columns. The pointer changes to a resize arrow

3. Double-click the column heading dividing line to make the selected columns optimal width (see Figure 2.29)

FIGURE 2.29

Optimizing columns' widths

selected columns whose width is changed

	A	B	C	D	E	F	G	H	I	J
1	0.02	per can								
3				Aluminum Can Recycling Contest						
5	City	Population	Jan	Feb	Mar	Total	Per Capita			
6	Arcata	15,855	10,505	24,556	12,567	47,628	3.00			
7	Los Gatos	28,951	24,567	21,777	26,719	73,063	2.52			
8	Pasadena	142,547	102,376	105,876	121,987	330,239	2.32			
9	San Diego	2,801,561	2,714,664	2,503,344	1,999,877	7,217,885	2.58			
10	Sunnyvale	1,689,908	1,523,665	1,487,660	1,002,545	4,013,870	2.38			
11		Total	4,375,777	4,143,213	3,163,695	11,682,685				
13		Minimum	10,505	21,777	12,567					
14		Average	875,155	828,643	632,739					
15		Maximum	2,714,664	2,503,344	1,999,877					
17	Potential Revenue		$ 87,516	$ 82,864	$ 63,274					

4. Click any cell to deselect the columns. Notice that all the computed results display in the worksheet. The Potential Revenue row values contain commas and currency symbols, just as Kelly wanted

You learned in Chapter 1 how important page headers and footers are in identifying printed output. Kelly wants you to add a header with the title "Aluminum Can Recycling Contest Results" centered on the page. In addition, she wants the worksheet footer to contain your first and last names to identify the worksheet's author.

Creating a worksheet header and footer:

1. Click **View** on the menu bar and then click **Header and Footer**

2. Click **Custom Header,** click in the **Center section,** type **Aluminum Can Recycling Contest Results**, and click **OK**

3. Click **Custom Footer,** click in the **Center section,** type your first and last names, and click **OK**

4. Click the **Print Preview** [icon] button on the Standard toolbar to preview the worksheet complete with the new header and footer

5. After you have examined the output to ensure that it looks as you expected, click the **Close** button to close the Preview window and return to the worksheet window

---

The output looks great. Save the worksheet and then print it so that Kelly can scan the worksheet before you make it available to the public.

Printing a worksheet:

1. Click **File** on the menu bar

2. Click **Print**

3. Click **OK** to print the worksheet

ADJUSTING PAGE SETTINGS

You give the worksheet printout to Kelly so that she can comment on it. She is pleased with your work and suggests that you change the left margin to 1.5 inches and set the top, bottom, and right margins to one inch. She wants another printout that contains only rows 3 through 11 of the worksheet.

Setting the Print Area

Unless you specify otherwise, Excel prints the entire worksheet, including any incidental or scratch areas of the worksheet you may have used. Many times, you want to print just a selected part of a worksheet. To restrict the print output to part of a worksheet, you select the area to be printed and then execute the Excel Set Print Area command to tell Excel the print range.

Setting a worksheet's print area:

1. Drag the mouse pointer through the cell range **A3:G11** to select it

2. Click **File,** point to **Print Area**, and then click **Set Print Area**

3. Click **File,** and then click **Print Preview** to examine the output prior to printing it. Notice that the statistics do not appear in the output. Neither does the value per can assumption cell in row 1 of the worksheet

4. Click **Close** to return to the worksheet, and click any cell to deselect the area

---

To print the entire worksheet after you have set the print area, you must remove the print area before printing the worksheet. A worksheet's print area is stored with the worksheet, so Excel remembers if a print area is set or not. Remove the print area by clicking **File**, point to **Print Area,** and click **Clear Print Area**. Once you remove the print area, the entire worksheet will print.

Setting Print Margins

Print margins define the area of a printed page in which a worksheet appears. The left, right, top, and bottom margins define the area. The *left margin* defines the size of the white space between a page's left edge and the leftmost edge of the print area. Similarly, the *right margin* defines the white space between the print area's rightmost position and the right edge of a printed page. Header information appears within the *top margin,* which is the area between the top of the page and topmost edge of the print area. The *bottom margin* is the area at the bottom of the page between the bottommost portion of the print area and the bottom edge of the page. A worksheet's page footer, if any, appears in the bottom margin.

You can set each worksheet's page margins independently using several techniques. Set the margins by executing the Page Setup command in the File menu and clicking the Margins tab. Alternatively, you can click the Margins button in the Print Preview window and move any margin by dragging the dashed line representing each margin.

Setting a worksheet's print margins:

1. Click **File** on the menu bar

2. Click the **Page Setup** command. The Page Setup dialog box opens

3. Click the **Margins** tab

4. Type **1.5** in the Left spin control box. This sets the left margin to 1½ inches

5. Type **1** in the Top, Right, and Bottom spin control boxes (see Figure 2.30). This sets the margins to 1 inch

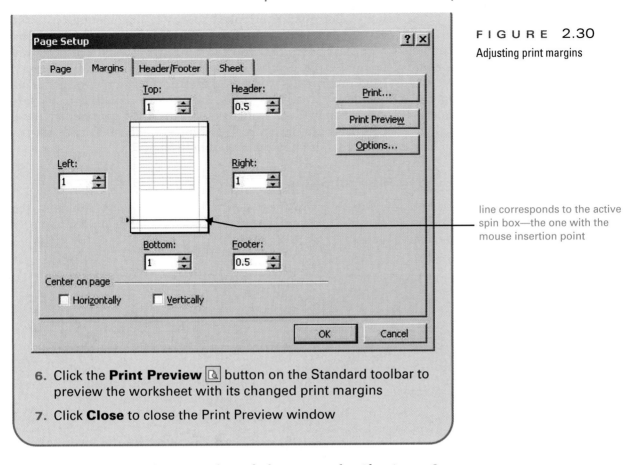

FIGURE 2.30
Adjusting print margins

line corresponds to the active
spin box—the one with the
mouse insertion point

6. Click the **Print Preview** button on the Standard toolbar to preview the worksheet with its changed print margins

7. Click **Close** to close the Print Preview window

You have made a large number of changes to the Aluminum Can Recycling Contest worksheet since you last saved it. It is time to save your work so that you preserve all the changes.

Saving your worksheet:

1. Click **File** on the menu bar

2. Click **Save**

DOCUMENTING THE WORKBOOK

It is always smart to document your work so that the next person assigned to modify or extend your work can easily and quickly understand the purpose and use of your worksheet. Besides external documentation such as printouts of worksheet formulas and your own notes, you can create internal documentation. As you recall, the first page of a workbook can contain extensive documentation including the author's name, the dates of major changes to the worksheet, and instructions on how to input data and use the worksheet. Small simple worksheets such as the Recycling worksheet require simple instructions. Larger more complex worksheets require more extensive instructions including which cells comprise the input area, which cells contain formulas whose results depend on the input area(s), and which workbook worksheets contain additional information or instructions.

EXCEL

One valuable but often overlooked source of documentation is the Properties dialog box found on the File menu. The ***Properties dialog box*** contains several text boxes that you can fill in with helpful information including the fields Title, Subject, Author, Manager, Company, Category, Keywords, and Comments. A workbook's creator can enter his or her name in the Author field. Another way to document a workbook is to include internal notes on individual worksheet cells. Called ***comments,*** these worksheet cell notes are particularly helpful to indicate special instructions about the contents or formatting of individual cells.

Setting File Properties

Kelly wants you to fill in the Title, Author, and Manager fields of the Property dialog box to record within the worksheet these important pieces of documentation.

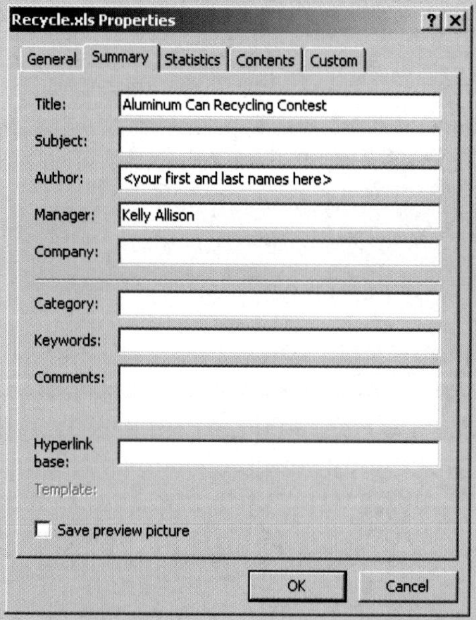

FIGURE 2.31

Completed Properties dialog box

> ## *Documenting a worksheet using the Properties dialog box:*
>
> 1. Click **File** on the menu bar, click **Properties,** and click the **Summary** tab, if necessary
>
> 2. In the Title text box, type **Aluminum Can Recycling Contest** and then press the **Tab** key twice to move to the Author text box
>
> 3. Type your first and last names in the Author text box and then press the **Tab** key
>
> 4. In the Manager text box, type **Kelly Allison** (see Figure 2.31)
>
>
> 5. Click **OK** to close the Properties dialog box

Adding Cell Comments

Kelly also wants you to place a note in cell A1 indicating that the two-cent per can recycling value is approximate. This will help others who use the worksheet in the future to understand that the value is a variable that anyone can change to observe changes in potential revenue from recycling. In cell B5, Kelly wants you to place a comment indicating the source of the population numbers—the World Wide Web.

Cell comments are analogous to sticky notes on which you can write reminders and attach to paper. Like sticky notes, cell comments can remind a worksheet developer or user about special conditions attached to a worksheet or cell, explain any restrictions on user input values, or provide an outline of the steps required to complete an unfinished worksheet.

---

task reference

Inserting a comment

- Click the cell to which you want to add a comment
- Click **Insert** and then click **Comment** to display the comment text box
- Type the comment
- Click any other cell to close and store the comment

Create the cell comment that Kelly asked you to insert in cells A1 and B5.

Insert comment in cells:

1. Click cell **A1** to make it the active cell

2. Click **Insert** and then click the **Comment** command. The comment text box opens

3. If the comment text box contains text, such as a user or computer name, delete the text.

4. Type **Kelly Allison:** (type a space after the colon)

5. Continue by typing the text **Per can value is an approximation. Change it for revenue what-if analysis.** (Be sure to include a period to end the comment's second sentence)

6. Click cell **B5,** click **Insert,** and click **Comment**

7. Repeat steps 3 and 4

8. Type **Population figures obtained from the World Wide Web.** and click any cell besides cell B5 to complete the comment and close the text box

9. View the hidden comment by hovering the mouse pointer over cell **A1.** The Comment text box pops up (see Figure 2.32)

10. Hover the mouse pointer over cell **B5** to view that cell's comment

FIGURE 2.32

Viewing a cell comment

red triangle indicates cell
contains a comment

comment text box

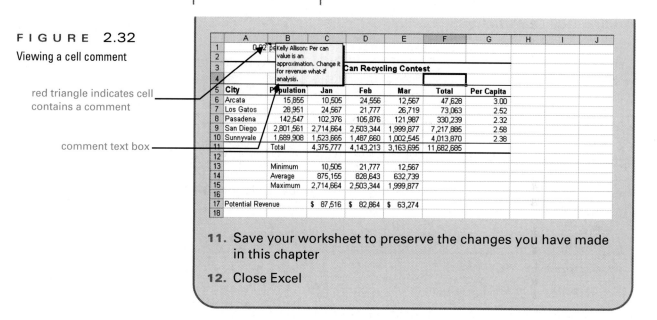

	A	B	C	D	E	F	G	H	I	J
1	0.02	Kelly Allison: Per can								
2		value is an								
3		approximation. Change it		an Recycling Contest						
4		for revenue what-if analysis.								
5	City	Population	Jan	Feb	Mar	Total	Per Capita			
6	Arcata	15,855	10,505	24,556	12,567	47,628	3.00			
7	Los Gatos	28,951	24,567	21,777	26,719	73,063	2.52			
8	Pasadena	142,547	102,376	105,876	121,987	330,239	2.32			
9	San Diego	2,801,561	2,714,664	2,503,344	1,999,877	7,217,885	2.58			
10	Sunnyvale	1,689,908	1,523,665	1,487,660	1,002,545	4,013,870	2.38			
11		Total	4,375,777	4,143,213	3,163,695	11,682,685				
12										
13		Minimum	10,505	21,777	12,567					
14		Average	875,155	828,643	632,739					
15		Maximum	2,714,664	2,503,344	1,999,877					
16										
17	Potential Revenue		$ 87,516	$ 82,864	$ 63,274					
18										

11. Save your worksheet to preserve the changes you have made in this chapter

12. Close Excel

To delete a comment, select the cell containing the comment you wish to delete. Then click Edit on the menu bar, point to Clear, and click Comments to delete the selected cell's comment.

SESSION 2.3 SUMMARY

Enter a value or text into an Excel cell by selecting the cell and typing the value or text. Excel formulas such as =D3−B4 begin with an equal sign to indicate the entry is not text. Excel provides AutoSum to automatically build a SUM function whose argument is an adjacent, contiguous row or column of values or expressions resulting in values. When necessary, you can adjust the AutoSum cell range suggested by Excel.

Excel provides standard mathematical operators of exponentiation, multiply, divide, add, and subtract. The mathematical operators conform to a precedence order that dictates which parts of an expression are evaluated before other parts. When you want to alter the order in which Excel evaluates expressions in a formula, you can use parentheses to group parts of the formula. For example, you use parentheses to cause Excel to evaluate the expression A1+B2 first in the formula =B17*(A1+B2) even though addition has lower precedence than multiplication.

Three other important statistical functions Excel provides are MIN, AVERAGE, and MAX. MIN determines the smallest value of its arguments. AVERAGE calculates the average value of its argument list. MAX displays the largest value in its list of arguments. Similar to other functions, these three statistical functions ignore empty cells or text cells in argument cell ranges. You can write arguments in the argument list in any order.

Most spreadsheet projects include formulas that are similar to one another. Take advantage of Excel's ability to quickly create formulas by copying a formula to other cells. When you copy a formula such as =SUM(A1:A4) to another cell, Excel creates a copy of that formula and *adjusts* all cell references to reflect the copied formula's new position. Cell adjustment is automatic when you use *relative* cell references. When you do not want Excel to adjust selected cell references in a copied formula, then you must use either *mixed* or *absolute* cell references. Moving a cell's contents to another location has no effect on the formula—all cell references remain unaltered.

making the grade

1. Briefly describe how you might test a worksheet to determine whether its formulas are correct.

2. If you make a mistake in entering a formula, you can reverse the operation by executing the _____ command on the _____ menu.

3. Which of the following is the correct formula to add cells B4 and A5 and multiply the sum by cell C2?
   a. =C2*B4+A5
   b. =B4+A5*C2
   c. =(B4+A5)*C2
   d. =B4+(A5*C2)
   e. none of the above is correct

4. Suppose cell A5 contains the formula =C1+D12 and you *move* that cell's contents to cell C6. After the move, what is the formula in cell C6?
   a. =E2+F3
   b. =C1+D2
   c. =B1+D12
   d. =none of the preceding

5. Modify the recycle worksheet, **Recycle.xls,** in the following ways. In cell **G11** write a formula that will compute the overall average per capita values stored in cells G6 through G10. Move the Total label in cell **B11** to cell **A11.** (You notice that moving a cell's contents removes the source cell's formatting. You will restore that in a moment.) Type a formula in B11 that will compute the total population of the five cities in the contest. Write a formula in cell **F17** to sum the potential revenue row. In **F16,** type **Total Revenue** to identify the summation of revenue. Clear the Print Area so that the entire worksheet prints. Select the cell range **A3:G11** and reformat it with the AutoFormat Simple style. Click cell **A1** to deselect the cell range. Save the worksheet under the name **Recycle2.xls.** Print the worksheet and then print the worksheet formulas.

Insert additional rows or columns into a worksheet wherever needed. Select a cell above which you wish to insert additional rows or to the left of which you wish to insert additional columns and then execute the Insert Rows or Insert Columns command. Excel automatically adjusts all formulas affected by the Insert procedure to reflect the new location of referenced cells, regardless of whether the cell references are relative, mixed, or absolute. Deleting one or more rows or columns is equally simple. Select the row(s) or column(s) to delete and then execute the Edit menu Delete command. When you delete cells, Microsoft Excel removes them from the worksheet and shifts the surrounding cells to fill the space.

Formatting modifies the appearance of cells, but not their contents. AutoFormat provides a predefined set of formats you can apply to a cell range, or you can format cells individually with the Format menu. Correct any mistakes, including unwanted formatting, by executing the Undo command in the Edit menu. If pound signs (#) appear in a cell indicating a column is too narrow to display the formatted numeric value, widen the

EXCEL

column or columns by dragging the column heading dividing line located on the right side of the column's label.

Before printing a worksheet, preview your output. If necessary, adjust a worksheet's print margins by executing Page Setup in the File menu and clicking the Margins tab. Set a worksheet's Print Area to specify printing less than all the non-empty worksheet cells. Document a workbook by filling in the text boxes found in the Properties dialog box that you access from the File menu. In addition, you can use comments to attach internal notes to worksheet cells to explain any unusual circumstances or remind the worksheet user or developer about the content of selected cells.

MOUS OBJECTIVES SUMMARY

- Create formulas containing cell references and mathematical operators (MOUS Ex2002-5-1)
- Write functions including Sum, Average, Max, and Min (MOUS Ex2002-5-2)
- Differentiate between absolute, mixed, and relative cell reference (MOUS Ex2002-5-1)
- Adjust column widths (MOUS Ex2002-3-2)
- Set a print area (MOUS Ex2002-3-7)
- Move text, values, and formulas (MOUS Ex2002-1-1)
- Insert and delete rows and columns (MOUS Ex2002-3-2)
- Format cells (MOUS Ex2002-3-1)
- Create cell comments (MOUS Ex2002-7-3)

task reference roundup

Task	Location	Preferred Method
Writing formulas	EX 2.9	• Select a cell, type **5**, type the formula, press **Enter**
Modifying an AutoSum cell range by pointing	EX 2.11	• Press an arrow key repeatedly to select leftmost or topmost cell in range, press and hold **Shift**, select cell range with arrow keys, release **Shift**, press **Enter**
Writing a function using the Paste Function button	EX 2.17	• Select a cell, click **Paste Function**, click a function category, click a function name, click **OK**, complete the Formula Palette dialog box, click **OK**
Copying and pasting a cell or range of cells	EX 2.21	• Select source cell(s), click **Edit**, click **Copy**, select target cell(s), click **Edit**, click **Paste**
Copying cell contents using a cell's fill handle	EX 2.23	• Select source cell(s), drag the fill handle to the source cell(s) range, release the mouse button
Changing relative references to absolute or mixed references	EX 2.27	• Double-click the cell, move insertion point to the cell reference, press **F4** repeatedly as needed, press **Enter**
Moving cells' contents	EX 2.29	• Select the cell(s), move the mouse pointer to an edge of the selected range, click the edge of the selected cell or cell range, drag the outline to the destination location, release the mouse
Spell-checking a worksheet	EX 2.31	• Click cell **A1**, click the **Spelling** button, correct any mistakes, click **OK**
Inserting rows	EX 2.34	• Click a cell, click **Insert**, click **Rows**
Inserting columns	EX 2.34	• Click a cell, click **Insert**, click **Columns**
Applying AutoFormat to cells	EX 2.36	• Select a cell range, click **Format**, click **AutoFormat**, select a format style, click **OK**
Modifying a column's width	EX 2.39	• Select the column heading(s), click **Format**, point to **Column**, click **Width**, type column width, and click **OK**
Inserting a comment	EX 2.45	• Click a cell, click **Insert**, click **Comment**, type a comment, and click another cell

EXCEL

CROSSWORD PUZZLE

Across

5. This list is enclosed in parentheses
7. A mathematical _____ that represents an arithmetic operation
9. General name for cells to which other cells are copied
11. This dialog box contains fields such as Title and Subject that you fill in to provide additional documentation

Down

1. Type of internal documentation, or note, attached to a cell
2. Rules governing the way you write Excel functions
3. A _____ cell is a cell upon which a formula depends
4. When you do this to cells, it changes their appearance but not their contents
6. General name for cells that are being copied
8. The _____ finder color codes cells referenced by the formula you are editing
10. This value occurs when you make a mistake writing a formula

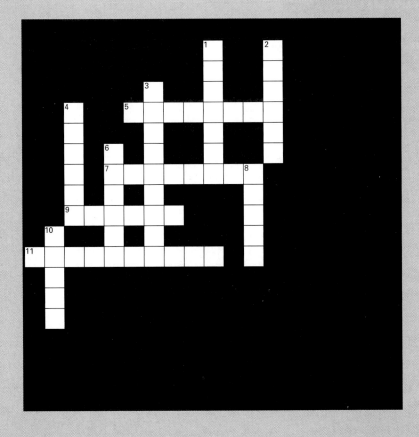

FILL-IN

1. The _____ function totals one or more cells.

2. While writing a formula, you can use a technique called _____ to select a cell range rather than using the keyboard to type the cell range.

3. _____ order determines the sequence in which Excel evaluates expressions containing addition, subtraction, multiplication, division, or exponentiation.

4. If you copy a formula such as =B4−C9, Excel does what to the copied formula's cell references?

5. There are three types of cell references: relative, _____, and _____.

6. The Standard toolbar _____ _____ button helps you write a function and fill in the arguments.

REVIEW QUESTIONS

1. Suppose cell D1 contains 0.14, the proposed salary percentage increase for next year, and cells B5 through B8 contain current salaries. Next year's increased salaries—computed from formulas—are in cells C5 through C8. All other cells are empty. You write the formula **=B5*(1+D1)** in cell C5 and then copy that formula to cells C6 through C8. Explain, briefly, what is wrong with the original formula in cell C5 and how you would correct it before recopying the formula.

2. If Excel did not have an AVERAGE function, how would you write an expression to compute the average of cells A5 through A10 using other Excel functions?

3. Describe in two or three sentences what Excel does to modify *copied* formulas.

4. Briefly describe what Excel does, if anything, to the contents of a formula that you *move* to another location. What happens, if anything, to formulas that refer to a moved cell?

5. Does formatting a cell alter its contents? Explain.

6. Experiment with Excel to answer this question. Describe what happens when you enlarge or narrow a column having an unformatted cell whose formula is =1/7?

CREATE THE QUESTION

For each of the following answers, create an appropriate, short question.

ANSWER	QUESTION
1. Builds a SUM function automatically	_____
2. Provides a variety of predefined formats	_____
3. Do this to view worksheet output before printing	_____
4. Set this to restrict the cells that Excel prints	_____
5. This command can reverse a mistake you made in the previous operation	_____
6. Dragging this object copies formulas to other cells	_____

1. Managing Employees' Work Hours

You are a project manager for Wexler's Tool and Die Manufacturing and manage a group of five people. Each employee in your group has a different hourly rate, and you must record on a weekly basis the number of hours each employee works, the total wages per employee, and percentage of the whole group's wages that each employee's weekly wage represents. Keeping the information on a worksheet is the most efficient way to record and report employee activity. Alan Gin, the company's Chief Operating Officer, wants you to prepare an Excel worksheet to report your group's weekly hours and gross wages. You create a worksheet to track the hours and wages.

1. Open the workbook **ex02Wages.xls** and save it as **Wages2.xls**
2. Review the Documentation sheet and then click the **Sheet2** tab to move to that worksheet
3. Widen column A so that all the employees' names are entirely visible
4. Insert two new rows above row 1: Click cell **C1,** drag through cell **C2,** and release the mouse. Click **Insert** on the Menu bar and then click **Rows**
5. Click cell **A1** to deselect the range and type **Employee**
6. Click cell **B1,** type **Rate,** click cell **C1,** type **Hours,** click cell **D1,** type **Wages,** click cell **E1,** and type **Percentage**
7. Type the following employee hours in the corresponding cells:
    Cell B3: **25**
    Cell B4: **40**
    Cell B5: **30**
    Cell B6: **20**
    Cell B7: **35**
8. Click cell **D3,** type **=B3*C3,** the formula to compute Bushyeager's wage, and press **Enter**
9. Copy Bushyeager's wage formula to the cell range **D4:D7**
10. Click cell **B8** and type **Totals**
11. Select cell range **C8:D8** and click the **AutoSum** Σ · button

12. Click cell **E3** and type the formula that represents the employee's percentage of the total wages: **=D3/D$8*100**
13. Copy the formula in cell E3 to the cell range **E4:E7**
14. Select cell range **A1:E8,** click **Format,** click **AutoFormat,** select the **Simple** format, and click **OK**
15. Select cell range **E3:E7** and click the **Decrease Decimal** button enough times to reduce the displayed percentages to two decimal places
16. Click cell **A10** and type your first and last names
17. Set the left, right, top, and bottom margins to two inches
18. Either execute **Print** or execute **Save As,** according to your instructor's direction

2. Creating an Invoice

As office manager of Randy's Foreign Cars, one of your duties is to produce and mail invoices to customers who have arranged to pay for their automobile repairs up to 30 days after mechanics perform the work. Randy's invoices include parts, sales tax on parts, and labor charges. State law stipulates that customers do not pay sales tax on the labor charges. Only parts are subject to state sales tax. State sales tax is 6 percent. Create and print an invoice whose details appear below.

1. Open the workbook **ex02Randys.xls** on your student disk in folder **Ch02**
2. Insert rows in which you can enter the customer's name and address: Click cell **A5,** drag the mouse down through cell **A8,** and release the mouse
3. Click **Insert** and then click **Rows**
4. Type the following in the indicated cells:
    cell A5: **Customer**:
    cell B5: **Craig Shaffer**
    cell B6: **21121 Bluff Place**
    cell B7: **Lincoln, NE**
5. Click cell **E11** and type the extended price (unit price times quantity) formula:
    =A11*D11

6. Select **E11** and drag its fill handle to copy the formula in E11 to cells **E12** through **E15**

7. Click cell **E17,** drag the mouse down to cell **E18,** release the mouse, click **Insert,** and then click **Rows**

8. Click cell **D17** and type **Subtotal.** Click cell **D18** and type **Tax.** Click Cell **D24** and type **Subtotal,** and click cell **D26** and type **Total**

9. Widen column C by moving the mouse to the dividing line between columns C and D. When the mouse pointer changes to a resize arrow, double-click the mouse

10. Click cell **E17** and type **=SUM(E11:E15)**

11. Click cell **E18** and type **=E17*B1**

12. Click cell **E24** and type **=D21+D22**

13. Click Cell **D26** and type **=SUM(E17,E18,E24)**

tip: *Typing commas between the single-cell references allows you to sum cells that are not adjacent to one another*

14. Click cell **E11** and drag through cell **E26** to select the cell range

15. Click once the **Increase Decimal** button on the Formatting toolbar

16. Select cell range **A2:E26** and then click **File, Print Area, Set Print Area**

17. Click cell **D5**, type your first and last names, and save the worksheet as **Randys2.xls**

18. Either **Print** the worksheet or execute **Save As,** according to your instructor's direction

1. Building a Product Comparison Worksheet

Jacob's Fine Stationers carries different lines of fine pens. You have been asked to help them figure out the profits the store generates from pen sales. The information is as follows: The store has 20 Stylo pens in stock, which sell for $27 each and cost the store $8 each. There are 15 Royal pens in stock, which sell for $45 and cost the store $12. There are 50 Hans pens in the store, which sell for $78 and cost the store $50. There are 6 Tower pens in stock, which sell for $120 and cost the store $60.

Create a spreadsheet with the following column labels: **Pen, Quantity, Cost,** and **Price.** Enter the pen names Stylo, Royal, Hans, and Tower in the column headed by the label "Pen." Write formulas below the Quantity, Cost, and Price columns that indicate the minimum, average, and maximum values for Quantity, Cost, and Price. Create a column labeled **Profit per Pen.** Create a formula and copy it to fill in these cells with the difference between price and cost. Create a column labeled **Total Profits per Pen.** Fill the cells in this column with formulas that multiply profit per pen by quantity in stock for each pen. Add a formula below the last entry in the Total Profits per Pen to compute total profits for all pens, assuming all pens in stock sell.

Widen any columns as needed to view column-top labels. Insert two rows at the top of the worksheet and type your first and last names. Select all numeric cells and then click the Increase Decimal button enough times to display two decimal places for numbers. Print the worksheet.

Change a cell in the worksheet to answer this question: If the store decides not to sell any of their Royal pens, how will total profits be affected? (Type 0 in the Quantity cell for the Royal pen.) Add text to the worksheet indicating that this shows what happens to the total profits if Royal pens are not sold. Print the worksheet.

2. Writing a Payroll Worksheet

Bateman Leisure Properties wants you to create a payroll worksheet that provides management with an overview of the hourly workers' pay and taxes. Alicia Hernandez, the human resources manager, provides you with a preliminary worksheet containing employee names—there are quite a few—column labels, and some tax rate information. She asks you to complete the worksheet and save it under a new name when you are done. She would like you to document the tax rate cell and the overtime rate cell with short comments. In preparation for this exercise, open the workbook **ex02Payroll.xls** stored on your disk (see Figure 2.33).

Start by writing a formula for Patti Stonesifer's gross pay. Compute gross pay as regular pay plus overtime pay. Regular pay is the employee's pay for up to 40 hours and is computed as hourly rate times hours worked. Overtime pay is paid for overtime hours—any hours over 40. Compute overtime pay at an hourly rate that is 1.5 times the regular rate times the overtime hours. Be sure to reference cell C2 in the gross pay formula using a mixed cell reference form, C$2 instead of using the constant 1.5. When her gross pay formula is correct, copy it down through the remaining employees' gross pay cells.

In the Federal Tax column, write one formula and copy it to the other employees' rows. Federal tax is gross pay times the federal tax rate found in

FIGURE 2.33

Payroll worksheet

	A	B	C	D	E	F	G	H	I
1		Fed. Tax R	0.25						
2		Overtime r	1.5						
3				Hourly	Regular	Overtime	Gross	Federal	Net
4	ID	First Name	Last Name	Rate	Hours	Hours	Pay	Tax	Pay
5	1301	Patti	Stonesifer	23.10	40	13			
6	1364	Kevin	Pruski	17.00	22				
7	1528	Luca	Pacioli	19.70	40	8			
8	1695	Ted	Nagasaki	21.80	40				
9	2240	Sharon	Stonely	20.30	13				
10	2318	Helen	Hunter	19.50	40	18			
11	2754	Phillipe	Kahn	16.20	40	19			
12	3370	David	Kole	18.70	19				
13	3432	Melinda	English	24.70	40	16			
14	3436	William	Gates	22.50	14				
15	3458	Alanis	Morrison	25.00	26				
16	3609	Annie	Chang	16.40	17				
17	3692	Steve	Ballmer	18.20	40	11			
18	3700	Larry	Ellison	18.80	24				
19	3892	Brad	Shoensteir	18.60	30				
20	3943	Barbara	Watterson	24.30	40	12			
21	4012	Barbara	Minsky	23.10	40	15			
22	4029	Sharad	Manispour	16.60	32				
23	4057	Giles	Bateman	17.60	40	4			
24	4058	Whitney	Halstead	24.20	24				
25	4062	Hillary	Flintsteel	22.00	40	19			
26	4112	Ted	Goldman	23.90	13				

cell C1. Be sure to reference cell C1 using the mixed reference, C$1. Otherwise, you will not get the correct answer. Write a formula for net pay, remembering that net pay is gross pay minus federal tax (in this example). Copy the net pay formula to other employees' cells.

Next, widen columns B and C so that all names and tax rates are completely visible. Add a blank row between the column labels and the first employee row. Select the Federal Tax Rate value stored in cell C1 and type this comment: **This is a flat tax rate for experimentation.** Click the overtime rate cell and type the comment **Normal overtime rate is 1.5 times regular rate. Change this value to review overall changes to gross pay.** (If the comments remain visible after you press Enter, you can make them disappear by clicking **Tools** on the menu bar, clicking **Options,**

clicking the **View** tab, and clicking the **Comment indicator only** option button in the Comments section.) Select all cells in the Gross Pay, Federal Tax, and Net Pay columns displaying values, click the Decrease Decimals button once, and then click the Increase Decimal button once to display two decimal places for all selected cells.

Create a header in page setup, placing your name in the worksheet header (in the Center section), and then print the worksheet. Print the Gross Pay, Federal Tax, and Net Pay formulas for all employee rows. (Hint: Check the Formulas option on the View tab of the Options dialog box. Set the print area to include only the three columns containing formulas.). Save the worksheet under the name **Payroll2.xls.**

1. Selecting an Online Broker

Erik Engvall is trying to decide which online brokerage firm he should use for trading stocks. After some research, he came up with the following list of five online brokerages that are highly rated. The brokerages are Ameritrade, Charles Schwab & Co., Datek Online Brokerage Services, DLJ Direct, and Fidelity. Figure 2.34 shows the Web addresses of each of these online brokers. To help Eric, you will use the Web to look up how much each service charges for stock transactions. The annual fees vary and are sometimes difficult to find. Assume that the annual charges are as follows: Ameritrade—$49, Charles Schwab—$35, Datek—$20, DLJ Direct—$40, and Fidelity—$50. (The preceding fees are contrived costs—the listed online brokers have different annual fees or none at all.) Arrange this information in columns, with each brokerage firm in a separate row.

Label the columns the following way: **Company, Price per Trade,** and **Annual Fee.** In a cell, enter **4**, which is the number of brokerage transactions per month that Erik estimates he executes with a broker. (That number will be the what-if analysis value you can change to determine the overall cost differences between the brokers you have selected.) Write formulas to compute the minimum, average, and maximum charge per transaction and formulas to compute the minimum, average, and maximum annual fee. Create a column labeled **Total Cost per Month** and label another column to the right of the monthly cost column called **Total Yearly Cost.** Beneath the Total Cost per Month column, write a formula for each brokerage indicating the cost for four transactions (refer to a cell containing 4 that you created earlier). Write formulas for each brokerage row indicating the total annual cost, assuming Erik continues to execute four transactions per month for the year. Remember to add the annual fee.

You forgot to include another important brokerage, E*Trade. Insert a new row between DLJ Direct and Fidelity and enter **E*Trade** under the Company column. Complete the information in the E*Trade row including Price per Trade. Assume they do not charge an annual fee. Copy formulas from DLJ Direct to complete E*Trade's missing formulas.

Use the **Increase Decimal** button on the Formatting menu to cause all numeric entries to display two decimal places. Widen columns as necessary so all entries including brokerage names and column labels display completely. Place your name in your worksheet to identify it and then print the worksheet. Save your worksheet in the Ch02 folder as **Brokerage2.xls.** Based on this information, which online broker is the least expensive?

FIGURE 2.34

Brokerage Web addresses

Brokerage	Web Address
Ameritrade	www.ameritrade.com/
Charles Schwab	www.schwab.com/
Datek	www.datek.com/
DLJ Direct	www.dljdirect.com/
E*Trade	www.etrade.com/
Fidelity	www.fidelity.com/

e-business

1. Investigating E-Commerce Service Providers

Green Gardens is a one-stop gardening store located in Lincoln, Nebraska. They have been a successful brick-and-mortar store for over 22 years, but their owner, Orlando Madrigal, wants to create an online store that will complement their existing store. Because they do not have room nor the expertise to buy computing equipment and software to create an online store, Orlando wants to locate a commerce service provider (CSP) to host the store and provide a complete menu of online services. The CSP provides computer hardware, commerce software, and merchant account processing (to process credit cards). There are several hosting plans available, and each one offers the same basic service. Orlando wants you to find a least-cost provider.

Your investigation reveals that most CSPs charge a one-time setup fee when you sign up for their service, monthly store rental fee to pay for disk space, and transaction fees charged when a customer submits his or her credit card to pay for a purchase. You have found four representative CSPs and want to create a worksheet to compare your costs. Orlando estimates that the online store can sell approximately 10,000 items each month for the first year. Each sale, he estimates, will average $50. Armed with those sales assumptions, you build a worksheet to compare CSP costs.

Figure 2.35 shows the partially complete worksheet. You are to complete the sheet by filling in formulas for the estimated annual cost, the minimum annual cost, and the six statistics showing the minimum, average, and maximum setup fees and monthly rental fee.

Begin by opening the E-Commerce worksheet **ex02E-Merchant.xls** in the folder Ch02 on your student disk. Save the file under the name **E-Merchant2.xls**. Annual costs consist of the sum of the one-time setup fee (for the first year), 12 times the monthly rental fee, and the transaction costs. The transaction costs consist of a fixed per-transaction charge, shown in Column D of Figure 2.35, and a percentage charge for each transaction. For example, Yoddle charges 15 cents for each transaction plus 2.1 percent of the transaction value. In other words, Yoddle charges a transaction cost for selling one $10 garden implement of $0.15 + 0.021 * 10, or a total of $0.36. The four formulas for estimated annual cost should reference the monthly transactions value in cell B1 and the average transaction value, $50, in cell B2.

Print the worksheet and print the worksheet formulas. Based on Orlando's transaction volume and per-transaction value assumptions, which CSP is the least expensive? Which one is the most expensive?

FIGURE 2.35

E-Commerce hosting cost comparison

	A	B	C	D	E	F
1	Monthly Transactions:	10000				
2	Average Trans. Value: ($)	50				
3						Estimated
4		One-time	Monthly	Per-Transaction Costs		Annual
5	Host	Setup Fee	Rental Fee	Fixed ($)	Variable (%)	Cost
6	ClickEnsure	500	200	0	0.016	
7	HostWay	200	400	0.25	0.015	
8	ShopSmart	0	250	0.12	0.017	
9	Yoddle	125	100	0.15	0.021	
10						
11	Minimum				Minimum	
12	Average					
13	Maximum					

write formulas for estimated annual cost

write a formula for minimum annual cost

write statistical formulas for setup and monthly rental

1. Comparing Living Expenses Around the World

What does it cost to live for a month in a foreign country? You've been considering living in Europe or South America for a month next summer and want to know the total cost of living abroad. Costs include an apartment locator agency fee, one month's rental charges, the cost of food, utilities, transportation to the foreign country, and transportation costs within the country for the month. Using the Web, research the cost of renting a one-bedroom apartment in Florence (Italy), Paris, Buenos Aires, and Santiago. Include cell comments for each city indicating the source—Web URL or other reference—for your rental cost information. Document the workbook by entering information in the Properties dialog box. Print the worksheet.

running project

Pampered Paws

Besides providing pet sitting services, Pampered Paws has a complete line of pet products. Grace Jackson, the company founder and owner, wants to compare the profitability of five different dog food products she's interested in selling. There are several costs associated with purchasing dog food in bulk. A wholesaler, from which Grace purchases the dog food, charges a fixed order fee of $100, a one-time fee charged for each order any customer places with the wholesaler. Bags of dog food costs vary, depending on brand. Shipping costs $0.10 per pound, and the shipper charges $25 to deliver the product to the store. Figure 2.36 shows Pampered Paws' cost and the retail price Pampered Paws can charge for each of the five dog food products in 10-pound bags.

Create a worksheet showing the total cost of each of the products if Grace orders 50 bags of each of the five products. Compute the total profit Grace's store can realize if she sells 50 bags of each of the products. Remember to include the shipping and delivery charges in your calculations. Figure 2.37 displays one way you might organize your worksheet. Wherever the notation *xxxxx* appears in the worksheet, you should create a formula.

FIGURE 2.36
Dog food cost comparison

Brand	Wholesale cost per bag	Retail price per bag
Eukanuba	16.09	22.99
Iams	12.71	16.95
Nutro	12.67	19.49
Pro Plan	11.01	18.99
Vita Rx	13.93	16.99

FIGURE 2.37
Example dog food comparison

	A	B	C	D	E	F
1	Dog Food Cost Comparison					
2						
3	Assumptions:					
4	Order fee ($):	100				
5	Shipping/lb. ($)	0.1				
6	Delivery ($)	25				
7						
8	Purchase				Extended	Extended
9	Quantity (bags)	Brand	Cost	Price	Cost	Price
10	50	Eukanuba	16.09	22.99	xxx.x	xxx.x
11	50	Iams	12.71	16.95	xxx.x	xxx.x
12	50	Nutro	12.67	19.49	xxx.x	xxx.x
13	50	Pro Plan	11.01	18.99	xxx.x	xxx.x
14	50	Vita Rx	13.93	16.99	xxx.x	xxx.x
15				Subtotal	xxxx.x	xxxx.x
16						
17			Order fee	xxx		
18			Shipping	xx		
19			Delivery	xx		
20			Subtotal	xxx		
21						
22			Total	xxxx.x		xxxx.x
23						
24			Net Profit			xxxx

did you
know?

the *city in the United States that purchases the most ice cream on a per capita basis is Portland, Oregon.*

the *Great Lakes have a combined area of 94,230 square miles — larger than the states of New York, New Jersey, Connecticut, Rhode Island, Massachusetts, and Vermont combined.*

"However *fascinating it may be as scholarly achievement, there is virtually nothing that has come from molecular biology that can be of any value to human living."—Nobel Prize-winning immunologist Frank MacFarlane Burnett (1899–1985) whose work made organ transplantation possible.*

paul Saffo, *a director of the Institute for the Future, in February 1996 predicted the Web would mutate into "something else very quickly and be unrecognizable within 12 months."*

bricks *are the oldest manufactured building material still in use. Egyptians used them 7,000 years ago.*

you *can attach graphic objects to your worksheet. Read this chapter to find out how.*

Chapter Objectives

- Left-, center-, and right-align text (MOUS Ex2002-3)

- Apply currency and accounting formats to numbers (MOUS Ex2002-3-1)

- Modify the typeface and point size of text and numbers (MOUS Ex2002-3-1)

- Apply boldface, italic, and underline to cells (MOUS Ex2002-3-1)

- Clear all formatting from selected cells (MOUS Ex2002-3; Ex2002-1-2)

- Modify column widths and row heights (MOUS Ex2002-3-3)

- Hide and reveal rows and columns (MOUS Ex2002-3-2)

- Remove worksheet gridlines

- Modify a worksheet's print characteristics (MOUS Ex2002-3-7)

CHAPTER

3

three

Formatting a Worksheet

chapter case

The Exotic Fruit Company

The Exotic Fruit Company is a wholesale exotic fruits, nuts, and roots distributor headquartered in La Mesa, California. Exotic Fruit's customers include most of the large grocery store chains in the western United States. Corporate buyers for the grocery stores contract with Specialty Fruits to supply and ship exotic fruits to stores' warehouses scattered throughout the West. Exotic Fruit's chief procurement officer, Nancy Carroll, oversees the purchase and distribution operations for all divisions from her La Mesa office.

Exotic Fruit also maintains a small Web site from which it sells exotic fruit to consumers. While the online store is not a large part of their revenue stream, it is an essential and growing part of Exotic Fruit's business. Nancy has asked her financial analyst to quickly develop a sales forecast for the coming year of selected exotic fruits, using the previous year's figures as the basis of the projection. Nancy wants to investigate sales predictions based on the assumption that next year's wholesale sales will increase by approximately 10 percent for each product included in the projection.

Due to time constraints, her financial analyst, Angel Hernandez, did not have time to format the worksheet. Consequently, the worksheet looks unprofessional and, frankly, it is a little difficult to read and understand. While Nancy understands that Angel is stretched to the limit and has little time to format the projection, Nancy wants to improve the worksheet's appearance. She asks you to spend a little time formatting it so that the labels and numbers are easier to read and the entire worksheet is ready for presentation at the annual board meeting next month.

Figure 3.1 shows the completed Exotic Fruit Sales Forecast worksheet. You will be developing the worksheet in this chapter beginning with a fundamental worksheet that Nancy and Angel provide for you.

FIGURE 3.1

Exotic Fruit Sales Forecast worksheet

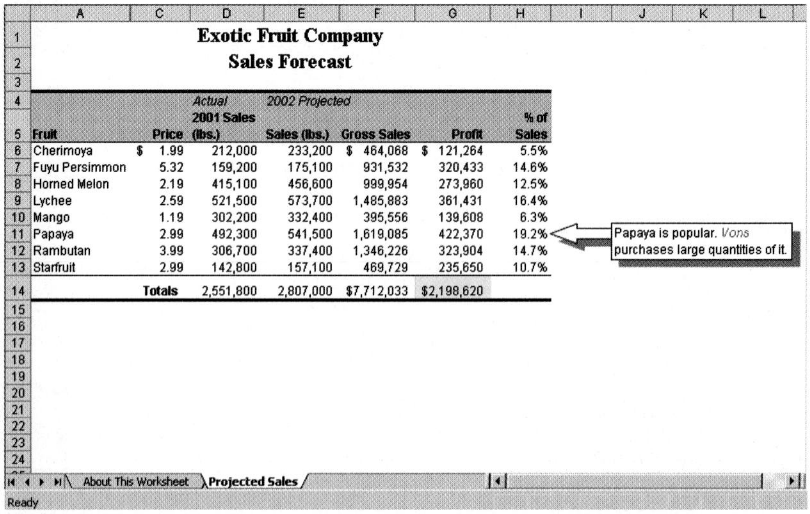

Exotic Fruit Company

Sales Forecast

Fruit	Price	*Actual* 2001 Sales (lbs.)	*2002 Projected* Sales (lbs.)	Gross Sales	Profit	% of Sales
Cherimoya	$ 1.99	212,000	233,200	$ 464,068	$ 121,264	5.5%
Fuyu Persimmon	5.32	159,200	175,100	931,532	320,433	14.6%
Horned Melon	2.19	415,100	456,600	999,954	273,960	12.5%
Lychee	2.59	521,500	573,700	1,485,883	361,431	16.4%
Mango	1.19	302,200	332,400	395,556	139,608	6.3%
Papaya	2.99	492,300	541,500	1,619,085	422,370	19.2%
Rambutan	3.99	306,700	337,400	1,346,226	323,904	14.7%
Starfruit	2.99	142,800	157,100	469,729	235,650	10.7%
	Totals	2,551,800	2,807,000	$7,712,033	$2,198,620	

INTRODUCTION

Chapter 3 covers formatting. In this chapter you will open and use an existing worksheet—complete with formulas, text, and values—and apply various formats to its cells. Formats that you will apply include aligning numeric results in columns by their decimal places, controlling the number of decimal places that display, and displaying currency symbols for column-heading monetary values. Other formatting you will apply includes indenting a label and formatting the worksheet title and subtitle by merging several cells and centering the title in the merged cells. Drawing objects can add interest to a worksheet, and Excel has several drawing objects from which you can choose. You will add two of the available objects—an arrow and a text box—to the highlighted example used in this chapter. The chapter concludes by describing ways to customize printing a worksheet including selecting either landscape or portrait orientation, centering output on the page, and printing multiple worksheets at once.

SESSION 3.1 ALIGNING DATA AND APPLYING CHARACTER FORMATS

In this section, you will learn how to render your worksheets more professional looking by using various formatting methods. You will format text so that it wraps to a new line within a cell, indent text, format numeric cells with currency and accounting numbers, paint existing formats over other cells, and explore other numeric formatting details. You will align data on the right and left edges of cells and across several cells. This section introduces how to modify typefaces, apply boldface, apply underline, and modify a typeface point size.

LOCATING AND OPENING THE WORKBOOK

After Nancy outlines what she wants you to do to the Exotic Fruit worksheet to improve it, you outline what your goal and plans are to complete the worksheet as follows:

- Goal: Format the Exotic Fruit worksheet, without changing any formulas or values, so that it is easier to read and looks professional.
- Information needed to complete the work: Exotic Fruit worksheet and Nancy's outline of the changes she wants.
- New formulas or values needed: None. The worksheet's contents are complete and correct.

Angel has entered all the formulas, values, and text. Consequently, Nancy wants you to focus on formatting the cells to maximize their visual impact. You can accomplish this by formatting individual cells and columns so that numbers and text are formatted and by providing visual cues about data and labels that are related. Nancy wants selected areas of the worksheet to draw the reader's attention—to be formatted to attract attention without overwhelming the worksheet and without making the overall design look garish.

You begin by formatting individual cells and columns to maximize their impact. Then you plan to move on to providing larger, worksheet-wide improvements to help readers discern the different sections of the worksheet and how they are related. Begin by opening the worksheet.

> ### Starting Microsoft Excel:
>
> 1. Start Excel
> 2. Ensure that the Excel application window is maximized

You can open the worksheet. Angel cautioned you that she wants to preserve the original worksheet, **ex03Fruit.xls,** just in case she needs to adjust some of the formulas. She asked you to save the worksheet under a different name before beginning work on it. You will save the worksheet under the name **ExoticFruit.xls,** as a safety measure, before you get deeply involved with worksheet formatting changes.

> ### Opening the ex03Fruit.xls worksheet and saving it under a new name:
>
> 1. Click **File** and then click **Open** to display the Excel Open dialog box
> 2. Locate and then double-click the worksheet **ex03Fruit.xls** to open it. The first sheet, Documentation, opens (see Figure 3.2)

FIGURE 3.2

Exotic Fruit documentation worksheet

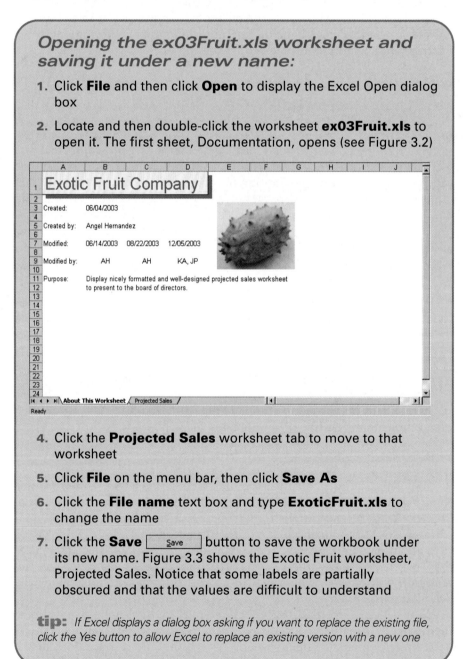

> 4. Click the **Projected Sales** worksheet tab to move to that worksheet
> 5. Click **File** on the menu bar, then click **Save As**
> 6. Click the **File name** text box and type **ExoticFruit.xls** to change the name
> 7. Click the **Save** [Save] button to save the workbook under its new name. Figure 3.3 shows the Exotic Fruit worksheet, Projected Sales. Notice that some labels are partially obscured and that the values are difficult to understand
>
> **tip:** *If Excel displays a dialog box asking if you want to replace the existing file, click the Yes button to allow Excel to replace an existing version with a new one*

FIGURE 3.3

The unformatted worksheet, Projected Sales

	A	B	C	D	E	F	G	H	I	J	K	L
1	Exotic Fruit Company											
2	Sales Forecast											
3												
4				Actual	2002 Projected							
5	Fruit	Cost	Price	2001 Sale	Sales (lbs.	Gross Sale	Profit	% of Sales				
6	Cherimoya	1.47	1.99	212000	233200	464068	121264	0.055155				
7	Fuyu Pers	3.49	5.32	159200	175100	931532	320433	0.145743				
8	Horned Me	1.59	2.19	415100	456600	999954	273960	0.124605				
9	Lychee	1.96	2.59	521500	573700	1485883	361431	0.16439				
10	Mango	0.77	1.19	302200	332400	395556	139608	0.063498				
11	Papaya	2.21	2.99	492300	541500	1619085	422370	0.192107				
12	Rambutan	3.03	3.99	306700	337400	1346226	323904	0.147322				
13	Starfruit	1.49	2.99	142800	157100	469729	235650	0.107181				
14			Totals	2551800	2807000	7712033	2198620					
15												
16												
17												
18												
19												
20												
21												
22												
23												
24												
25												

About This Worksheet \ **Projected Sales** /

Ready

FORMATTING DATA

Formatting a worksheet is the process of altering the appearance of data in one or more worksheet cells. Formatting is purely cosmetic—changing only the *appearance,* not the contents—of the formulas, values, or text stored in cells. Using the appropriate formatting renders a worksheet easier to read and understand and enhances a worksheet's overall appearance, making it more professional looking. Choosing inappropriate formatting has the opposite effect. It distracts the reader and creates a bad impression that extends beyond the worksheet to the company or activity illustrated by the worksheet.

You have already formatted some cells in the previous chapter. Recall that you used AutoFormat to format both numeric and text cells in one operation. Additionally, you used the increase decimal and decrease decimal buttons to increase or decrease the number of decimal places displayed by cell calculations and values alike. Although AutoFormat is simple to apply, it lacks versatility.

Often, you can provide the exact appearance you desire only by executing particular formatting commands that each make small changes to the appearance of cells. For example, you can apply a currency format with zero decimal places to the value 1234.5678 so that the cell displays $1,234, but the underlying value—the value you typed into the cell—remains unchanged. Only the cell's *appearance* changes. Suppose a cell contains the formula =A1*25.89 and it displays the result 0.6789945. You can format the cell using the Percentage format with two decimal places so that the cell's appearance changes—it displays 67.90% in the cell. When you apply formatting changes to a worksheet carefully, the changes enhance the worksheet tremendously.

By default, Excel formats all worksheet cells with a standard format called General. The *General* format aligns numbers on the right side of a cell, aligns text on the left side, indicates negative numbers with a minus sign on the left side of a number, and displays as many digits in a number as a cell's width allows. When you clear a cell's format, it takes on the General format. General format and no format are synonymous.

You have many ways to format one or more cells. The process begins by selecting the cell range you want to format. Then you can click one or more of the Formatting toolbar buttons to apply various formats to the selected cells or click Format on the menu bar to select formatting alternatives from the menu. Alternatively, you can right-click within the selected range of cells and click Format Cells from the shortcut menu that opens. Applying several formats is a cumulative process of applying one format followed by other formats. For example, you apply bold, italic, and underscore if you want a cell or cell range to display all three formatting characteristics.

Many of the more popular formatting operations appear as buttons on the Formatting toolbar. While many Formatting toolbar icons' graphics adequately describe the formats they apply, others may not. If you have trouble remembering what a particular Formatting toolbar button does, hover the mouse pointer over it and observe the ToolTip that appears within a few seconds. The ToolTip text tersely describes the format that a button applies. Figure 3.4 shows the Formatting toolbar.

FORMATTING NUMERIC ENTRIES

Excel's default numeric format General is not always the best format choice. Numeric entries and formulas that display values should have commas, or thousand separators, every three digits to make the numbers easier to read. The topmost number in a column of numbers representing money should display the currency symbol. Optionally, all values representing money could display the currency symbol. Some values in the Exotic Fruit worksheet represent percents and would look better if they were formatted as percentages with one or two decimal places. Excel provides these formatting choices for cells containing values and many format choices for a wide variety of situations.

Common format choices for numeric entries include General (the default format), Accounting, Currency, Date, Number, Percentage, Scientific, and formats you build yourself called Custom.

- General format displays numbers without commas or currency symbols (the dollar sign in the United States).
- Accounting provides left-aligned dollar signs, comma separators, a specified number of digits after the decimal place, and displays negative numbers inside a pair of parentheses.
- Currency is similar to Accounting, except the currency symbol is just to the left of the most significant digit and negative values are enclosed in parentheses.

FIGURE 3.4

The Formatting toolbar

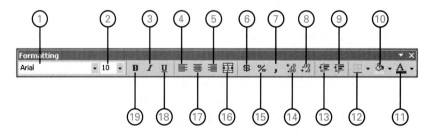

1	Font Style box	6	Currency Style	11	Font Color	16	Merge and Center
2	Font Size box	7	Comma Style	12	Borders	17	Center
3	Italic	8	Decrease Decimal	13	Decrease Indent	18	Underline
4	Align Left	9	Increase Indent	14	Increase Decimal	19	Bold
5	Align Right	10	Fill Color	15	Percent Style		

- Date provides special formats to display month, day, and year. Number format lets you designate the number of digits following the decimal place and the option to use comma separators. Negative values display a leading minus sign.

- Percentage inserts a percent sign to the right of the least significant digit and allows you to set the number of decimal places.

- Scientific displays a number between 1 and 10 followed by the letter E representing 10 raised to the exponent that follows E. For example, the number 123.45 formatted with Scientific displays 1.2345E+02, which reads "1.2345 times 10 to the 2nd power." This format is not used much in nonscientific applications.

- Customer allows you to create your own format when none of Excel's built-in number formats is suitable. Consisting of four sections separated by semicolons, you can specify how positive, negative, zero, and text appears with a custom format.

---

task reference

Formatting Numbers

- Select the cell or cell range to which you will apply a format

- Click **Format**, click **Cells**, and click the **Number** tab

- Click the format category you want and then select options for the format choice

- Click **OK** to finalize your format choices and format the selected cell(s)

If you change your mind and decide another format is better, simply select the cell or cell range whose format you want to change, click Format, click Cells, select the new format choices, and click OK.

anotherword

. . . on removing all formatting from a cell or cell range

If you decide to remove all formatting from a cell or cell range, select the cell(s) whose formatting you want to remove, click **Edit** on the menu bar, point to **Clear,** and click **Formats.**

Applying Accounting and Currency Formats

Reviewing Nancy's Exotic Fruit worksheet, you can see several distinct groups of numeric formats that will improve the worksheet. Columns B, C, D, F, and G all contain money values and should be formatted with commas. The first entries in those columns and the totals row entries should display currency symbols—a generally accepted format that accountants frequently prefer. Because the values in columns D through G represent relatively large numbers, you will format them so that they do not display any decimal places. Columns B and C, however, represent small numbers and should display two decimal places to represent dollars and cents. Column H represents percentages and should be formatted to look like percentage values. You begin by formatting the whole dollar columns with the Accounting format, no decimal places, and no currency symbol. Then you will come back and add the currency symbol to the top and bottom cells in the range.

Formatting columns D through G with the Accounting format:

1. Select cell range **D6:G14**

2. Click **Format** on the menu bar and click **Cells.** The Format Cells dialog box opens

3. Click the **Number** tab if necessary

4. Click **Accounting** in the Category list box. The Number tab display changes to display options appropriate for the Accounting selection including a list box for decimal places and the currency symbol. Notice that the default number of decimal places (displayed in the Decimal places list box) is 2

4. Type **0** in the Decimal places list box. The default currency symbol is the dollar sign if you installed the U.S. version of Excel

5. Click the **Symbol list box arrow** and then click **None** in the drop-down list (see Figure 3.5)

FIGURE 3.5

Format Cells dialog box

click the Number tab to display numeric format choices

choose Accounting format category from this list

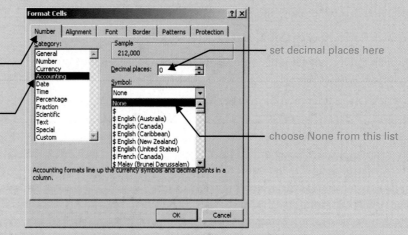

set decimal places here

choose None from this list

6. Click the **OK** button to affirm your formatting choices. The values in the formatted cell range display comma separators and are offset from the right cell wall by one character (see Figure 3.6)

FIGURE 3.6

Cells with Accounting format and no decimal places

formatted cells

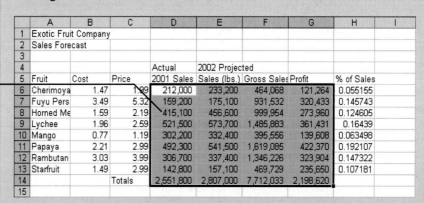

	A	B	C	D	E	F	G	H	I
1	Exotic Fruit Company								
2	Sales Forecast								
3									
4				Actual	2002 Projected				
5	Fruit	Cost	Price	2001 Sales	Sales (lbs.)	Gross Sales	Profit	% of Sales	
6	Cherimoya	1.47	1.99	212,000	233,200	464,068	121,264	0.055155	
7	Fuyu Pers	3.49	5.32	159,200	175,100	931,532	320,433	0.145743	
8	Horned Me	1.59	2.19	415,100	456,600	999,954	273,960	0.124605	
9	Lychee	1.96	2.59	521,500	573,700	1,485,883	361,431	0.16439	
10	Mango	0.77	1.19	302,200	332,400	395,556	139,608	0.063498	
11	Papaya	2.21	2.99	492,300	541,500	1,619,085	422,370	0.192107	
12	Rambutan	3.03	3.99	306,700	337,400	1,346,226	323,904	0.147322	
13	Starfruit	1.49	2.99	142,800	157,100	469,729	235,650	0.107181	
14			Totals	2,551,800	2,807,000	7,712,033	2,198,620		
15									

7. Click any cell to deselect the cell range

Recall from Chapter 2 that a cell displaying a series of pound signs ("#######") indicates that the column is too narrow to display the values in the cells as *formatted*. If your display shows a series of pound signs, you must widen the column to see the full formatted number. It is best to wait to widen the columns until you have formatted the remaining numeric values in a column that requires widening. Subtotals and totals, for example, usually are wider than other values because they are the sum of a possible large list of numbers.

Accountants, financial analysts, and others often format the top cell in a column of currency values with the currency symbol. The same is true for cells containing subtotals or totals. Displaying currency symbols on every value in a column creates visual clutter and is distracting.

Next, you will format cells F6 and G6 so that they display leading dollar signs. You want the dollar signs not to appear right next to the most significant (leftmost) digit of the numbers. You choose the Accounting number format with the currency symbol because the currency symbol appears near the left edge of the cell,

Formatting selected cells with the Accounting format and currency symbol:

1. Select cell range **F6:G6**

3. Click **Format** on the menu bar and then click **Cells**

4. Click the **Number** tab if necessary. Notice that the Category list highlights the Accounting category because that is the format assigned to all the selected cells. Notice also that the number of decimal places (displayed in the Decimal places list box) is 0—the formatted number of decimal places of the current cell selection

6. Click the **Symbol list box arrow** and click **$** appearing just below None in the Symbol drop-down list

7. Click **OK** to finalize your formatting selections

8. Click any cell to deselect the range. Figure 3.7 shows the worksheet with currency symbols displayed in cells F6 and G6

	A	B	C	D	E	F	G	H	I
1	Exotic Fruit Company								
2	Sales Forecast								
3									
4				Actual	2002 Projected				
5	Fruit	Cost	Price	2001 Sales	Sales (lbs.)	Gross Sales	Profit	% of Sales	
6	Cherimoya	1.47	1.99	212,000	233,200	$ 464,068	$ 121,264	0.055155	
7	Fuyu Pers	3.49	5.32	159,200	175,100	931,532	320,433	0.145743	
8	Horned Me	1.59	2.19	415,100	456,600	999,954	273,860	0.124605	
9	Lychee	1.96	2.59	521,500	573,700	1,485,883	361,431	0.16439	
10	Mango	0.77	1.19	302,200	332,400	395,556	139,608	0.063498	
11	Papaya	2.21	2.99	492,300	541,500	1,619,085	422,370	0.192107	
12	Rambutan	3.03	3.99	306,700	337,400	1,346,226	323,904	0.147322	
13	Starfruit	1.49	2.99	142,800	157,100	469,729	235,650	0.107181	
14			Totals	2,551,800	2,807,000	7,712,033	2,198,620		
15									

FIGURE 3.7

Worksheet with some currency symbols in place

cells display the currency symbol

Painting Formats onto Other Cells

You recall Nancy's advice that values (or formulas that display values) representing subtotals and totals usually display a currency symbol. Cells F14 and G14 display totals for their respective partial columns. Instead of repeating the command sequence you used above for cells F6 and G6, to save time and effort you will copy the cell format (but not the contents) from cell F6 to the two cells containing sales and profit totals. The Format Painter ⬐ button, located on the Standard toolbar, is a quick and convenient way to copy one cell's format to another cell or cell range. The advantage of painting a format instead of using formatting commands is that the painter duplicates *all* of a cell's formats at once.

---

task reference

Copying a Cell Format to a Cell or Cell Range

- Select the cell whose format you want to copy
- Click the **Format Painter** ⬐ button
- Click the cell where you want to paint the format, or click and drag the cell range where you want to paint the format

---

Rather than repeat the formatting sequence to apply the currency symbol to cells F14 and G14, you will copy the format with the Format Painter.

Formatting cells with the Accounting format and currency symbol and widening columns:

1. Click cell **F6,** the cell whose format you want to copy to another cell or cells
2. Click the **Format Painter** ⬐ button on the Standard toolbar
3. Click and drag the cell range **F14:G14** (see Figure 3.8) to copy the format to those cells. The newly formatted cells probably display ########. Recall that this indicates a formatted numeric value wider than the column can display. You need to widen the columns to accommodate the sums
4. With F14 and G14 still selected, click **Format** on the menu bar, point to **Column,** and click **AutoFit Selection.** Excel widens columns F and G to accommodate formatted cells F14 and G14
5. Click any cell to deselect the cell range

---

*another***way**

. . . to Copy a Cell's Format to Noncontiguous Cells

Click the cell whose format you want to copy

Double-click the **Format Painter** button to permanently engage it

Select a cell or cell range to which you want Excel to copy the format

Select other cells or cell ranges to receive a copied format

When done, click the **Format Painter** button to disengage it

---

OTHER NUMBER FORMATS

You can apply other number formats by using buttons on the Formatting toolbar, shown in Figure 3.4, such as Currency Style, Percent Style, Increase Decimal, or Decrease Decimal. Many other formatting options are available in the Format Cells dialog box, shown in Figure 3.5. Number format options allow you to select whether or not to display a comma to

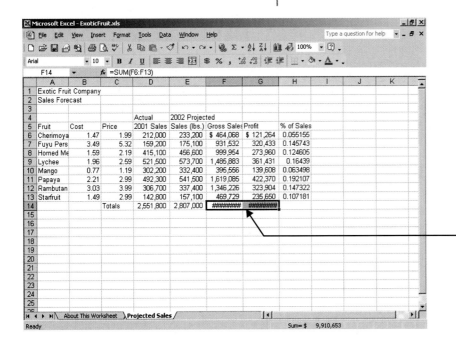

FIGURE 3.8
Worksheet totals with copied format

pound signs signal that a column is too narrow to display formatted numeric value

delimit numbers every three digits, to select the number of decimal places that display, and the exact format of negative numbers.

Percent Style

Column H displays values beneath the column label "% of Sales." These values are percentages, although they are somewhat difficult to interpret because they display five or six decimal places. Nancy wants you to format these column values (such as 0.107181, the Starfruit percentage) to display 10.7% instead—a percentage displaying one decimal place.

Formatting column H with percent and one decimal place:

1. Click and drag the cell range **H6:H13**

2. Click the **Percent Style** % button to apply the Percent Style format to the selected cell range. The default for the Percent Style is to display zero decimal places

3. With the cell range H6:H13 still selected, click the **Increase Decimal** button on the Formatting toolbar to increase, by one, the number of decimal places the selected cells display

tip: *If the Increase Decimal button is not visible on the Formatting toolbar, it is farther right on the Formatting toolbar and out of sight—probably sharing space with the Standard toolbar. If so, drag the Formatting toolbar below the Standard toolbar and to the left edge to view the entire toolbar. Then click the Increase Decimal button*

4. Click any cell to deselect the range (see Figure 3.9)

EXCEL

FIGURE 3.9

Worksheet cells formatted with the Percent Style

	A	B	C	D	E	F	G	H	I
1	Exotic Fruit Company								
2	Sales Forecast								
3									
4				Actual	2002 Projected				
5	Fruit	Cost	Price	2001 Sales	Sales (lbs.)	Gross Sales	Profit	% of Sales	
6	Cherimoya	1.47	1.99	212,000	233,200	$ 464,068	$ 121,264	5.5%	
7	Fuyu Pers	3.49	5.32	159,200	175,100	931,532	320,433	14.6%	
8	Horned Me	1.59	2.19	415,100	456,600	999,954	273,960	12.5%	
9	Lychee	1.96	2.59	521,500	573,700	1,485,883	361,431	16.4%	
10	Mango	0.77	1.19	302,200	332,400	395,556	139,608	6.3%	
11	Papaya	2.21	2.99	492,300	541,500	1,619,085	422,370	19.2%	
12	Rambutan	3.03	3.99	306,700	337,400	1,346,226	323,904	14.7%	
13	Starfruit	1.49	2.99	142,800	157,100	469,729	235,650	10.7%	
14			Totals	2,551,800	2,807,000	$7,712,033	$2,198,620		
15									

Percent Style applied to column H values ⎯

Nancy has reviewed your formatting work and suggests that you format the values at the top of the Cost and Price columns to display a currency symbol and two decimal places.

> **Formatting selected cells with the Accounting format and currency symbol:**
>
> 1. Click cell **B6** and drag the mouse through cell **C6**
> 2. Click the **Currency Style** button on the Formatting toolbar
> 3. Click any cell to deselect the range

Look carefully on your screen at the cell range B6 through C13. Do you notice that cell B6 is not aligned on the right side with cell B7 or the remainder of the cells in the Cost column? Similarly, Cell C6 is no longer aligned on the right side with the other cells in the Price column? This is because the Currency Style also adds one character, a space, to the right side of all values so that there is room for a right parenthesis. Under the Accounting format, negative numbers are surrounded with parentheses.

It is sloppy to leave the values beneath the formatted cell out of alignment with the top value in the column. You can correct this by applying a comma format to the remaining cells in the Cost and Price columns.

Comma Style

Even though commas are not needed for values less than 1000, comma formatting also aligns values the same way the Currency format does—by adding a character to the right side of each value. You will format cells B7 through C13 with the Comma format to align those values the same as the first two entries in each column.

> **Formatting cells with the Comma Style:**
>
> 1. Click cell **B7** and drag the mouse through cell **C13**
> 2. Click the **Comma Style** , button on the Formatting toolbar

3. Click any cell to deselect the range. Notice that all values in the Cost and Price columns are aligned (see Figure 3.10)

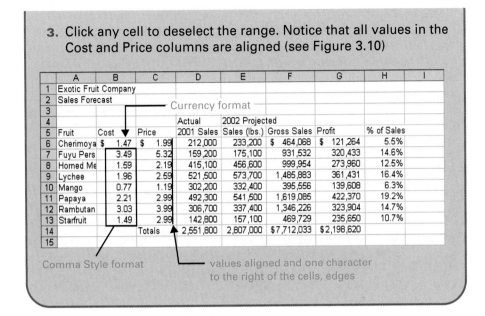

FIGURE 3.10

Applying the Comma Style to numeric values

ALIGNING DATA

Excel allows you to align data within a cell. Data **_alignment_** refers to the position of the data relative to the sides of a cell. You alter a cell's alignment with formatting commands. You can align data on the left or right sides of a cell, or you can center it between the two cell walls. A special center alignment command called Merge and Center allows you to center data across several cells in a single row—to create a heading over several columns of numbers, for example. Figure 3.11 shows examples of these four alignment options.

General rules about aligning data have evolved over time. As you know, Excel automatically aligns text on the left side and aligns values or formulas that result in values on the right side. While you certainly can choose data alignment that suits your style and taste, here are some suggestions about cell alignment. Align a column of text on the left side, the default alignment provided by Excel. If you align text on the right, the result can be a disorienting ragged left edge down the column. You can center numeric values if all values have the same number of digits. Examples are employee identification numbers that are all the same

FIGURE 3.11

Cell alignment examples

number of digits long. In a column of numeric values that are not all the same size, align the values so that their decimal places are lined up vertically (column D, Figure 3.11). To do so, you may have to format values to display the same number of decimal places. Text that labels a column of values below it should be right aligned, the same way the values are. This makes the number column easy to identify. For example, column D is easier to interpret than column C, which contains the same values but whose column top label is left aligned. It is often best to center a worksheet title or a text label describing several columns over those columns. In this case, you use the Merge and Center to accomplish the task. Row 1 in Figure 3.11 is an example. The title "1st Quarter Sales" is centered over four columns.

Before altering the alignment of any text or values, you widen column A to accommodate the widest entry in the list of fruit. Notice that two labels identifying the worksheet, "Exotic Fruit Company" and "Sales Forecast," are also in column A (Figure 3.10). This is important because you want to enlarge the column enough to display the fruit names in cells C6 through C13, but the column need not be as wide as the text in cell A1. Widening the column to completely contain the text in cell A1 would make the column far too wide.

Widening column A to accommodate the longer fruit names:

1. Select cells **A6** through **A13**

2. Click **Format** on the menu bar, point to **Column,** and then click **AutoFit Selection.** The column widens to one character wider than the widest entry in the selected cells, Fuyu Persimmon

3. Click any cell to deselect the range. Now each fruit name is visible

Centering Data Across Columns

You will want to center text across multiple columns periodically. A worksheet title or a label that identifies a group of columns is an example. A worksheet title aligned across the columns of the worksheet it identifies can look especially nice. Nancy wants you to center the worksheet title and subtitle found in cells A1 and A2, respectively, across columns A through H.

Centering a worksheet title and subtitle across several columns:

1. Select the cell range **A1:H2**

2. Click **Format** and then click **Cells**

3. Click the **Alignment** tab in the Format Cells dialog box

4. Click the **Horizontal list box arrow** to display a list of alignment choices (see Figure 3.12)

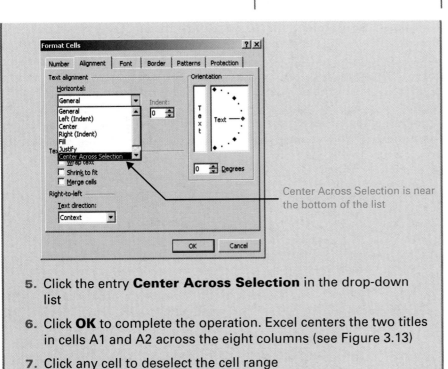

FIGURE 3.12

Format Cells dialog box

Center Across Selection is near the bottom of the list

5. Click the entry **Center Across Selection** in the drop-down list

6. Click **OK** to complete the operation. Excel centers the two titles in cells A1 and A2 across the eight columns (see Figure 3.13)

7. Click any cell to deselect the cell range

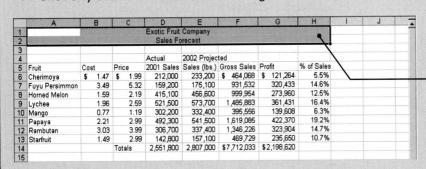

	A	B	C	D	E	F	G	H	I	J
1				Exotic Fruit Company						
2				Sales Forecast						
3										
4				Actual	2002 Projected					
5	Fruit	Cost	Price	2001 Sales	Sales (lbs.)	Gross Sales	Profit	% of Sales		
6	Cherimoya	$ 1.47	$ 1.99	212,000	233,200	$ 464,068	$ 121,264	5.5%		
7	Fuyu Persimmon	3.49	5.32	159,200	175,100	931,532	320,433	14.6%		
8	Horned Melon	1.59	2.19	415,100	456,600	999,954	273,960	12.5%		
9	Lychee	1.96	2.59	521,500	573,700	1,485,883	361,431	16.4%		
10	Mango	0.77	1.19	302,200	332,400	395,556	139,608	6.3%		
11	Papaya	2.21	2.99	492,300	541,500	1,619,085	422,370	19.2%		
12	Rambutan	3.03	3.99	306,700	337,400	1,346,226	323,904	14.7%		
13	Starfruit	1.49	2.99	142,800	157,100	469,729	235,650	10.7%		
14			Totals	2,551,800	2,807,000	$7,712,033	$2,198,620			
15										

FIGURE 3.13

Centering titles across several columns

labels centered across columns A through H

Right Aligning Data

Text labels that appear above columns containing values often look best if the text labels align the same way as the data beneath them. There are three labels in the Exotic Fruit worksheet, shown in Figure 3.13, which should be right aligned to match the data columns beneath the labels. They are the text in cells B5, C5, G5, and H5. (It is difficult to tell that the text in cell H5 is left aligned, but it is.)

Right aligning text:

1. Click and drag the cell range **B5:C5**

2. Press and hold the **Ctrl** key, click cell **G5,** click cell **H5,** and then release the Ctrl key

3. Click the **Align Right** button on the Formatting toolbar. Excel right-aligns the selected text labels

4. Click any cell to deselect the range

Upon close examination, you notice that the labels Excel right-aligned actually appear one character to the right of the values beneath each text label in columns B, C, and G. You ask Nancy how to correct this, and she tells you that you can use the Accounting format to align text as well as numbers. The advantage of using Accounting format is that it matches the format you applied earlier to the numbers. She explains that the Accounting format adds a space on the right side of the label just as it does for numbers. You change the formatting to improve the worksheet's appearance.

Applying the Accounting format to text:

1. Click and drag the cell range **B5:C5**

2. Press and hold the **Ctrl** key, click cell **G5,** click cell **H5,** and then release the Ctrl key

3. Click **Format**, click **Cells**, click the **Number** tab, click **Accounting** in the Category list, and click **OK** to complete the reformatting process (see Figure 3.14)

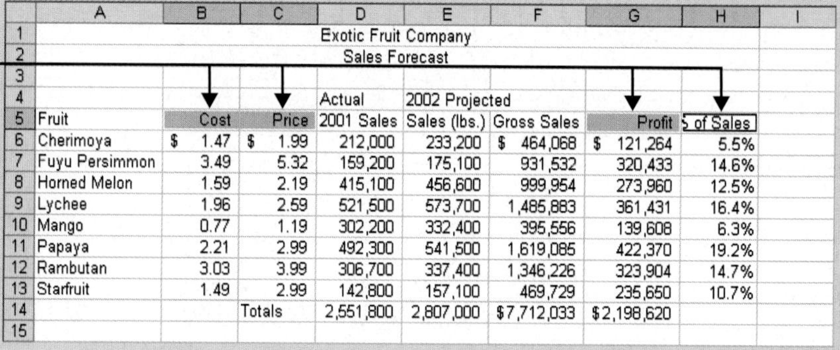

FIGURE 3.14

Applying the Accounting format to text cells

Accounting format aligns text to match formatting of numbers beneath

4. Click any cell to deselect the range

That looks better. Now you are ready to modify the format of the remaining column labels.

Wrapping Data in a Cell

Recall that text that is too long to display in a cell extends beyond the cell into the adjacent cell as long as the adjacent cell is empty. If it is not, the long label is visually truncated at the cell boundary. Labels in cells D5, E5, F5, and H5 are all longer than their respective columns are wide. One solution would be to increase the width of the three columns until the labels completely fit within the cells. However, this is not always the best solution because especially long labels force their columns to become exceptionally wide, wider than is attractive. An alternative solution is to format long labels so they appear in multiple rows *within* a cell, much the same way that a text line in a word-processed document wraps around to the next line when it approaches the right margin. Excel uses the same term as Word—**wrap text**—to describe what happens to long text that continues onto the next line of the same cell.

---

task reference

Wrapping Long Text Within a Cell

- Select the cell or cell range to which you will apply a format
- Click **Format,** click **Cells,** and click the **Alignment** tab
- Click the **Wrap text** check box
- Click **OK** to finalize your format choice

Wrapping the text within cells D5, E5, F5, and H5 will make each label visible and eliminate the need to increase the column widths. It will be a good improvement toward making the worksheet more professional looking.

Wrapping text within a cell:

1. Click and drag the cell range **D5:F5**

2. Press the **Ctrl** key, click cell **H5,** and release the Ctrl key. This adds H5 to the list of selected cells

3. Click **Format,** click **Cells,** and then click the **Alignment** tab

4. Click the **Wrap text** check box, in the Text control panel, to place a checkmark in it

5. Click **OK** to complete the format operation and close the Format Cells dialog box

6. Click any cell to deselect the range (see Figure 3.15)

	A	B	C	D	E	F	G	H	I
1				Exotic Fruit Company					
2				Sales Forecast					
3									
4				Actual	2002 Projected			% of	
5	Fruit	Cost	Price	2001 Sales (lbs.)	Sales (lbs.)	Gross Sales	Profit	Sales	
6	Cherimoya	$ 1.47	$ 1.99	212,000	233,200	$ 464,068	$ 121,264	5.5%	
7	Fuyu Persimmon	3.49	5.32	159,200	175,100	931,532	320,433	14.6%	
8	Horned Melon	1.59	2.19	415,100	456,600	999,954	273,960	12.5%	
9	Lychee	1.96	2.59	521,500	573,700	1,485,883	361,431	16.4%	
10	Mango	0.77	1.19	302,200	332,400	395,556	139,608	6.3%	
11	Papaya	2.21	2.99	492,300	541,500	1,619,085	422,370	19.2%	
12	Rambutan	3.03	3.99	306,700	337,400	1,346,226	323,904	14.7%	
13	Starfruit	1.49	2.99	142,800	157,100	469,729	235,650	10.7%	
14			Totals	2,551,800	2,807,000	$7,712,033	$2,198,620		
15									

FIGURE 3.15

Wrap text format

Wrap text format

Indenting Text

You can indent text within a cell by clicking the Increase Indent or Decrease Indent buttons on the Formatting toolbar. Indenting text allows finer control over text placement within a cell, somewhere between the extremes of left-aligning and right-aligning data. Each time you press the Increase Indent button, Excel moves the text or a value within a cell to the right a few character spaces. Pressing the Decrease Indent button does the opposite: It moves a value or text in a cell to the left a few spaces. You decide to move the label "Totals" in cell C14 right a few spaces.

> **Indenting text within a cell:**
>
> 1. Click cell **C14**
> 2. Click the **Increase Indent** ⊞ button on the Formatting toolbar to indent "Totals" within cell C14
> 3. Since it has been a while since you saved your worksheet, click the **Save** 🖫 button to save your workbook

The basic formatting looks good. All the numbers are visible and contain commas, and selected cells contain the currency symbol. Percentages are formatted to display one decimal place and the percent symbol. Next, you want to alter the typeface and font style of the column headings as well as the worksheet title and subtitle.

CHANGING FONT AND FONT CHARACTERISTICS

Excel allows you to select from a wide variety of typefaces, character formatting characteristics, and point sizes. A *font* is the combination of typeface and qualities including character size, character pitch, and spacing. Typefaces have names such as Garamond, Times Roman, and Helvetica. The height of characters in a typeface is measured in *points,* where a point is equal to 1/72 of an inch. Characters' widths are measured by *pitch,* which refers to the number of characters horizontally per inch. A font is *fixed pitch* (or monospace) if every character has the same width, whereas a font is called a *proportional* font if characters' pitches vary by character. Most people agree that proportional fonts are easier to read than fixed pitch fonts. (The typeface in this book is a proportional font.) Excel provides a large number of fonts from which you can format text and numbers.

Excel also provides the font styles regular, bold, and bold italic. Most fonts are available in a variety of sizes, and you can apply special effects to fonts such as strikethrough, superscript, subscript, a variety of colors, and various types of underlines. You access all of the preceding—fonts, font styles, and font special effects—through the Format Cells dialog box, which opens when you click Format and then Cells. Applying font characteristics is straightforward.

---

task **reference**

Applying Fonts and Font Characteristics

- Select the cell or cell range that you want to format
- Click **Format,** click **Cells,** and click the **Font** tab
- Select a typeface from the Font list box
- Select a font style and a font size
- Click **OK** to finalize your choices

Applying Boldface

Applying font size and characteristic changes to the worksheet title, subtitle, column headings, and selected cells in the Exotic Fruit worksheet will yield a more professional worksheet. Column labels in row 5 will look better if they stand out, and the label in cell C14 will improve too. Applying boldface to them is just the touch needed to distinguish the labels from the data and enhance the worksheet's appearance.

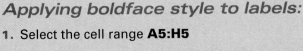

Applying boldface style to labels:

1. Select the cell range **A5:H5**

2. Click and hold the **Ctrl** key and then click cell **C14**

3. Release the **Ctrl** key

4. Click the **Bold** B button on the Formatting toolbar. Excel applies the boldface style to the selected labels (see Figure 3.16). Excel also increased the row height of row 5. Notice that the Bold formatting toolbar button is outlined and light blue, indicating that the style is active for <u>all</u> cells in the selected range. The style buttons and the alignment and numeric formatting buttons indicate the formats applied to selected cells in the same way

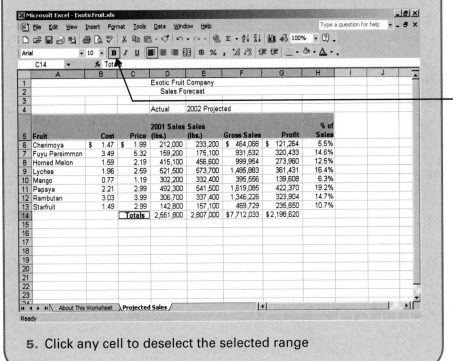

FIGURE 3.16
Bolding column labels

indicates selected range is bold

5. Click any cell to deselect the selected range

Applying Italic

Next, you will italicize the column labels in cells D4 and E4 and the numeric cells D14 through G14 for emphasis.

Applying italic to column labels and values:

1. Select the cell range **D4:E4**

2. Press and hold the **Ctrl** key and click the cell range **D14:G14**

3. Release the Ctrl key

4. Click the **Italic** button I on the Formatting toolbar. Excel applies the Italic style to the two labels and four numeric cells

5. Click any cell to deselect the two cell ranges

Applying Boldface and Changing Point Size and Typeface

The worksheet title and subtitle would look better bolded and with a larger point size. You also want to change the typeface from Arial to Times New Roman. You make those changes in the following steps.

Applying boldface style and modifying the point size and typeface:

1. Select the cell range **A1:A2.** Though the worksheet title and subtitle are centered across several columns, they are actually stored in cells A1 and A2, respectively. To alter their formats, you must click the cells in which they are stored

2. Click **Format** on the menu bar, and then click **Cells**. The Format Cells dialog box opens

4. Click the **Font** tab

5. Drag the mouse across the typeface name displayed in the Font list box to select it and type **Times New Roman.** Notice that the list scrolls automatically to the Times New Roman entry after you type the word *Roman*

6. Click **Bold** in the Font style list box

7. In the Size list box, click the **down-pointing scroll arrow** to locate and then click **16** (see Figure 3.17)

FIGURE 3.17

Setting typeface and font characteristics

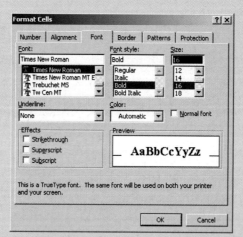

8. Click **OK** to confirm your choices and close the Format Cells dialog box

9. Click any cell to deselect the cell range

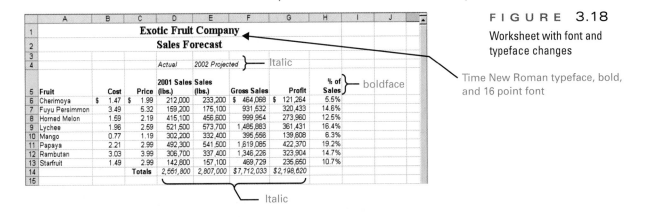

FIGURE 3.18
Worksheet with font and
typeface changes

The title and subtitle look better with the larger point size, Times New Roman typeface, and boldface applied (see Figure 3.18).

Removing Selected Formats

Nancy reviewed your worksheet and is pleased with it. However, she believes that the italic style applied to the values appearing in cells D14 through G14 is distracting. She asks you to remove that formatting entirely but to maintain the Accounting format.

Removing one style while retaining others:

1. Select the cell range **D14:G14.** Notice that the Italic button is outlined and light blue, indicating the entire range has the Italic format

2. Click the **Italic** button to remove the Italic format from the selected cells. The Italic button is no longer highlighted. (Bold, Italic, and Underline buttons are toggle buttons: You click a button once to activate it and click it again to deactivate it.) The Italic style is removed from the selected cells

3. Click any cell to deselect the cell range

Clearing Formats

When you want to remove all formatting from a cell or cell range, you use the Clear Formats command. Doing so clears all formats, returning the selected cells to their default, General format.

---

task reference

Clearing Formats From a Cell, a Cell Selection, Rows, or Columns

- Select the cell, cell range, rows, or columns whose format you want to clear

- Click **Edit,** point to **Clear,** and then click **Formats** to remove all formatting

---

EXCEL

Although you do not need to clear any formats, experiment with the procedure in the following steps. Then you can click Edit, Undo to restore or cancel the Format Clear operation and restore the original formatting.

Clearing one or more cells' formatting:

1. Select the cell range **A5:H5**

2. Click **Edit** on the menu bar, point to **Clear,** and click **Formats.** The cell range formats all return to the General format. Notice that the cells' contents are unaffected. Only the cells' appearances change

3. After observing the cleared formats, reverse the effects of step 2 by clicking **Edit** and then clicking **Undo Clear.** The cell range displays its bold and wrapped text formats

4. Click any cell to deselect the cell range

You have made several changes to your worksheet since you last saved it. Save your worksheet before continuing.

Saving your workbook under a new name:

1. Click **File** on the menu bar

2. Click **Save As**

3. Type **ExoticFruit2.xls** in the File name list box and then click the Save button. Excel saves your workbook under its new name

---

Nancy reviews your progress on the Exotic Fruit worksheet. She's pleased with the worksheet's appearance and makes some suggestions that you note. You will implement her suggested enhancements in the next section of this chapter.

SESSION 3.2 ADVANCED FORMATTING

In this session, you will continue formatting a worksheet. You will alter the row height of a row, enlarging it to add emphasis. Borders delineate particular areas of a worksheet, and you will learn how to apply borders for maximum effect. In order to provide information protection, you will hide information in a column. You will use the Drawing toolbar to add text boxes and arrows to the worksheet to draw attention to especially important elements on it. Finally, you will learn how to add and remove gridlines on the screen and on the printed output and how to specify important print settings such as repeating rows and columns.

CONTROLLING ROW HEIGHTS

Earlier in this chapter, you adjusted several columns' widths. You can adjust the height of rows to provide more room for labels or values or to

making the grade

1. What does formatting do to the contents of a cell?

2. By default, Excel worksheet cells are formatted with what format?

3. Excel aligns numbers on the _____ and aligns text on the _____ by default.

4. The Accounting format allows you to specify an optional _____ symbol, specify the number of _____ _____, and adds a space on the right side of all entries.

5. Modify the Exotic Fruit Company Sales Forecast worksheet, **ExoticFruit2.xls,** in the following ways. First, save the workbook under the name **ExoticFruitModified.xls** to preserve the original **ExoticFruit2.xls** for the next Session. Make these changes. Change the point size of all labels in row 4 to 12 points. Italicize all labels in row 5, and insert your name in the worksheet's header. Save the workbook and then print the worksheet.

simply add emphasis. When you enlarged the worksheet title and subtitle, Excel compensated for the taller characters by increasing the rows' heights automatically. You can increase or decrease the height of one or more rows manually in several ways.

task reference

Modifying a Row's Height

- Click the row heading to select the row whose height you want to modify

- Click **Format,** point to **Row,** and click **Height**

- Type the row height in the Row height text box

- Click **OK** to finalize your choices

You decide that row 14 containing totals would look better if it were taller. Increase the row's height by following these steps.

Increasing a row's height:

1. If you took a break at the end of the last session, make sure Excel is running and then open the **ExoticFruit2.xls** workbook that you saved at the end of Session 3.1

2. Click row 14's **row heading,** which is located to the left of column A in row 14. Excel selects the entire row

3. Click **Format,** point to **Row,** and click **Height.** The Row Height dialog box appears

FIGURE 3.19

Row Height dialog box

new row height ——

selected row
whose height is
being altered ——

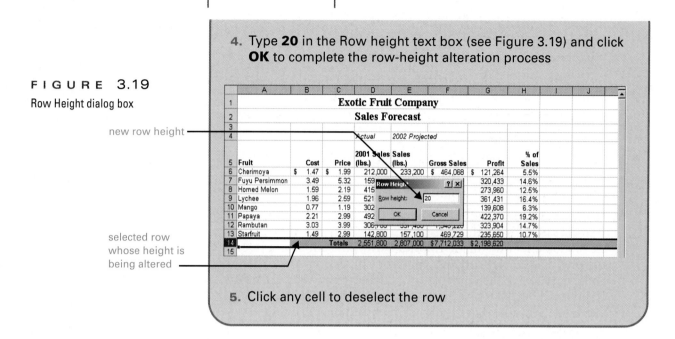

4. Type **20** in the Row height text box (see Figure 3.19) and click **OK** to complete the row-height alteration process

5. Click any cell to deselect the row

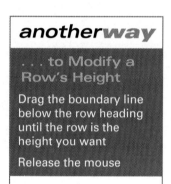

anotherway

. . . to Modify a
Row's Height

Drag the boundary line
below the row heading
until the row is the
height you want

Release the mouse

EMPLOYING BORDERS, A TEXT BOX, AN ARROW, AND SHADING

Like many worksheets, the Exotic Fruit Sales Forecast worksheet has distinct regions or zones that contain groups of related information. Using lines to delineate these groups adds impact to your worksheet and makes the groups easier to identify.

Adding Borders

A *cell border* is a format that applies lines of various types to one or more edges (left, right, top, bottom) of the selected cell(s). You create borders among or around selected cells by selecting the Borders button on the Formatting toolbar or by selecting options on the Border tab of the Format Cells dialog box. Using the Outline option, you can place a border around one cell or the rectangle created by a selection of several cells. You can create a horizontal line by selecting cells in the same row and then formatting either the top or bottom edge with a border. Similarly, you create a vertical line by formatting a border on the left or right side of a selection of cells in a single column.

Using the Formatting dialog box, you have several border styles available, including solid lines of various thicknesses, dashed lines, and double lines. The Border button provides a few of the more popular border options. Removing borders from a cell is straightforward with the Format Cells dialog box. You select the cell(s) whose borders you want to remove, click the Border tab of the Format Cells dialog box, and click None.

You want to place a thick line above the column headings in row 4 and a thinner line below the column headings in row 5 to set off the column headings.

Adding a thick line above column labels will help establish the column labels and data beneath them as a separate area. When you want to add a border whose style is not available in the Borders list, you customize border choices by using the Format menu. Next, you will add a border above row 4.

---

task reference

Adding a Border to a Cell

- Click the cell to which you want to add a border
- Click **Format,** click **Cells,** and click the **Border** tab
- Click the line style in the Style list that you want to apply to the selected cell or cells
- Click one or more of the buttons indicating which cell walls you want to format with a border
- Click **OK** to apply your border formatting choices

  or

- Click the cell to which you want to add a border
- Click the Formatting toolbar **Borders list box arrow** and click the type of border you want

---

Formatting a border below the column headings:

1. Select the cell range **A5:H5**

2. Click the **Borders button list arrow** ⬜▾ on the Formatting toolbar. A series of borders appears (see Figure 3.20)

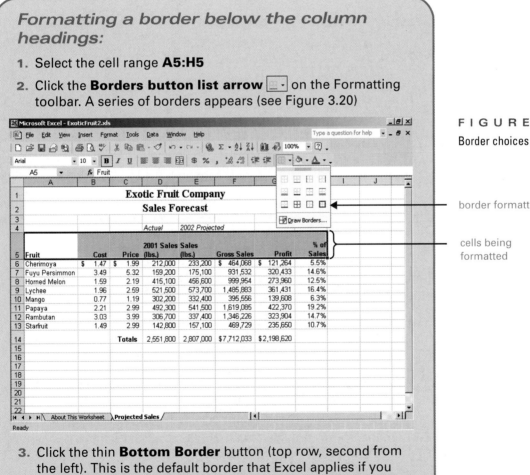

FIGURE 3.20
Border choices

border formatting choices

cells being formatted

3. Click the thin **Bottom Border** button (top row, second from the left). This is the default border that Excel applies if you click the Borders button on the Formatting toolbar. It is helpful for you to view the predefined border sets available from the Borders button list

4. Select any cell to deselect the range

Formatting a border above column headings:

1. Select the cell range **A4:H4**

2. Click **Format,** click **Cells,** and click the **Border** tab on the Format Cells dialog box

3. Click the **thick line** in the Line Style box (the second line from the bottom on the right side of the Line Style box)

4. Click the **top border** button. Excel places a thick line at the top of the Border preview window indicating the relative position of the line in the selected cell range (see Figure 3.21)

FIGURE 3.21

Selecting a border style and positioning it

border in position

top border button

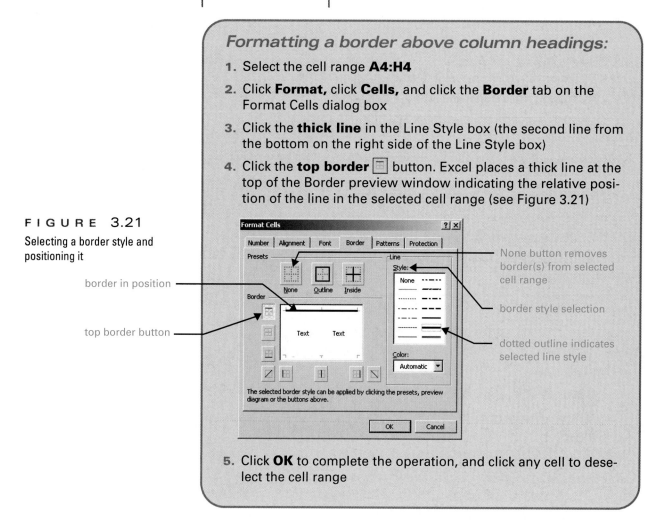

None button removes border(s) from selected cell range

border style selection

dotted outline indicates selected line style

5. Click **OK** to complete the operation, and click any cell to deselect the cell range

The last pair of borders will be similar to the first two you created. A thin line will separate product information from totals in row 14. Finally, you will format the bottom edge of row 14 with a thick border to enclose the product sales information in a pair of thick lines.

Adding a thin and thick border to row 14:

1. Select the cell range **A14:H14**

2. Click **Format,** click **Cells,** and then click the **Border** tab on the Format Cells dialog box

3. Click the **thin line** in the Line Style box (the bottom line on the left side of the Line Style box)

4. Click the **top border** button. Excel places a thin line at the top of the Border preview window indicating the relative position of the line in the selected cell range

5. Click the **thick line** in the Line Style box and then click the **bottom border** button. Excel places a thick button at the bottom of the Border preview window indicating the position of the line in the selected cell range

6. Click **OK** to complete the border formatting procedure and then click any cell to deselect the cell range

Adding and Removing Toolbars

Excel provides several useful drawing tools that allow you to create graphic elements on a special drawing layer of a worksheet. Drawing elements float over the top of a worksheet. They include arrows, text boxes, various lines and connector lines, over 30 basic shapes such as rectangles and trapezoids, WordArt, and clip art. You access these features on the Drawing toolbar.

You are already familiar with Excel's Standard toolbar and Formatting toolbar. In addition, Excel has other toolbars, including the Chart toolbar, Database toolbar, Forms toolbar, and Visual Basic toolbar. Usually only the Standard and Formatting toolbars are visible. To use any toolbar's menus, you must make it appear. If many toolbars are visible simultaneously, there is little room for a worksheet. Normally you make a toolbar visible, use its features, and then remove the toolbar when you are done with it. That way, toolbar clutter is not a problem. *Activating a toolbar* is the process of making it appear on the desktop.

FIGURE 3.22

Excel toolbar shortcut menu

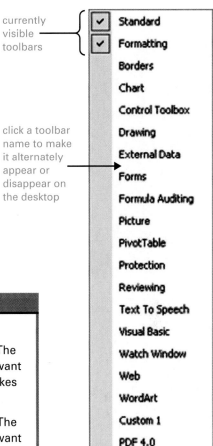

currently visible toolbars

click a toolbar name to make it alternately appear or disappear on the desktop

task reference
Activating or Removing a Toolbar

- Activate a toolbar by **right-clicking** any toolbar or the menu bar. The toolbar shortcut menu appears. Click the name of the toolbar you want to use, which places a checkmark next to the toolbar name and makes the toolbar appear

- Remove a toolbar by **right-clicking** any toolbar or the menu bar. The toolbar shortcut menu appears. Click the name of the toolbar you want to remove, which removes the checkmark next to the toolbar name and makes the toolbar disappear

If your worksheet is obscured by too many toolbars, you can selectively remove the toolbars you do not want. You can remove all toolbars, leaving only the menu bar visible if you choose. However, in order to use the Drawing toolbar features, you must ask Excel to display the Drawing toolbar. If the Drawing toolbar is not visible, do the following

Displaying the Drawing toolbar:

1. **Right-click** the menu bar. The toolbar shortcut menu appears (see Figure 3.22)

2. Click **Drawing** in the shortcut menu. The Drawing toolbar appears. Usually Excel docks the Drawing toolbar at the bottom of the screen

tip: *If a toolbar is **floating** on the worksheet, it can appear anywhere in the worksheet window. If so, you can dock it on any of the four edges of your display. (When you **dock** a toolbar, it clings to the edge of the window.) Simply click the toolbar's title bar and drag it toward an edge of the worksheet window. It will dock on the edge when the mouse nears it.*

*another*way

. . . to Display or Remove the Drawing Toolbar

Click the **Drawing** button on the Standard toolbar

EXCEL

Adding a Text Box

Excel's *text box* is a rectangular-shaped drawing object that contains text. It floats above a worksheet's cells and is useful to annotate an especially important point. It draws the worksheet reader's attention to the text box and its comments. Excel has other drawing objects including lines, ovals, circles, rectangles, and arrows. All of these graphic elements provide ways to enhance your worksheet. You can move or delete an object easily. First, move the pointer over the object and click it to select it. An object displays small square *selection handles* around its perimeter or on its ends to indicate it is selected. Once you select an object, you can press the Delete key to delete it or click within the object and drag it to a new location. You can adjust the size of an object by clicking one of its selection handles and dragging until the object obtains the desired size.

task reference

Adding a Text Box to a Worksheet

- Activate the Drawing toolbar and then click the **Text Box** 📄 button
- Click the worksheet in the location where you want the text box
- Drag an outline away from the initial point until the text box outline is the right size and shape
- Type the text you want to appear in the text box
- Click anywhere outside the text box to deselect it

Exotic Fruit's best-selling product this year and projected bestseller next year is Papaya. You want to draw attention to the projected profit and overall percentage of sales for Papaya. A text box is a good way to emphasize the projected sales of Papaya.

Adding a text box to a worksheet:

1. With the Drawing toolbar visible, click the **Text Box** 📄 button, and then move the mouse over any cell in the worksheet. Notice that as you move the mouse pointer on the worksheet, the mouse shape changes to ⬓

2. Move the mouse pointer to the upper-left corner of cell **J11** and then click the mouse to establish the upper-left corner of the text box. (You may have to scroll the worksheet to the left so that columns J, K, and L are in view.) A narrow box appears with four circular selection handles—one at each corner of the box

3. Move the mouse to the lower-right text box selection handle. The mouse pointer changes to a two-headed arrow ⬔

4. Click and drag the mouse to the right until you reach the lower-right corner of cell **L11,** and then release the mouse

5. Type **Papaya is popular. Vons purchases large quantities of it**

6. Carefully move the mouse pointer to any border of the text box until the pointer changes to a four-headed pointer and then **right-click** the border. A shortcut menu appears

7. Click **Format Text box** in the shortcut menu, click the **Colors and Lines** tab, click the **Color** list box found in the Fill section, and click **Automatic,** which appears above the color palette

8. Click the **Color** list box in the Line section of the Format Text Box dialog box, click **Automatic,** which appears above the color palette, and then click **OK** to apply the text box formatting and close the dialog box. Excel places a border around the text box

You can see that the message is longer than the text box can display and it appears that only part of the message is available. Therefore, you need to enlarge the text box just enough so that the entire message is visible.

Modifying the Size of a Text Box:

1. Click the **text box** to select it. Six circular selection handles appear around the text box indicating it is selected

2. Move the cursor until it is directly above the center handle on the bottom edge of the text box. The pointer changes to a double-headed arrow

3. Click and drag the selection handle so that the bottom edge of the text box is aligned with the bottom edge of row 12 so that the text box covers approximately two rows

4. Release the mouse. The text box is large enough to display the entire message (see Figure 3.23)

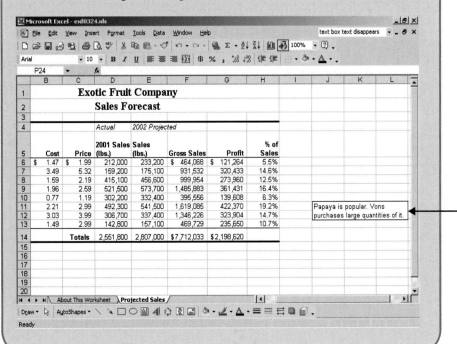

FIGURE 3.23
Adding a text box for emphasis

text box spans approximately two rows

EXCEL

You want to emphasize the word *Vons*, the name of a grocery store chain, with italic and a splash of color.

Italicizing a text box word and changing its font color:

1. Double-click the mouse inside the text box and then use the arrow keys to move the insertion point just ahead of the word "Vons"

2. Hold down the Shift key and press the right arrow key four times to highlight the entire word "Vons"

3. Click the Formatting toolbar **Italic** $\boxed{I}$ button

4. Click the Formatting toolbar **Font Color list arrow** $\boxed{\underline{A} \cdot}$. The color palette opens (see Figure 3.24)

5. Click the **Red** button in the color palette (see Figure 3.24)

6. Click any cell to deselect the text box. The font color of the word "Vons" changes to red and is italicized

---

Adding an Arrow

The text box adds just the right emphasis without overpowering the worksheet. You decide to add an arrow leading from the text box to the right end of the Papaya row—to cell H11—so that it is clear to which row the text box refers. There are several arrows available in the Drawing toolbar from which you can choose.

Adding an arrow graphic and placing it in a layer behind the text box:

1. Click the **AutoShapes** menu on the Drawing toolbar

2. Point to **Block Arrows** and then click the **Left Arrow** (see Figure 3.25), which is in the top row, second arrow from the left. The mouse pointer changes to a small plus sign

3. Move the mouse pointer ⊞ just to the right of the word *Papaya* in the text box

4. Click and drag the mouse to the left and down so that the outline of the arrow completely fills cell **I11** and covers the word Papaya and the tip of the arrow just touches the right edge of cell **H11**. Release the mouse

tip: *If you are dissatisfied with the arrow for any reason (its right end does not cover Papaya, it is too skinny, for example), then select the arrow, press the* **Delete** *key, and repeat the preceding steps until you are pleased with the arrow.*

5. With the arrow selected, move the mouse pointer *inside* the arrow and **right-click** the mouse. A shortcut menu appears

6. Point to **Order** on the shortcut menu and click **Send to Back**. Excel places the arrow in a layer beneath the text box and the word *Papaya* becomes visible again (see Figure 3.26)

7. Click in any cell to deselect the arrow

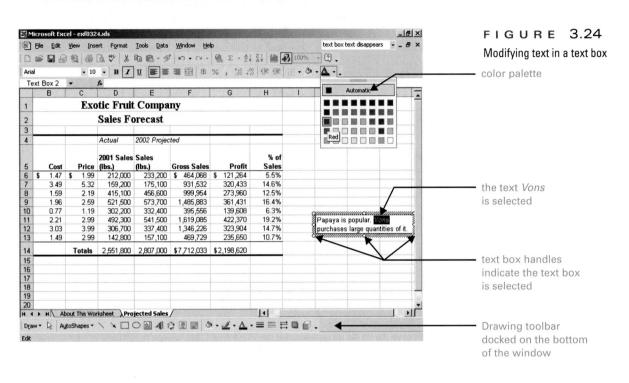

F I G U R E   3.24

Modifying text in a text box

color palette

the text *Vons* is selected

text box handles indicate the text box is selected

Drawing toolbar docked on the bottom of the window

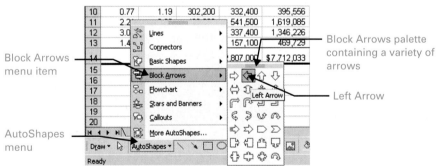

F I G U R E   3.25

Selecting an arrow from the AutoShapes menu

Block Arrows menu item

AutoShapes menu

Block Arrows palette containing a variety of arrows

Left Arrow

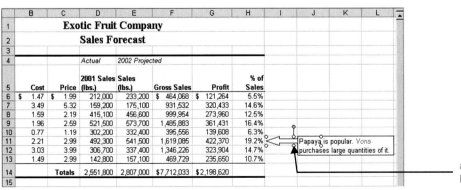

F I G U R E   3.26

Placing an arrow behind a text box

arrow is partially behind the text box

Grouping Drawing Objects

You can move the arrow and text box graphics independently of each other. If you selected the text box and moved it to another location, the arrow would remain where it is. It is better if the two objects are combined into one object. That way, if you choose to move the graphics around, you can select the combined arrow and text box graphic and move it as one unit. Joining two graphics into one object is called *grouping.* Once grouped, multiple objects act as one and one set of selection handles surround the larger grouped object. You can ungroup objects later if you want to adjust their position and then regroup them.

FIGURE 3.27

Grouped objects

Grouping two graphic objects:

1. Click the **text box** to select it. Selection handles appear around the text box

2. Press and hold the **Shift** key

3. Move the mouse over the arrow graphic and **click** the mouse to select the arrow graphic. Both objects should be selected. If not, repeat steps 1 through 3

4. With the mouse within the arrow graphic (the mouse pointer displays the four-headed arrow pointe ⊹) **right-click** the mouse. A shortcut menu appears

5. Point to **Grouping** in the shortcut menu and then click **Group.** The two objects are grouped, and one set of selection handles surrounds the grouped graphic (see Figure 3.27)

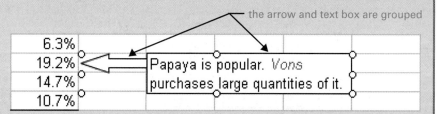

6. Click any cell to deselect the grouped objects

Adding a Drop Shadow

You can make some drawing objects look three-dimensional by adding a drop shadow. A *drop shadow* is the shadow that is cast by the object. Adding a drop shadow to the grouped object—the arrow and text box—enhances the object and adds a little flair.

Adding a drop shadow to a drawing object:

1. Ensure that the Drawing toolbar is visible and then click the arrow and text box grouped object to select it. Selection handles appear around the object

2. Click the **Shadow Style** button on the Drawing toolbar. A palette of drop shadow choices appears (see Figure 3.28)

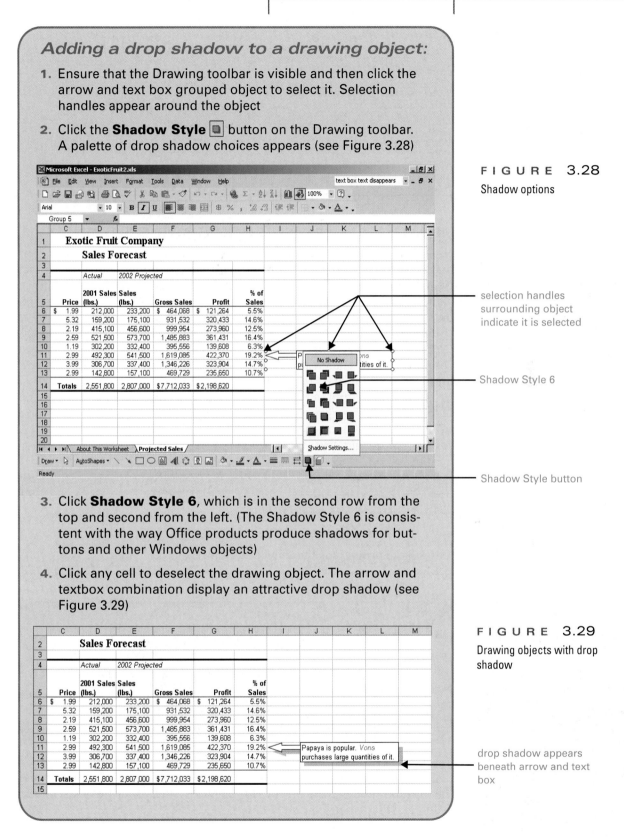

FIGURE 3.28
Shadow options

selection handles surrounding object indicate it is selected

Shadow Style 6

Shadow Style button

3. Click **Shadow Style 6**, which is in the second row from the top and second from the left. (The Shadow Style 6 is consistent with the way Office products produce shadows for buttons and other Windows objects)

4. Click any cell to deselect the drawing object. The arrow and textbox combination display an attractive drop shadow (see Figure 3.29)

FIGURE 3.29
Drawing objects with drop shadow

drop shadow appears beneath arrow and text box

Because you do not need to use the Drawing toolbar in the remainder of this chapter, you can hide it. Doing so provides a little more room for your worksheet.

EXCEL

> **Remove the Drawing toolbar from the work surface:**
>
> 1. Click the **Drawing** 🖉 button on the Standard toolbar. The Drawing toolbar disappears from the work surface and the Drawing button no longer appears highlighted (selected)
>
> 2. Just to be safe, save your worksheet by clicking the **Save** button on the Standard toolbar

HIDING AND UNHIDING ROWS AND COLUMNS

Nancy reviewed the worksheet and is pleased with the way you have formatted it. It is really taking shape. The Cost column contains prices that Exotic Fruit Company pays to its suppliers and is company confidential. Nancy wants you to somehow make that column not appear in any printouts you or any of the managers produce. Naturally, you cannot delete the column from the worksheet because the Profit column depends on the Cost column. The Percent of Sales column depends indirectly on the Cost column. If you deleted the Cost column, Excel would display the error message #REF! in the Profit column and the Percent of Sales column.

Hiding a column is the best solution. Any columns or rows that you hide remain in the worksheet but they are not displayed. When you hide a column, Excel sets its column width to zero. Similarly, when you hide a row, its row height is set to zero.

> **task reference**
>
> **Hiding Rows or Columns**
>
> - Select the rows or columns you want to hide
> - Click **Format,** point to **Row** (or **Column**), and click **Hide**

anotherway

. . . to Hide Rows or Columns

Select the rows or columns you want to hide

Right-click the selected rows or columns to display a shortcut menu

Click **Column Width** in the shortcut menu

Type **0** in the Column width text box and click **OK**

> **Hiding the Cost column:**
>
> 1. Click the **column B header.** Excel selects the entire column
>
> 2. Click **Format,** point to **Column,** and then click **Hide.** Excel hides column B (see Figure 3.30)
>
> 3. Click any cell to deselect the hidden column

Column B disappears, although it is still part of the worksheet because the formulas that depend on column B entries, such as formulas in column G and H, still display correct values.

USING COLOR FOR EMPHASIS

Using colors and patterns carefully can emphasize areas of the worksheet, highlight input areas where users type assumption values, or provide an attractive design element to your worksheet. An important key to effective

column B is hidden

use of color is restraint. Use color sparingly. Too much color or too many colors in a worksheet can yield a garish, unattractive, or confusing overall appearance. On the other hand, the subtle use of color results in an attractive worksheet that others can easily understand and use. If you plan to make color transparencies from your worksheet output, you will need a color printer. However, you can print out color-enhanced worksheets on a noncolor printer. Be aware that black text in cells containing a colored background may not be legible. Experiment with different text and cell background colors if you cannot print your worksheet on a color printer. Generally, lighter colors work better on noncolor printers. As an alternative, you can use patterns to emphasize areas when the output device is a noncolor printer.

Nancy's office has both color printers and noncolor printers (sometimes called monochrome printers or black-and-white printers). She wants you to add a splash of color to the worksheet that looks good on both types of printers. After consulting other people in the office, you decide to use light colors such as pale yellow and light gray for emphasis. Those colors don't obscure black text and look good on both types of printers.

task reference

Applying Color or Patterns to Worksheet Cells

- Select the cells to which you want to apply a color or pattern

- Click **Format,** click **Cells,** and click the **Patterns** tab in the Format Cells dialog box

- If you want to apply a pattern, click a pattern from the Pattern list box

- If you want the pattern to appear in color, click the Pattern list box again and click a color from the Pattern palette

- If you want to apply a colored background, click a color in the Cell shading color palette in the Format Cells dialog box

You decide to apply two separate colored backgrounds, but not patterns, to two worksheet areas. A light gray background color would enhance the column labels in rows 4 and 5. To draw the worksheet reader's eye to the important projected profit value in cell G14, you decide to apply a yellow background to that cell.

Applying a background color to column labels:

1. Click and drag the cell range **A4:H5**

2. Click **Format** on the menu bar, click **Cells,** and then click the **Patterns** tab on the Format Cells dialog box (see Figure 3.31)

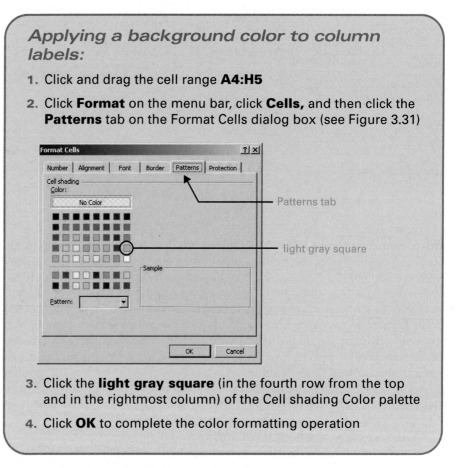

3. Click the **light gray square** (in the fourth row from the top and in the rightmost column) of the Cell shading Color palette

4. Click **OK** to complete the color formatting operation

Next, you will apply another background color to the total profit cell, G14, to highlight that value. Instead of using the Format menu to apply a color, you will use the Fill Color button on the Formatting toolbar, a faster alternative for this type of formatting.

Applying a background color to the total profit cell:

1. Click cell **G14**

2. Click the **Fill Color** button list arrow to display the cell shading color palette

3. Click the **Yellow** color square found in the fourth row from the top and the third square from the left. The background of cell G14 changes to yellow. Figure 3.32 shows the two color formatting changes you have made

4. Press **Ctrl+Home** to make cell A1 active

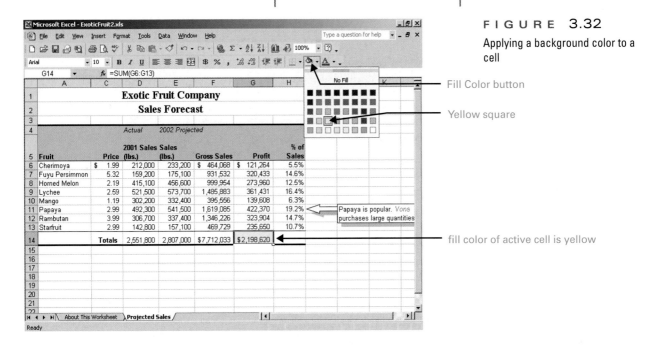

FIGURE 3.32

Applying a background color to a cell

You have finished applying the formatting changes to the Exotic Fruit worksheet. Nancy has reviewed the worksheet and is very pleased with its overall look. She wants you to make one more change to it, however. Nancy thinks that the gridlines that Excel displays onscreen by default are distracting and lessen the visual impact of the worksheet. She asks you to remove the gridlines displayed onscreen.

CONTROLLING GRIDLINES

Excel normally outlines worksheet cells in black. The black gridlines are very handy because they help you locate cells as you are building your worksheet models. When your worksheet is complete, you may wish to eliminate the onscreen gridlines. Consider the example Exotic Fruit documentation worksheet shown in Figure 3.2. That worksheet page would be much less attractive and a bit confusing if the page displayed gridlines.

You can also control whether Excel displays gridlines on output or not. Normally Excel does not display gridlines on output. However, you may want to display them for documentation or demonstration purposes. Whether or not gridlines display onscreen or in output is completely under your control. Next, you will remove the gridlines from the onscreen display of the Projected Sales worksheet.

Removing and Displaying Gridlines Onscreen

Gridline display is an option that you can set for each worksheet or for all worksheets at once. If you remove the gridlines from one worksheet, they need not be removed from other worksheets in the same workbook.

Removing gridlines from the Projected Sales worksheet:

1. Click **Tools** on the menu bar and then click **Options.** The Options dialog box opens

2. If necessary, click the **View** tab

3. Click the **Gridlines** check box in the Window options section to remove the checkmark and remove the onscreen gridlines

4. Click **OK** to complete your changes, close the Options dialog box, and display the worksheet without gridlines (see Figure 3.33)

F I G U R E 3.33

Worksheet without gridline display

	A	C	D	E	F	G	H	I	J	K
1				**Exotic Fruit Company**						
2				**Sales Forecast**						
3										
4			Actual	2002 Projected						
5	Fruit	Price	2001 Sales (lbs.)	Sales (lbs.)	Gross Sales	Profit	% of Sales			
6	Cherimoya	$ 1.99	212,000	233,200	$ 464,068	$ 121,264	5.5%			
7	Fuyu Persimmon	5.32	159,200	175,100	931,532	320,433	14.6%			
8	Horned Melon	2.19	415,100	456,600	999,954	273,960	12.5%			
9	Lychee	2.59	521,500	573,700	1,485,883	361,431	16.4%			
10	Mango	1.19	302,200	332,400	395,556	139,608	6.3%			
11	Papaya	2.99	492,300	541,500	1,619,085	422,370	19.2%			
12	Rambutan	3.99	306,700	337,400	1,346,226	323,904	14.7%			
13	Starfruit	2.99	142,800	157,100	469,729	235,650	10.7%			
14		Totals	2,551,800	2,807,000	$7,712,033	$2,198,620				

Papaya is popular. *Vons* purchases large quantities

About This Worksheet   Projected Sales
Ready

anotherword

. . . on Adding or Removing Onscreen Gridlines

If you want to remove gridlines from more than one worksheet, Shift-click a range of worksheet page tabs or Ctrl-click noncontiguous worksheet tabs

Click **Tools** and then click **Options**

Click the **View** tab

Click the **Gridlines** check box to check it, and click **OK**

Restoring worksheet gridlines is the reverse of the preceding steps. That is, you click Tools, click View, click the Gridlines check box to check it, and click OK.

Removing and Displaying Gridlines on Output

When you want to display worksheet gridlines in *output pages*, set that option prior to printing a page. While output worksheets containing gridlines are not as professional looking as those without gridlines, you may want to print out the worksheet with gridlines as well as the row and column headers as documentation.

Nancy wants you to document the worksheet in hard copy by printing gridlines and row and column headers. First, you will set the option that prints gridlines. Then, you can set another option to print row and column headers. In the steps that follow, you will preview the output but not actually print it. Then you will reset the options so that no gridlines or row and column headings appear.

Adding gridlines and row and column headings to a worksheet to be printed:

1. Click **File** on the menu bar and then click **Page Setup.** The Page Setup dialog box opens

2. Click the **Sheet** tab in the Page Setup dialog box and then click the **Gridlines** check box (in the Print section) to place a checkmark in it. The Gridlines option controls whether or not gridlines print

3. Click **Row and column headings** check box to place a checkmark in it. The Row and columns headings check box controls whether or not worksheet row and column headings appear in printed worksheet pages (see Figure 3.34)

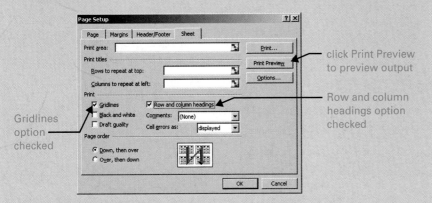

Gridlines option checked

click Print Preview to preview output

Row and column headings option checked

F I G U R E   3.34
Setting print options

4. Click the **Print Preview** button (see Figure 3.34) to preview the output. Examine the preview for a few moments. Notice the gridlines and row and column headings

5. Click the **Setup** [Setup...] button in the Print Preview toolbar to redisplay the Page Setup dialog box

6. Click the **Gridlines** check box to clear it and then click the **Row and column headings** check box to clear it. You don't want to print the worksheet gridlines or the row and column headings at this time

7. Click **OK** in the Page Setup dialog box

8. Click the **Close** [Close] button on the Print Preview toolbar to return to your worksheet

PRINTING

When you are ready to print a worksheet, you should preview the output using the Print Preview command first. That way, you can check to ensure that the worksheet looks right or check to make sure the output is not several pages long. Keep in mind the rule: Preview before printing. That can save both time and effort. Print Preview shows margins, page breaks, headers and footers, and other elements that you do not see in the worksheet window.

EXCEL

FIGURE 3.35

Print Preview window

an available Next button means there is another page

indicates number of pages to print

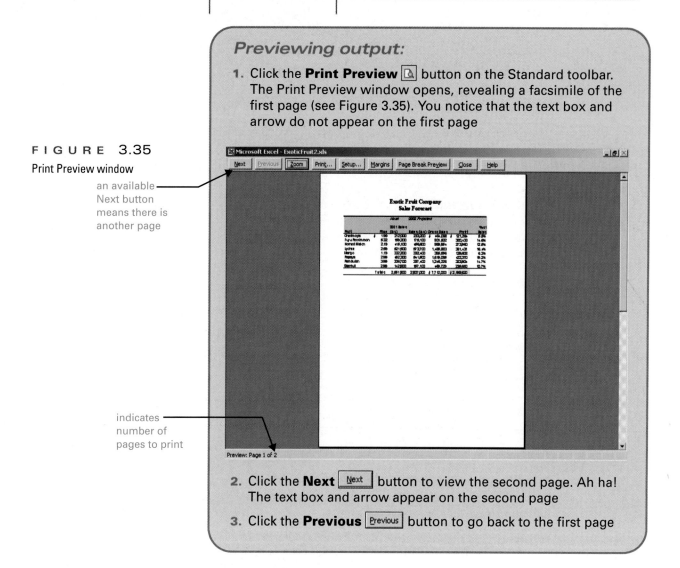

Previewing output:

1. Click the **Print Preview** 🔍 button on the Standard toolbar. The Print Preview window opens, revealing a facsimile of the first page (see Figure 3.35). You notice that the text box and arrow do not appear on the first page

2. Click the **Next** button to view the second page. Ah ha! The text box and arrow appear on the second page

3. Click the **Previous** button to go back to the first page

Previewing the output reveals that the worksheet is slightly larger than can currently fit on one page. There are several ways to remedy this. One possibility is to reduce the left and right margins until there is enough room to fit all the output on one page. As in this case, this may not be the solution. Another possibility is to reduce the font size of the entire worksheet until it is small enough to squeeze the entire worksheet on one page. This is not often a good choice. An alternative is to reorient the worksheet printout.

Controlling Print Orientation

Excel provides two print orientations called portrait and landscape. *Portrait* orientation prints a worksheet so that the paper is taller than it is wide—the standard way books and notebook paper is written. It borrows its name from the way artists paint portraits. *Landscape* orientation prints a worksheet that is wider than it is tall. The term landscape reminds you of an artist's painting depicting a landscape, which is often wider than it is tall. The Exotic Fruit is a worksheet that should be printed in landscape orientation to fit nicely on a printed page.

Changing an output orientation to landscape:

1. With the Print Preview window still open, click the **Setup** Setup... button, which opens the Page Setup dialog box

2. Click the **Page** tab and then click the **Landscape** option button in the Orientation section to select Landscape orientation

3. Click **OK** to return to Print Preview (see Figure 3.36). Notice that the entire worksheet fits on the page and the Next button is dimmed, which indicates there is only one output page

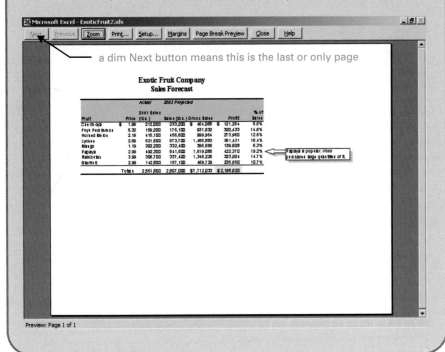

FIGURE 3.36
Landscape orientation

Centering Output on a Page

Before printing the worksheet, you can center the worksheet on a page and add a header and footer. First, center the worksheet.

Vertically centering worksheet output:

1. With the Print Preview window still open, click the **Setup** Setup... button

2. Click the **Margins** tab in the Page Setup dialog box. On this page, you can set left, right, top, bottom, header, and footer margins. In addition, you can check options to center a page horizontally or vertically on a page

3. Click the **Vertically** check box to place a checkmark in the check box (see Figure 3.37)

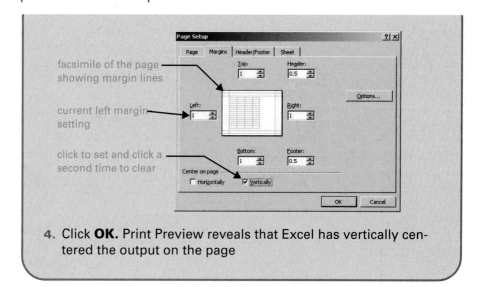

4. Click **OK.** Print Preview reveals that Excel has vertically centered the output on the page

You should place some documentation on the worksheet. In an e-mail message she sent a week ago, Nancy requested that you print the worksheet with the header "Company Confidential" in the center and a footer containing your name and the current date. Nancy did not specify the exact placement of the footer information, so you decide to place your name on the left side of the page and the current date on the right side. You are familiar with worksheet headers and footers, because you have used them in previous chapters.

Placing information in a worksheet header and footer:

1. With the Print Preview window still open, click the **Setup** button

2. Click the **Header/Footer** tab in the Page Setup dialog box

3. Click the **Custom Header** [Custom Header...] button and click in the **Center section**

4. In the Center section, type **Company Confidential** and then click **OK**

5. Click the **Custom Footer** [Custom Footer...] button, click in the **Left section,** and type your first and last names

6. Click in the **Right section** and click the **Date** 🔲 button to insert the current date

7. Click **OK** to close the Footer dialog box

8. Click **OK** again to close the Page Setup dialog box. The Print Preview window redisplays and shows the header and footer information you entered

9. Click the **Close** [Close] button in the Print Preview toolbar to close the window. The worksheet window opens

Unhiding a Column

Your work on the Exotic Fruit Sales Forecast worksheet is almost done, and you are ready to give Nancy the printed copy for her to check before her presentation next week. Before you print the worksheet, unhide column B, check the output once more in the Print Preview window, and make any necessary output adjustments. Then you can save the worksheet and exit Excel.

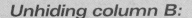

Unhiding column B:

1. Position the mouse pointer over the column A header

2. Click and drag the mouse through the **column C header** to select the three columns (column A, hidden column B, and column C). Notice that the two visible columns are highlighted

3. Right-click anywhere inside the selected columns. A shortcut menu appears

4. Click **Unhide** in the shortcut menu. Column B reappears

5. Click any cell to deselect the three selected columns

6. Click the **Print Preview** button to check the output (see Figure 3.38)

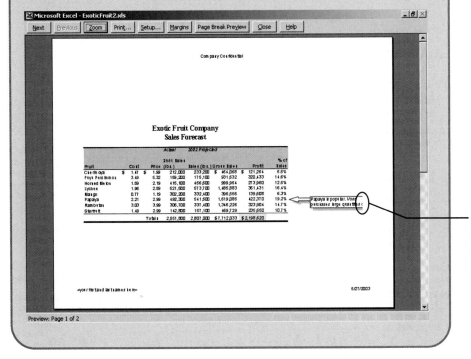

FIGURE 3.38
Preview of expanded worksheet

part of the drawing object may be on the second page (yours may vary)

Depending on where you positioned the drawing objects in the steps presented earlier in this chapter, your output may (still) not fit on one page. The example shown in Figure 3.38 shows a tiny part of the graphic missing from the right end of the text box. One way to handle this kind of problem is to enlarge your worksheet page by adjusting the left and right margins. Any space released by left and right margins is allocated to the worksheet printing area, just enough to print the entire worksheet and drawing object on one page.

Modifying the left and right margins:

1. With the Print Preview window still open, click the **Setup** button. The Page Setup dialog box opens

2. Click the **Margins** tab and double-click the **Left spin control box** to highlight the current left margin number

3. Type **0.5** to set the left margin to one-half inch

4. Double-click the **Right spin control box** to highlight the current right margin number

5. Type **0.5** to set the right margin to one-half inch

6. Click **OK** to close the Page Setup dialog box. The Print Preview window is visible. Unless your arrow and text box drawing boxes are unusually large, the entire grouped drawing object should be visible

tip: *If you still cannot see the entire worksheet on one page, you can force the worksheet to fit by clicking the **Page** tab in the Page Setup dialog box and then click the **Fit to** option button in the Scaling section of the Page tab settings. This shrinks the overall worksheet so that it fits on a single page*

7. Click the **Close** button on the Print Preview toolbar to close the window and return to the worksheet

---

Printing Several Worksheets

Your work on the Exotic Fruit worksheet is complete. Always save your work when you have completed a significant number of changes. That way, your work is safely stored in case you need to open the latest version of the workbook.

Saving your worksheet:

1. Click the **File** on the menu bar

2. Click **Save**

Nancy asks you to print not only the main worksheet, which you have been working to perfect, but also the documentation sheet. You have printed single worksheets before, but not multiple worksheets in one print statement.

Printing multiple worksheets is almost the same process as printing a single worksheet. There is only one small difference in the procedure: You press and hold the Ctrl key and then click the worksheet tabs corresponding to all the worksheets you want to print. Then release the Ctrl key. Then you print as usual.

When you click multiple worksheet tabs, they turn white to indicate they are selected. You probably noticed that there are three option buttons available in the *Print what* section of the Print dialog box. The default option selected is *Active sheets*, which instructs Excel to print all selected sheets. Selected sheets are called ***active sheets.***

task reference

Printing multiple worksheets

- Press and hold the **Ctrl** key
- Click the sheet tabs of each sheet you want to print
- Release the **Ctrl** key
- Click the **Print** button on the Standard toolbar

Printing multiple Exotic Fruit worksheets:

1. Press and hold the **Ctrl** key

2. With the Projected Sales worksheet displayed (active), click the worksheet tab **About This Worksheet**. Both worksheet tabs turn white, indicating both worksheets are active (see Figure 3.39)

white sheet tabs indicate active worksheets

3. Release the **Ctrl** key

4. Click the **Print** button on the Standard toolbar. Both worksheets print

5. Click the **About This Worksheet** tab to deselect the multiple active worksheets. Only the About This Worksheet tab is active

FIGURE 3.39

Selecting multiple worksheets

---

another word

. . . on Selecting and Deselecting Multiple Worksheets

Select multiple worksheets in a contiguous group by clicking the leftmost worksheet tab in the group

Then press and hold the **Shift** key and click the rightmost worksheet tab in the group (using the tab scroll buttons if necessary)

Ctrl-clicking worksheet tabs allows you to select noncontiguous worksheets

Deselect multiple worksheet tabs by clicking any worksheet tab that is *not* selected

If all worksheet tabs are selected, click any one of the worksheet tabs to deselect all the other tabs

EXCEL

SESSION 3.2   *making the grade*

1. Describe how to modify a row's height.

2. Click the _____ tab in the Format Cells dialog box to add borders to selected cells.

3. Activate the Drawing toolbar by right-clicking any _____ or the _____ bar and then clicking Drawing in the list.

4. When you click a drawing object such as a text box, _____ _____ appear around the object.

5. Modify the **ExoticFruit2.xls** worksheet in the following ways. Hide the Cost and Price columns (columns B and C). Change the typeface of the worksheet title and subtitle (cells A1 and A2) to Arial and change the point size of the worksheet title to 18 point and the subtitle to 14 point. Change the worksheet header to **Copyright Exotic Fruit Company, Inc**. Change the formatting of the Gross Sales and Profit numbers to Currency Style with zero decimal places. Modify the % of Sales column to display percentages with two decimal places instead of one. Format the background of each total in row 14 with the color Yellow. Modify the page footer to display the page number in the Center section. Remove the arrow and text box objects from the worksheet. Change the left and right margins to 1.5 inches and center the output horizontally and vertically. Place your name in the Left section of the footer of the *About This Worksheet* page. Save the worksheet as **ExoticFruit3.xls**. Print both worksheet pages.

SESSION 3.3 SUMMARY

Formatting worksheet entries alters the appearance of labels and values but does not alter the cells' contents. By default, Excel formats all cells with the General format. The General format displays values right aligned in a cell and displays text left aligned in a cell. Clicking Clear and then Formats from the Edit menu restores selected cells to an unformatted state. Selected popular format commands appear as buttons on the Formatting toolbar to make them easier to use. Nearly all worksheets contain some formatting. Formatting yields professional-looking worksheets that are suitable for publication in sales brochures and accounting statements that always accompany company annual reports.

Common formatting choices display values with leading currency symbols, allow you to select the number of decimal places to display, and provide comma separators for larger numbers. Formatting can display negative numbers enclosed in parentheses or with a leading minus sign. Other formats present numbers as percentages or dates in a variety of forms. Scientific formats are convenient for engineering and scientific applications in which large numbers display with a number and an exponent. Scientific notation represents the value 123.436 as 1.23E+02, where E+02 means multiply the number preceding E by 100. Applying an Accounting format to numbers displays a left-aligned dollar sign, commas when necessary, and any number of decimal places, including zero.

Excel repeats the symbol # in formatted numeric cells in which the values are larger than the column can display. In that case, widen the column until the # symbols disappear. When possible, delay altering column widths until you complete all formatting. Use the Format Painter button to apply one cell's format characteristics to other cells. Doing so relieves you from executing several multistep formatting commands to apply a series of formats. Other time-saving formatting buttons on the Formatting toolbar include Currency Style, Percent Style, Increase Decimal, and Decrease Decimal. Select a cell or cell range and click the Increase Decimal button to increase the number of displayed decimal places, for example.

Several data alignment formats allow you to align numbers or text on the left, center, or right side of a cell. The Merge and Center Formatting toolbar button centers text across multiple columns by merging the cells in a row and then centering text within the merged cells. You can format especially long labels to fit in narrower columns with the Wrap text option, which is found on the Alignment tab of the Format Cells dialog box. This option creates multiple lines within a cell and automatically increases the row height to accommodate multiline text. Excel includes a wide variety of typeface, point size, and character formatting choices. Typeface choices range from Arial to ZaphDingbats, and you can format text or numbers in point sizes ranging from 4 points to over 96, depending on the typeface you choose. Boldface, Italic, and Underline are popular character formatting choices that you can apply to any cells.

Change the height of a row by typing the new height in the Row Height dialog box, or drag the line between the row headings to adjust a row's height. Sparing use of cell border formatting visually enhances worksheets with vertical and horizontal lines following cell wall boundaries. Excel provides several line styles and widths from which you can choose.

Excel provides several toolbars whose name you can see by right-clicking in the menu or in any toolbar. You can activate a toolbar from the shortcut menu by clicking the toolbar's name. The Drawing toolbar contains graphic objects that you can place on a layer above the worksheet. Objects include arrows, connecting lines, callouts, various geometric shapes including squares and ovals, WordArt, fill colors, drop shadows, and other 3-D effects. A text box is one of the Drawing toolbar's objects. Text boxes contain text enclosed in a sizeable rectangle that you can place anywhere on the worksheet. Text boxes are handy for pointing out special worksheet features or simply noting important facts about the worksheet. Clicking an object selects it and selection handles appear around the object's perimeter. Move objects by selecting and then dragging them to their new locations. Group multiple objects into one object by shift-clicking each object and then grouping them.

Cell background colors, when used tastefully and sparingly, add emphasis and draw the eye to selected features. Colors can also visually group related areas of a worksheet. Foreground color does not affect the contents of cells, and a variety of colors is available. When color is not appropriate—especially for noncolor laser printers—you can pattern cell backgrounds for dramatic and eye-catching effects.

Clicking the Print Preview button allows you to preview output before you print it. If the worksheet is too wide to fit on a page, try landscape orientation rather than portrait. Landscape orientation is wider than it is tall. Print multiple pages of a worksheet by shift-clicking multiple tabs before printing. Modify page margins when needed to provide more space for worksheet output. Hide selected columns when necessary to prevent printing confidential or proprietary information. Select the column and select Column Hide from the Format menu. Hiding a column is synonymous with making its width equal to zero.

EXCEL

MOUS OBJECTIVES SUMMARY

- Left-, center-, and right-align text (MOUS Ex2002-3)
- Apply currency and accounting formats to numbers (MOUS Ex2002-3-1)
- Modify the typeface and point size of text and numbers (MOUS Ex2002-3-1)
- Apply boldface, italic, and underline to cells (MOUS Ex2002-3-1)
- Clear all formatting from selected cells (MOUS Ex2002-3; Ex2002-1-2)
- Modify column widths and row heights (MOUS Ex2002-3-3)
- Hide and reveal rows and columns (MOUS Ex2002-3-2)
- Modify the worksheet's print characteristics (MOUS Ex2002-3-7)

task reference round-up

Task	Location	Preferred Method
Formatting numbers	EX 3.7	• Select cell(s)
		• Click **Format**, click **Cells**, click **Number**
		• Click format category and select options
		• Click **OK**
Copying a cell format to a cell or cell range	EX 3.10	• Select the cell whose format you want to copy
		• Click the **Format Painter** button
		• Click (click/drag) the target cell(s)
Wrapping long text within a cell	EX 3.17	• Select the cell or cell range to which you will apply a format
		• Click **Format**, click **Cells**, and click the **Alignment** tab
		• Click the **Wrap text** check box
		• Click **OK**
Applying fonts and font characteristics	EX 3.18	• Select the cell or cell range that you want to format
		• Click **Format**, click **Cells**, and click the **Font** tab
		• Select a typeface from the Font list box
		• Select a font style and a font size
		• Click **OK**
Clearing formats from a cell, cell selection, rows, or columns	EX 3.21	• Select the cell, cell range, rows, or columns
		• Click **Edit**, point to **Clear**, and click **Formats**

task reference round-up

Task	Location	Preferred Method
Modifying a row's height	EX 3.23	• Click the row heading
		• Click **Format**, point to **Row**, and click **Height**
		• Type the row height in the Row height text box
		• Click **OK**
Add a border to a cell	EX 3.25	• Click the cell to which you want to add a border
		• Click the Formatting toolbar **Borders list box arrow**, and click the border you want
Activating/removing a toolbar	EX 3.27	• **Right-click** the menu bar
		• Click the name of the toolbar you want to activate or remove
Adding a text box to a worksheet	EX 3.28	• Activate the Drawing toolbar
		• Click the **Text Box** button
		• Click the worksheet in the location where you want the text box
		• Drag an outline away from the initial point until the text box outline is the right size and shape
		• Type the text you want to appear in the text box
Hiding rows or columns	EX 3.34	• Select the rows or columns
		• Click **Format**, point to **Row** (or **Column**), and click **Hide**
Applying color or patterns to worksheet cells	EX 3.35	• Select the cells to which you want to apply a color or pattern
		• Click **Format**, click **Cells**, and click the **Patterns** tab in the Format Cells dialog box
		• If you want to apply a pattern, click a pattern from the Pattern list box
		• If you want the pattern to appear in color, click the Pattern list box again and click a color from the Pattern palette
		• If you want to apply a colored background, click a color in the Cell shading color palette in the Format Cells dialog box
Printing multiple worksheets	EX 3.45	• Ctrl-click the sheet tabs of each sheet you want to print
		• Click the **Print** button

EXCEL

CROSSWORD PUZZLE

Across

2. Name for the combination of typeface, character size, and spacing
4. Print orientation for a narrow but long output
7. Type into the Excel _____ box drawing object
9. Name of the default format for cells
10. The process of making a toolbar appear on the desktop
13. General name for font if characters' pitches vary

Down

1. The cell _____ format applies lines to worksheet cell edges
3. Sheet is _____ when it is selected
4. Metric used to indicate the height of a character
5. The position of data relative the sides of a cell
6. The property of a toolbar that is not attached to one of the four window walls
8. Altering the appearance of data in one or more cells
11. Format drawing objects with 3-D effects with a _____ shadow
12. Name given to the width of a character

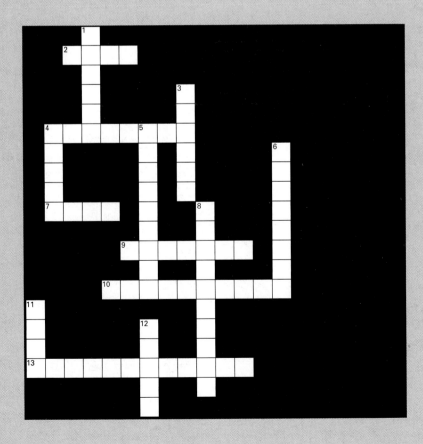

FILL-IN

1. Use the numeric format _____ when you want to format a value such as 0.3478 to display 34.78%.

2. Use the Format _____ to copy the format of one cell to another.

3. The _____ format displays a left-justified currency symbol for numeric entries.

4. Apply a cell _____ format to produce lines and to outline an area of related cells.

5. Click the _____ menu on the Drawing toolbar to display a palette of shapes such as Block Arrows and lines.

6. Select _____ orientation for wide worksheets. The default orientation, _____, is best for narrow worksheets.

REVIEW QUESTIONS

1. Suppose you have a column of numbers representing the wholesale cost of various quantities of produce, and suppose the label "Whole produce cost" heads the column. Discuss how you would format the numeric entries in the column and discuss which formats you might apply to the column's identifying label.

2. Discuss the impact of a worksheet in which five columns each are formatted with a different background color. Is such formatting suitable for professional presentations? What improvements, if any, would you suggest?

3. What are Excel drawing objects and how are they useful? Are drawing objects attached to particular cells, stored as part of the cells' contents, or in some other position in a worksheet? Explain.

4. Explain why you might want to hide one or more columns in a worksheet.

CREATE THE QUESTION

For each of the following answers, create an appropriate, short question.

ANSWER	QUESTION
1. So that the label and numeric values alignments match	_____
2. Selection handles appear when you do this	_____
3. Changes a cell's background color	_____
4. Proportional typeface	_____
5. Excel merges cells and centers text within the merged cells	_____
6. Excel sets the column width to zero	_____

1. Formatting a College Bookstore Book Order

Mr. Waldron Madden is an instructor in the Philosophy department at South-Western College. Each semester for more years than he can remember, Mr. Madden has ordered his books for each semester through the college bookstore using one of their multipart book order forms. A separate book order form is required for each course, although instructors can group courses together on one order form whenever multiple sections of the same course use the same books. While filling out a book order form is not difficult, Mr. Madden has often thought how much simpler it would be if he could simply fill out an electronic form and e-mail it to the bookstore.

This year the bookstore sent a notice to all instructors that the bookstore would accept book orders by fax or e-mail. However, all fax orders must use a copy of the old paper book order form. Instructors wanting to use e-mail could produce a reasonable facsimile of the paper book order form using Word or Excel. Mr. Madden decides to use Excel. He asks you to help him format the worksheet so that it resembles the paper form. Execute each of the steps that follow to create a book order form containing Mr. Madden's book request. First, ensure Excel is running and the application window is maximized.

1. Open the workbook **ex03Bookstore.xls** and then click **File,** click **Save As,** type **Bookstore2** in the File name text box, and click the **Save** button to save the file under a new name. Ensure that the Formatting toolbar is visible.
2. Type the following in the indicated cells:
    Cell B10: **Mr. W. Madden**
    Cell B11: **1, 2, 5**
    Cell F10: **Philosophy 101**
    Cell F11: **Spring, 2003**
    Cell H10: **10/17/2002**
3. Click cell **A1,** click the **Font Size list box arrow** on the Formatting toolbar, and click **36** in the Font Size list box (scroll it if necessary).

4. Click cell **A2,** click the **Font Size list box arrow** on the Formatting toolbar, and click **24** in the Font Size list box (scroll it if necessary).
5. Select cell range **A1:I1** ("eye-one") and then click the **Merge and Center** button on the Formatting toolbar.
6. Select cell range **A2:I2** and then click the **Merge and Center** button on the Formatting toolbar.
7. Alter the column widths of columns A through I by right-clicking each column heading in turn, clicking **Column Width,** and then typing a width—listed below for each column—and then clicking **OK.** Column A: **16,** column B: **21,** column C: **12,** columns D and E: **4,** column F: **21,** columns G and H: **10,** and column I: **12.**
8. Click and drag the cell range **A14:I20,** click the **Borders list box arrow,** and click the **All Borders** square to place borders around all cell walls of the selected cell range.
9. Click and drag the cell range **I21:I24** and click the **Borders** button (the All Borders button appears on the Borders button now).
10. Click and drag the cell range **A14:I14,** click the **Fill Color list box arrow,** and click the **Gray-25%** square to place a light gray background in the selected cells. Click the **Bold** button on the Formatting toolbar.
11. Click **B10,** press and hold the **Ctrl** key, click **B11, F10, F11,** and **H10,** and then release the Ctrl key.
12. Click the **Borders list box arrow** and click the **Bottom Border** square to place a line on the lower edge of each selected cell.
13. Click the cell range **B14:C14** and click the **Center** formatting toolbar button.
14. Click **D14,** press and hold the **Ctrl** key, and click cells **E14, G14, H14,** and **I14,** release the Ctrl key, and click the **Align Right** Formatting toolbar button.
15. Click and drag the cell range **I15:I24,** click **Format,** click **Cells,** click the **Number** tab, click **Accounting** in the Category list, click the **Symbol list box arrow,** and click **None.** Click the **Decimal places spinner** so that it displays 2 and click **OK.**

16. Click the **Format Painter** button and then select the cell range **H15:H20.**
17. Click **I15**, press and hold the **Ctrl** key, click **I21**, click **I24**, release the Ctrl key, click the **Currency Style** button on the Formatting toolbar, and press **Ctrl+Home** to deselect the cell range.
18. Click **View**, click **Header and Footer**, click the **Custom Header** button, replace the text in the Right section with your name, click **OK**, and click **OK** again.
19. Click the **Print Preview** button on the Standard toolbar. Then click the **Setup** button on the Print Preview toolbar, click the **Page** tab, click the **Landscape** option under the Orientation section, click the **Margins** tab, and change the Left and Right margins to **0.75.** Finally, click the Page Setup dialog box **OK** button and then click the Print Preview toolbar **Close** button.
20. Click the Save button on the Standard toolbar, print the worksheet, and close Excel.

2. Creating a Business Card

Carmen Cervantes is the president of the Professional Students Association, which is a club that meets once a month to hear a professional speaker from the community speak about various topics in both business and society. The association has almost 40 members, and Carmen thought it would be nice if the members had cards, similar in format to business cards, that identify each of them as members of the Professional Students Association (PSA). Unfortunately, PSA's budget is very limited. Therefore there is not enough money to supply each member with a set of business cards. As an interim measure, Carmen wants to make business cards using Excel. She can print the cards on heavier stock paper to give the printed output the feel of real business cards. Follow these steps to print a business card similar to Carmen's organization.

1. Start Excel and open a blank workbook.
2. Click **A1** and type **Professional Students Association.**
3. Click **B3** and type your first and last names.
4. Click **B4** and type your school's name.
5. Click **B5** and type the street address of your school.
6. Click **B6** and type the city and state, separated by a comma, where your city is located.
7. Click **B7** and type your telephone number, beginning with the area code. Enclose the area code in parentheses, type a space, and type the rest of your phone number.
8. Click **A1** and click the **Bold** button on the Formatting toolbar. Change the point size of the typeface to **14.**
9. Click **B3** and click the **Bold** button on the Formatting toolbar. Change the point size of the typeface to **12.**
10. Select the cell range **B4:B7** and click the **Increase Indent** button twice.
11. Click **B4** and click the Formatting toolbar **Italic** button.
12. Select cell range **A1:E11.**
13. Click the **Borders** button on the Formatting toolbar and then click the **Thick Box Border** square.
14. Click **File**, click **Save As**, type **BusinessCard** in the File name text box, and click **Save.**
15. Click **File**, click **Print**, and click **OK** to print your business card.

challenge!

1. Formatting a Class Schedule

You just received your Spring 2003 class schedule and you want to create a copy of it using Excel. Once you create the schedule, you can post it to the Web for others to view. Begin by loading the workbook **ex03Schedule.xls.** It contains an example class schedule containing a total of 17 credit hours.

Format and then print the schedule by doing the following. Set the title in A1 to **18** point **Times New Roman** typeface and merge and center it over columns A through E. Set row 1's Row Height to **24. Bold** cell range **A2:E2.** Change the column widths of column A to **5,** columns B and C to **8,** column D to **22,** and column E to **8.** Format cell range A2:E2 with wrap text alignment. Format cells A1 through E7 with the **All Borders** selection so that borders appear around each cell in the range. Remove the gridlines from the onscreen display. Center all entries in column E, and right-align labels in cells B2 and C2. Format the times in columns B and C to display AM or PM. Adjust column widths so that they are no wider than necessary to accommodate the existing data. Finally, color the background of cells A2 through E2 with **Yellow** and the background of cells A3 through E7 with **Light Yellow.** Place your name somewhere in the worksheet header or footer and then execute File, Save As, or print the worksheet according to your instructor's direction.

2. Formatting a Payment Ledger

John Kirry purchased a new automobile last year. He received a bank loan for $10,000 for the car and paid the dealer a down payment of just over $5,000. His bank sent a statement at the end of the year detailing all of his loan payments during 2001. The worksheet shows the amount of John's payment that is applied toward interest and the amount that reduces the outstanding loan balance. John, a commercial airline pilot, understands enough about spreadsheet programs to enter data and save workbooks, but he is reluctant to format the data. He calls you up and asks you to format it for him. (To return the favor,

John promises to take you up in a private plane for an hour to tour the city.) You agree to help John and ask him to send you the worksheet as an e-mail attachment. He does. The file is called **ex03Payment.xls.** You detach it from the e-mail message and load it into Excel. Figure 3.40 shows you the formatted version of the payment ledger.

Reproduce the formatting shown in that figure as accurately as you can. The font is Arial 10 point. Column labels are bold, some column labels are centered, but the labels above numeric values are right aligned. Column-top numeric values contain the Accounting format. Notice the Interest Payment label. It has a superscript—a footnote. Type the word **Payment1** and then highlight the digit 1. Click **Superscript** from the Font tab of the Format Cells dialog box. Follow the same procedure for the text box at the bottom of the figure. It contains the same superscript. The text box and the callout Drawing objects both have drop shadows. Remember to place your name in the header or footer. Set all margins to 1 inch. Use borders and shading as shown in the figure.

FIGURE 3.40

Formatting a payment ledger

www.mhhe.com/i-series

EX 3.55

EXCEL

on the web

1. Building and Formatting a Product Comparison Worksheet

Ernie Kildahl wants to open an online store to carry audio equipment. The real physical store he owns sells a variety of electronic equipment but has only a limited selection of audio equipment. Ernie is particularly interested in offering a variety of brand-name stereo headphones in his online store. He wants you to research a few brands on the Web, collect a bit of information about the headphones, and report back to him. He is interested in the following brands and models: AKG, Beyerdynamic, Etymotic Research, Grado, and Sennheiser. Using Web search engines, locate three prices for each headphone and model and compare their prices on these five brands. The particular models you are to price-shop—one per brand—are in the worksheet **ex03Headphones.xls**. Load and print the worksheet for reference as you conduct your Web research.

After you have collected three prices for each brand and model, format the worksheet with currency symbols, borders, bold, and at least two typefaces—one for the title (Headphone Price Survey) and a different font for the remainder of the worksheet. Bold column titles, and use a larger point size for the column titles than the five product rows. One Web location to get you started is www.headphone.com (what else!). Use one or more search engines such as www.hotbot.com and www.google.com to search for "headphone" to locate prices. If those search results are not satisfying, search for particular brand and model combinations. For example, search for "Grado SR224" and look for any vendor's prices. Identify your worksheet, save it when you are done as **Headphones2.xls**, and print the results.

2. Formatting an "Audio Rippers and Encoders" Comparison Worksheet

You have an extensive collection of MP3 files that you have purchased from various reputable online MP3 distribution sites. Now you want to convert several of your MP3 sound tracks into a CD-compatible format. First, do a little feature, cost, and popularity comparisons before choosing a conversion program by creating a worksheet with features across a row and different encoding and ripping program names down a particular column. Format the results into an attractive worksheet with commas where needed. Start your research by using any Web browser and going to www.download.com. Click the *Rippers and Encoders* link under the heading *MP3 and Audio*. After the browser displays the Rippers and Encoders page, click the Downloads link at the top of the column displaying the number of downloads. This sorts the resulting rows into descending order by popularity. Place the following information into a worksheet, format it, save it, and print it.

In column A (beginning in cell A4, for example), list at least five of the most popular entries in the sorted list of encoders. In row 3, beginning in cell B3, place the following labels left to right: **Software Cost, Date Added to List, Number of Downloads,** and **File Size (KB)**. Format these long labels by clicking Format, Cells, and then clicking the Alignment tab. Format the column labels wrap text so that they completely display. Next, fill in the rows and columns with information for each of the five products and their features (software cost, date added to list, etc.). Place a zero in a cell whenever the software cost indicates "free." For "shareware" or "check latest prices" software, determine the software's price by clicking the appropriate links and then insert the price into your worksheet. (Leave it blank if the price is not readily available.) Be sure the file sizes are in thousands of kilobytes so that the units are comparable in the File Size column. List the file size for a 2.9MB file as 2,900 or a 950K file as 950. Remember that 1MB is equal to 1000K. Use cell borders in any way you choose to enhance the worksheet.

Place a worksheet title (such as "Encoder Price Comparison") in row 1 and increase the title's font size. Bold the title to make it stand out. Center the title across all information-containing columns (product name, software cost, and so on). Insert a comment in the cell containing the File Size label. The comment should contain the statement "All information obtained from Download.com." Remember to label your output with your name in the header, footer, or in the worksheet itself. Execute either Print or Save As, according to your instructor's direction.

e-business

1. Developing a Rowing Product Worksheet

Marcia Sandoval was on the lightweight women's crew in college. She rowed for Radcliffe seven years ago and has maintained her passion for rowing ever since. Since she graduated from college, she has been rowing at an all-women's rowing club in Santa Monica. Marcia majored in journalism and she minored in business in college. She has always had an entrepreneurial spirit. Three years ago, she started a mail-order store from her garage selling rowing accessories and athletic equipment. She wants to open a rowing store on the Internet selling her rowing items that appeal to both recreational and competitive rowers. She has created a fundamental worksheet that she will present to her loan officer next Monday, but she has to format it to make it more professional looking.

Open the worksheet **ex03Rowing.xls** and format it to make it more attractive and professional looking. Make at least six formatting changes to the worksheet and print it. Marcia has introduced some indenting that is incorrect. All values should be formatted to two decimal places.

around the world

1. Investigating the Value of the U.S. Dollar

Format a table showing the exchange rate for $100 U.S. Start your research by loading your favorite Web browser. There are several exchange rate calculators on the Web, but you might find one particularly handy because it maintains a history of currency exchange rates. Go to www.exonofinance.com/xrates.html and use their Web pages to locate currency exchange rates. Specifically, you are to find the exchange rate of

$100 U.S. in the following currencies: Australian Dollar, French Franc, British Pound, Italian Lira, and Japanese Yen. Format the worksheet to resemble Figure 3.41. Select any three consecutive months and compute each currency's average value against the U.S. Dollar. Color the $100 red (second row of the figure), shade the column headers, use a background color, and format values in the four columns with commas and zero decimal places. Print your worksheet.

FIGURE 3.41

Formatting a foreign currency table

Value of U.S. Dollar

The value of $100 U.S. is:

Currency	Currency	9/1/2003	10/1/2003	11/1/2003	Average
Australia	Australian Dollar				
France	French Franc				
Great Britain	Pound				
Italy	Lira				
Japan	Yen				

fill in values in these three columns

write formulas for this column

Pampered Paws

Grace Jackson wants to assemble a worksheet showing the first-quarter sales and remaining inventory of dog and cat baked and bottled treats. The worksheet will help her order supplies next month based on sales for the previous period and the amount of inventory on hand. She has created a rudimentary worksheet called **ex03Paws.xls** that she wants you to format so that it is easier to understand and use.

Format the worksheet using borders, at least one text box and arrow combination that points out the inventory item on hand with the largest value, and use some foreground and background color to highlight the product that has the highest total sales. Format the Beginning Inventory, Ending Inventory, and the Units Sold columns using Accounting with zero decimal places. Format the Inventory Value and Total Sales columns with Accounting with two decimal places. Remember to place a dollar sign on each column-top numeric value per product category. Use at least two different typefaces but no more than four in the worksheet. Use foreground and background color for the three product category names and separate the categories with one blank row. Center the worksheet both horizontally and vertically on the worksheet. Save the workbook as **Paws33.xls.** Print the worksheet in landscape orientation.

did you
know?

the *"Cereal Bowl of America" is in Battle Creek, Michigan, where the most cereal in the United States is produced.*

oak *trees are struck by lightning more often than any other tree. Historians theorize that this is one reason why the ancient Greeks considered oak trees sacred to Zeus, god of thunder and lightning.*

on *a bingo card of 90 numbers, there are approximately 44 million ways to make B-I-N-G-O.*

ostriches *are such fast runners that they can outrun a horse. Male ostriches can roar like a lion.*

the *Sears Tower contains enough phone wire to wrap around the earth 1.75 times and enough electrical wiring to run a power line from Chicago to Los Angeles*

a *radar graph is a great way to represent what type of information? Read on and find out.*

Chapter Objectives

- **Define a data series and data categories**

- **Create an embedded chart and a chart sheet (MOUS Ex2002-6-1)**

- **Modify an existing chart by revising data, altering chart text, and labeling data (MOUS Ex2002-6-1)**

- **Use color and patterns to embellish a chart (MOUS Ex2002-6-1)**

- **Add a new data series to a chart (MOUS Ex2002-6-2)**

- **Alter a chart type and create a three-dimensional chart (MOUS Ex2002-6-1)**

- **Create a pie chart with a title, exploding slice, labels, and floating text (MOUS Ex2002-6-1)**

- **Add texture to a chart (MOUS Ex2002-6-1)**

- **Delete embedded charts and chart sheets (MOUS Ex2002-4-1)**

Big Wave Surfboards

Keoki Lahani founded Big Wave Surfboards in 1971 in his garage in Napili, Maui, Hawaii, where he designed and built his first surfboards. Keoki ships surfboards all around the world today. Since 1971, Keoki has enlarged his shop in Napili and created two more surfboard design and manufacturing facilities and accompanying outlet stores in Malibu, California, and Melbourne, Florida. A master board builder at each of his three stores oversees the design and manufacture of Keoki's surfboards, which bear his Big Wave logo.

Each facility builds surfboards from scratch using Keoki's time-honored hand craftsmanship and quality control methods. Starting with a foam blank, a shaper uses foam planers to create the rough shape for each custom-designed board to exacting customer specifications. If a board is going to contain a color or logo, it is applied after the blank is sanded. In the second major step of the four-step manufacturing process, a skilled technician applies fiberglass (called "glassing") followed by a coating of resin to hold the fiberglass in place to supply waterproofing and to give the board strength and integrity. The third step, called sanding, follows the glassing. An experienced sander carefully sands the board to remove any irregularities and ensures that the surface is smooth and even. The final step is called finishing. A finisher typically applies a gloss finish. The gloss finish supplies the final seal and gives the board a smooth, uniform, glossy look.

Big Wave offers a wide variety of surfboards ranging from smaller boards, called shortboards, that are as short as 5 feet long up to the largest surfboards, called longboards, that can be over 11 feet long. Each of the three manufacturing centers can build any surfboard from shortboards to longboards. Big Wave classifies the surfboards they sell into these groups: Shortboard, Fish, Funboard, Retro, and Longboard. Surfboard length, shape, and features classify them into the different groups.

Keoki and his chief financial officer, Stephen French, have created a worksheet summarizing sales for last year and broken out sales by sales outlet and board type. In this chapter, you will help Stephen create various charts from the raw worksheet data and enhance charts to convey sales information graphically. Charts provide the reader with a quickly understandable and simple picture of the sales patterns. Figure 4.1 shows the completed Big Wave Sales worksheet and accompanying embedded graph.

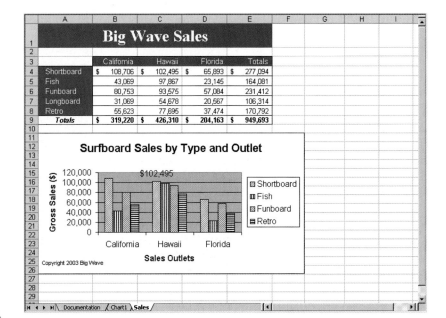

FIGURE 4.1

Completed Big Wave surfboard sales worksheet

INTRODUCTION

Chapter 4 covers creating Excel charts. In this chapter, you will use a worksheet from Big Wave, a surfboard manufacturer and seller. Using the sales values for three separate sales locations and several different surfboard categories, you will create graphs that pictorially display sales in a chart. Using the chart wizard and various chart formatting features, you will create and modify both an embedded chart and a chart stored on a separate worksheet. Formatting and graph features you will explore include altering a chart's title, legend, data markers, X- and Y-axis titles, background colors, and Y-axis scaling. Color and patterns add excitement to a chart. You will learn how to apply both. Three-dimensional charts simplify understanding the values in a worksheet, and you will create a 3-D pie chart with special features such as an exploded pie slice. The chapter concludes by describing how to add various text elements to charts, adding and modifying textures, printing chart sheets, and saving and deleting charts.

SESSION 4.1 CREATING AN EXCEL CHART

In this section, you will learn how to create your first Excel chart from existing sales data supplied in the Big Wave sales worksheet. First you will learn about data series and data categories. Then you will learn about the different chart types available in Excel and which situations favor one chart type over others. Using the Excel chart wizard, you will create an embedded chart displaying sales of different types of surfboards for each sales outlet. After creating a graph, you will update and modify it by changing the underlying data, changing text in the chart, and adding labels

CHAPTER OUTLINE

4.1 Creating an Excel Chart

4.2 Modifying and Improving a Chart

4.3 Summary

to the charted data. Next you will add color and modify color to enhance the chart's appearance. Finally you will preview the worksheet and chart and then print it.

DATA SERIES AND CATEGORIES

Two important terms you should understand before you work with charts are data series and categories. A *data series* is a set of values that you want to chart. For example, if you want to chart sales of Big Wave surfboards in California, the data series is the set of sales values under the column heading California. Similarly, if you want to chart temperatures in Nebraska for the month of January, the data series is the set of temperature readings for each day of January found in contiguous cells in a row or column. Each data series in a chart can have up to 32,000 values, or *data points,* for two-dimensional charts or 4,000 values for three-dimensional charts. You can chart as many as 255 data series in a chart, although a two-dimensional chart is limited to a total of 32,000 total data points.

You use *categories* to organize the values in a data series. For example, a data series of sales for surfboards sold in Florida contain the categories Shortboard, Fish, Funboard, Retro, and so on (see Figure 4.1). Similarly, the categories for a series of sales values for the past year are January, February, March, and so on—the month names under which sales are recorded. In a chart that plots value changes over time, such as fluctuating prices of a particular stock for the last month, the categories are always the time intervals (days, months, or years). To keep this clear in your mind, simply remember that the data series is the series of values you are charting and categories are the labels or headings under (or next to) which the values are stored.

LOCATING AND OPENING THE WORKBOOK

Stephen French, an avid surfer and Big Wave's chief financial officer, sits down with you and outlines what he wants you to do to the Big Wave sales worksheet. He sets milestones for you to complete in time for the important presentation coming up this month. The result of that meeting with Stephen are these points:

- Goal: Create charts from the Big Wave sales data in an attractive form ready for printing and presentation to the Board of Directors this month
- Information needed to complete the work: Sales data for California, Hawaii, and Florida by surfboard model for previous year
- New formulas or values needed: None. The worksheet data is complete as is. Only charts are missing from the workbook

With Keoki's guidance, Stephen has entered all the formulas, values, and text for the Big Wave workbook. It consists of one worksheet displaying sales for five categories of surfboards broken out by sales location. For example, the worksheet sales figures indicate that shortboard-style surfboards sold far more units in California last year than in either Hawaii or Florida. Similarly, longboards are more popular in Hawaii than they are in either Florida or California based on last year's sales. However, it takes careful study of the sales values to determine the preceding facts. A graph would make that fact obvious more quickly.

You begin by opening the Big Wave workbook.

Opening the Big Wave worksheet and saving it under a new name:

1. Start Excel
2. Open the workbook **ex04BigWave.xls.** The documentation sheet displays (see Figure 4.2)

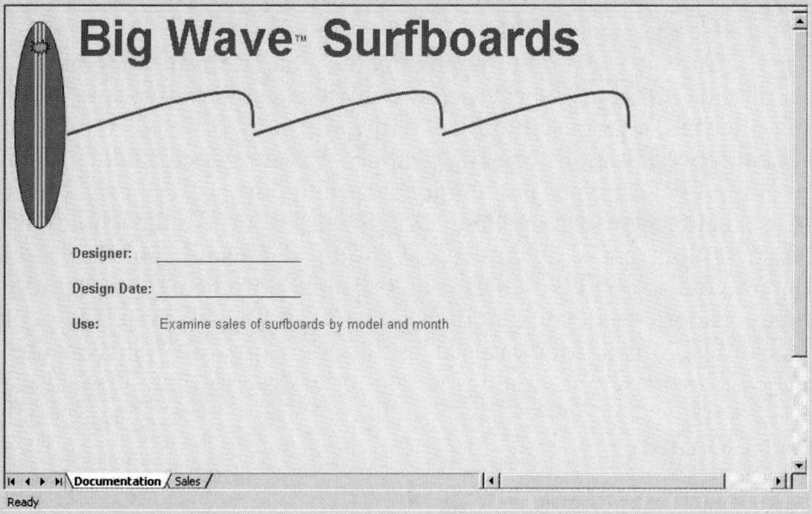

FIGURE 4.2
Big Wave documentation worksheet

3. Type your name in the cell to the right of the label Designer and type the current date in the cell to the right of the label Design Date. Notice that the Documentation worksheet does not display column and row headers
4. Save the worksheet as **BigWave2.xls** to preserve the original workbook in case you want to revert to that version
5. Click the **Sales** tab to display that worksheet (see Figure 4.3)

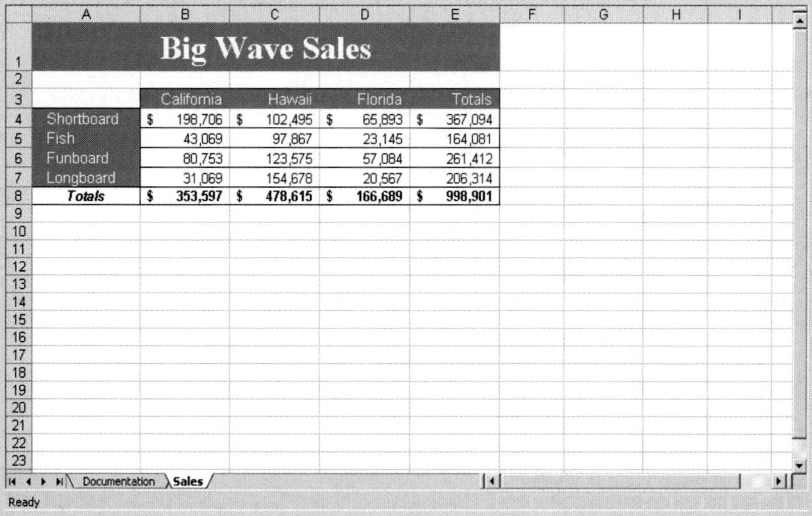

	California	Hawaii	Florida	Totals
Shortboard	$ 198,706	$ 102,495	$ 65,893	$ 367,094
Fish	43,069	97,867	23,145	164,081
Funboard	80,753	123,575	57,084	261,412
Longboard	31,069	154,678	20,567	206,314
Totals	**$ 353,597**	**$ 478,615**	**$ 166,689**	**$ 998,901**

FIGURE 4.3
Big Wave sales data worksheet

The Sales worksheet shows sales of four types of surfboards in the three states where Big Wave has outlets—California, Hawaii, and Florida. At the bottom of each state's column is the total value of sales for the year in that state's store. Details of individual models of each type of surfboard are not displayed in the worksheet because the Sales worksheet summarized sales for Keoki. Other worksheets maintained by store managers in each of the three states list each surfboard built and sold. Detailed information on each surfboard includes the exact dimensions, weight, construction, number and size of fins, sale price, and so on. Worksheet data arranged in row categories and column locations are ideal to graph.

CHOOSING A CHART TYPE AND FORMAT

Using Excel, you can create sophisticated charts from worksheet data. Excel provides 14 chart types, each of which has at least two subtypes providing alternative representations. While you may be used to calling the graphical representations of data "graphs," Excel refers to them as **charts.** Each of the 14 chart types has a unique use and purpose. For example, a pie chart is a better way to show the relationships of parts to the whole such as the distribution of tax dollars to education, defense, health and human resources, and so on. A bar chart is an excellent graphical representation to compare values of independent data such as sales by different salespersons or charitable contributions raised by different organizations. Figure 4.4 lists the Excel chart types and provides a brief description of their uses.

Chart Elements

Different chart types have different elements. A column chart is typical of an Excel chart. Figure 4.5 shows the elements of a column chart. All of a chart's elements reside in the **chart area.** Within the chart area is the **plot**

FIGURE 4.4

Excel chart types and their uses

Chart Type	Purpose	Identifying Icon
Area	Shows size of change over time	Area
Bar	Displays comparisons between independent data values	Bar
Bubble	A scatter chart showing relationships between sets of data	Bubble
Column	Displays comparisons between independent data values	Column
Cone	Displays and compares of data represented by each cone	Cone
Cylinder	Displays and compares of data represented by each cylinder	Cylinder
Doughnut	Shows the contribution of each part to a whole at the outer edge	Doughnut
Line	Shows a trend over time of a series of data values	Line
Pie	Shows the relative size of the parts to a whole	Pie
Pyramid	Displays and compares of data represented by each pyramid	Pyramid
Radar	Illustrates data change relative to a central point	Radar
Stock	Displays low, high, open, and close values for stock prices	Stock
Surface	Depicts relationships among large volumes of data	Surface
XY (scatter)	Shows the relationship between two sets of data points	XY (Scatter)

area, which is the rectangular area bounded by the X-axis on the left and the Y-axis on the bottom. By default the plot area is gray, but you can change the color. An *axis* is a line that contains a measurement by which you compare plotted values. The *X-axis* contains markers denoting category values, and the *Y-axis* contains the value of data being plotted. Normally the Y-axis is vertical. The *Y-axis title* identifies the values being plotted on the Y-axis. Above a chart is a *chart title,* which labels the entire chart. Below the X-axis are *category names,* which correspond to worksheet text you use to label data. Below the category names is the *X-axis title,* which briefly describes the X-axis categories. *Tick marks* are small lines, similar to marks on a ruler, that are uniformly spaced along each axis and identify the position of category names or values. *Gridlines* are extensions of tick marks that help identify the value of the data markers. A *data marker* is a graphic representation of the value of a data point in a chart; a data marker can be a pie slice, a bar, a column, or other graphic depending on the graph type. The data marker in the Big Wave sales chart is a column (see Figures 4.1 and 4.5). A chart's *legend* indicates which data marker represents each series when you chart multiple series. The legend in Figure 4.5 contains the series names (Shortboard, Fish, and so on) and the color-coded bar associated with that name. It is always a good idea to include a legend so that the reader can associate a particular data series with its assigned color or fill pattern.

Chart Placement Choices

You can place charts in one of two places: on a worksheet along with the data being charted or on a separate sheet. When you place a chart on a worksheet near the data you are charting, it is called an *embedded chart.* Embedded charts have the advantage that you can see the data and the accompanying chart on the same page. Often you can print both the data and chart on a single page. When you place a chart on a separate sheet, called a *chart sheet,* it is much larger and there are no other data on the chart sheet. In addition, a chart sheet contains no gridlines, which can distract from the chart's usefulness. Chart sheets are particularly handy when

FIGURE 4.5

Anatomy of an Excel column chart

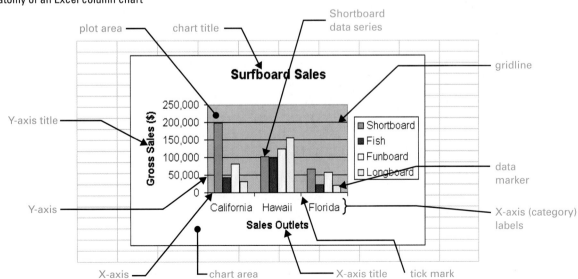

EXCEL

you want to print color transparencies for a presentation. In this first session, you will create an embedded chart. In the second section, you will create a chart sheet.

Developing and Planning a Chart

Prior to creating a chart, take time to plan what it is you want the chart to depict. Consider the following in developing and planning your chart(s):

- What data are to be represented by the chart?
- Which chart type is the best one to represent the data you want to plot?
- Where should the chart be placed—in a worksheet along with the data or on a separate sheet?
- What features should the selected chart type contain—what data markers, whether to include a legend, and what axis labels to include, for example?

Keoki wants you to create a chart summarizing the sales of surfboards. He wants a chart to show the sales by sales outlet and surfboard type. Another chart he'd like to have is total sales of each of the surfboard types, regardless of sales outlet. He has sketched the basic form of the two graphs on an output worksheet page containing sales data. Figure 4.6 shows

FIGURE 4.6

Sketch of two surfboard sales charts

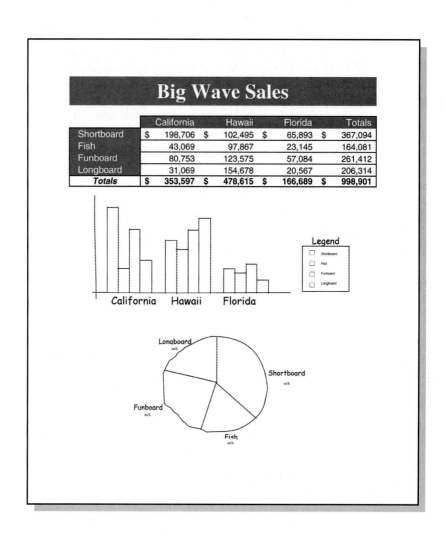

	California	Hawaii	Florida	Totals
Shortboard	$ 198,706	$ 102,495	$ 65,893	$ 367,094
Fish	43,069	97,867	23,145	164,081
Funboard	80,753	123,575	57,084	261,412
Longboard	31,069	154,678	20,567	206,314
Totals	$ 353,597	$ 478,615	$ 166,689	$ 998,901

Keoki's sketch. A column graph shows sales by surfboard type for each sales outlet. The pie chart is a good way to show overall sales by surfboard type.

CREATING AN EMBEDDED COLUMN CHART

After calling Keoki and discussing the drawing he faxed, you decide you have all the information you need to create a chart. Creating an Excel chart is a simple two-step process. First, select the worksheet cells you want to chart including any text cells containing row or column headings. Second, launch the Chart Wizard by clicking the Chart Wizard button and follow the multistep Chart Wizard's prompts. The Chart Wizard consists of four steps corresponding to four dialog boxes in which you make choices and proceed to the next step. Figure 4.7 outlines the choices you can make in each step.

Because Keoki wants a printout—on one page—of both the worksheet data and a chart, you choose to create an embedded chart so that both reside on the same page. Create a column chart using the Charting Wizard by selecting the data to be charted in the Big Wave surfboard sales worksheet and then invoking the Chart Wizard.

FIGURE 4.7
Chart Wizard steps and dialog boxes

Dialog box	Tasks and Choices
Chart Type	Select a chart type from a palette of choices
Chart Source Data	Specify or modify the worksheet cell range containing data to be charted
Chart Options	Alter the look of a chart by selecting from a tabbed set affecting gridlines, titles, axes, and data labels
Chart Location	Choose either an embedded chart or a chart sheet style chart

task reference

Creating a Chart

- Select the cell range containing the data you want to chart
- Click the Standard toolbar **Chart Wizard** button
- Respond to the series of Chart Wizard dialog box choices, clicking the **Finish** button on the last step

Invoking the Chart Wizard to create a column chart:

1. With the Sales worksheet displayed, drag the mouse to select the cell range **A3:D7,** which includes labels at the top of the sales columns and labels on the left of the surfboard data rows. The chart omits the totals column, because it cannot be compared easily to individual sales

EXCEL

FIGURE 4.8

Chart Wizard Step 1 dialog box

chart types

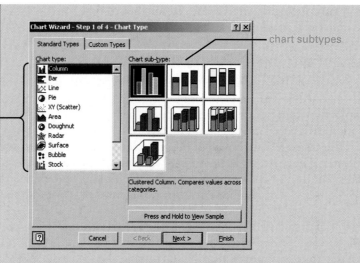

tip: *Do not include row 8 in the selected cell range. It contains totals for each numeric column and would be an inappropriate row to include or compare to individual sales.*

2. Click the **Chart Wizard** 📊 button located on the Standard toolbar. The first of several Chart Wizard dialog boxes opens (see Figure 4.8). The dialog box presents the chart types in a list along with a list of chart subtypes

tip: *If the Office Assistant appears, close it by clicking the button next to the message "No, don't provide help now."*

3. Click the **Column** chart choice in the Chart type list, if needed, to select it. In the Chart subtype panel are the seven column chart subtypes including clustered column, stacked column, and several 3-D subtypes of column charts

4. To view a sample of a subtype, click and hold the **Press and Hold to View Sample** button. A sample displays in the Chart subtype panel as long as you hold down the left mouse button. The default subtype, clustered column, is a good choice

5. Click the **Next** button, located at the bottom of the dialog box, to move to the next Chart Wizard dialog box

6. Ensure that the Data range text box displays "=Sales!$A$3:$D$7." The dialog box displays a preliminary chart of your data (see Figure 4.9)

Chart Wizard Step 2 allows you to modify the data series in case you selected an incorrect range accidentally. Notice that the preview of the chart looks different from the chart Keoki wants. Looking closely, you see that the series shown by each bar represent sales outlets, and the four groups represent the four surfboard types. You want just the reverse—series representing each surfboard type and three groups representing the three sales outlets. You modify the way the data series is represented—by rows or columns—with the ***Series in*** option. You will change this in the steps that follow.

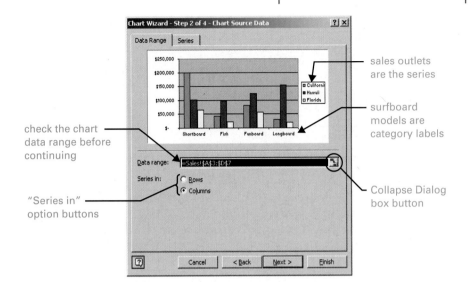

FIGURE 4.9
Chart Wizard Step 2 dialog box

sales outlets
are the series

surfboard
models are
category labels

check the chart
data range before
continuing

Collapse Dialog
box button

"Series in"
option buttons

Altering the data series and completing the Chart Wizard steps:

1. Click the **Rows** option in the "Series in" section of the Chart Wizard dialog box. Charting will produce a series for each surfboard type and form three groups, one for each sales outlet

2. Click the **Next** button to move to the next Chart Wizard step

3. If necessary, click the **Titles** tab to display chart title text boxes, click the **Chart title** text box, and then type **Surfboard Sales**. After a short pause, the title appears above the chart in the chart preview area of the dialog box

4. Click the **Category (X) axis** text box and then type **Sales Outlets**. After a brief pause, the category title appears below the X-axis in the chart preview area (see Figure 4.10)

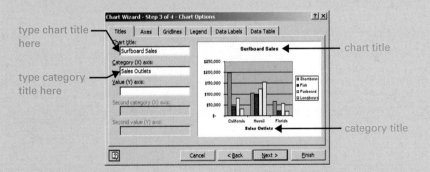

type chart title
here

type category
title here

chart title

category title

FIGURE 4.10
Chart Wizard Step 3 dialog box

5. Click the **Next** button to proceed to the final Chart Wizard step (see Figure 4.11). In this step, you choose whether to create an embedded chart or a chart sheet. Because you want an embedded chart, you leave unchanged the default option, <u>As object in</u>

EXCEL

FIGURE 4.11

Chart Wizard Step 4 dialog box

click for chart sheet ⎯⎯⎯

click for
embedded chart ⎯⎯

FIGURE 4.12

Finished column chart prior to placement

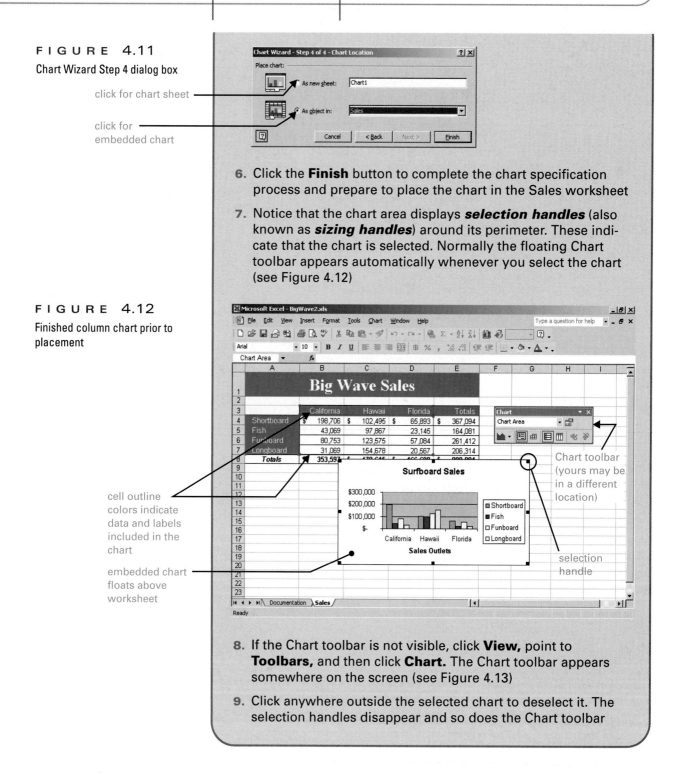

cell outline
colors indicate
data and labels
included in the
chart

embedded chart
floats above
worksheet

6. Click the **Finish** button to complete the chart specification process and prepare to place the chart in the Sales worksheet

7. Notice that the chart area displays **_selection handles_** (also known as **_sizing handles_**) around its perimeter. These indicate that the chart is selected. Normally the floating Chart toolbar appears automatically whenever you select the chart (see Figure 4.12)

8. If the Chart toolbar is not visible, click **View,** point to **Toolbars,** and then click **Chart.** The Chart toolbar appears somewhere on the screen (see Figure 4.13)

9. Click anywhere outside the selected chart to deselect it. The selection handles disappear and so does the Chart toolbar

MOVING AND RESIZING AN EMBEDDED CHART

The embedded chart you produced for Keoki is too small to distinguish sales details, and the labels are small as well. It would be nice to somehow enlarge the chart slightly. Because an embedded chart is an object, you can resize it or move it to another location. Like other Windows objects, you modify an object's size by selecting the object and then moving the mouse over one of the object's selection/resizing handles. When the mouse pointer changes to a double-headed arrow, you can drag any selection handle

FIGURE 4.13

Chart toolbar

Icon	Name	Meaning
Chart Area ▾	Chart Objects	List box contains names of all objects on the current chart
	Format	Displays Format dialog box for the selected object (plot area, chart area, and so on)
▲ ▾	Chart Type	List box contains list of chart types (radar, bar, etc.)
	Legend	On/off toggle that adds or removes the legend
	Data Table	On/off toggle that adds or removes a chart data table
	By Row	Displays data series using rows
	By Column	Displays data series using columns
	Angle Text Downward	On/off toggle to angle text down at a 45 degree angle
	Angle Text Upward	On/off toggle to angle text up at a 45 degree angle

away from the object's center to enlarge the object or toward the object's center to shrink it.

Sometimes you want to move an embedded chart to a specific position on a worksheet. For example, you may want to fit a chart exactly within a particular range of cells. Or you might want to modify several embedded charts so that they are the same height and width. In all these cases, you can use a handy Excel snap-to feature to place embedded charts precisely on a worksheet. Otherwise, you can move a chart by clicking the Chart Area and dragging the chart to a new location. (Be careful to click the Chart Area and not the Plot Area or other chart element.)

task reference

Snapping an Embedded Chart into Place

- Select the chart that you want to move or resize

- Press and hold down the **Alt** key

- Drag a chart left, right, up, or down until the chart edge snaps to a cell boundary

- Still holding down the **Alt** key, move the cursor to a chart selection handle

- Click and drag a chart selection handle until the chart's selected boundary snaps to a cell border

- Release the mouse and **Alt** key

Because the chart is too small and obscures part of the data area whose values it charts, you will move and resize the chart. You begin by moving the chart so that its upper-left corner is positioned below the worksheet data.

EXCEL

Moving an embedded chart to a cell boundary:

1. Click in any white area within the chart border, being careful not to click another chart object such as the chart title or the legend

tip: *Alternatively, you can click the **Chart objects** list box on the Chart toolbar and then select **Chart Area**. Selection handles appear around the border of the embedded chart.*

tip: *If the Chart toolbar is in your way, move it to another location by dragging it. You can dock the toolbar on the bottom of the window by dragging it close to the bottom of the screen until it automatically snaps into place.*

2. Press and hold the **Alt** key

3. Drag the chart down and to the left until the upper-left corner is positioned over cell A10 and the top edge of the chart aligns with the bottom edge of worksheet row 9. (The mouse pointer changes to ✥ as you drag the chart)

4. Release the mouse and then release the **Alt** key

Once you move the chart, it no longer obscures the data. However, the chart is still too small. The next task you want to accomplish is to enlarge the chart.

Resizing a chart:

1. Scroll the worksheet up on the screen so that the top of the embedded chart is near the top of the screen and row 25 is also visible

2. Click in any white area within the chart border, being careful not to click another chart object such as the chart title. Selection handles appear around the border of the chart

3. Position the mouse pointer on the bottom-right selection handle

4. When the mouse pointer changes to ◥, drag the selection handle down and to the right until it reaches the bottom of row 25 and the right edge of column F until the lower-right corner of the chart covers cell F25 (see Figure 4.14)

5. Click anywhere outside the chart area to deselect it

You show the Sales worksheet containing the embedded chart to Keoki. He's pleased with the chart but notices that there are three values in the worksheet that are incorrect. Luckily, Keoki catches the errors before you distribute a printed copy. The California Shortboard sales value should

FIGURE 4.14
Resized and relocated chart

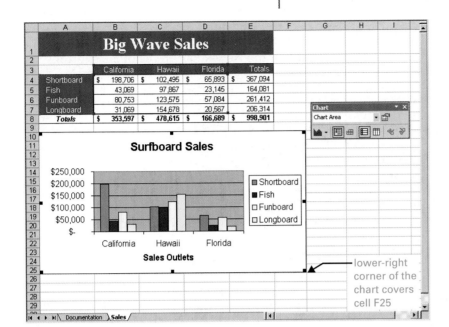

lower-right corner of the chart covers cell F25

be $108,706. The other two incorrect values are in the Hawaii sales column. Hawaiian Funboard sales should be $93,576, not $123,575. Hawaiian Longboard sales should be $54,678, not $154,678.

UPDATING A CHART

Charts are automatically linked to the data from which they have been created. Consequently, when you change a worksheet value, the portion of the chart representing that data point is automatically updated to reflect the new value. The same is true of worksheet labels that are in the range of cells you selected to create a chart. Any text values in a worksheet that are also part of a chart will change automatically when you change them in the worksheet. An example of this is the text "California" found in cell B3 of the Big Wave Sales worksheet. Changing that cell's contents would also cause the chart category label "California" to change to the new value.

You are ready to make changes to the erroneous data in cells B4, C6, and C7. Any changes you make to the data will change the chart also. Before continuing, notice the leftmost bar in the California category and the rightmost two columns in the Hawaii category. Those bars will decrease in size when you make the changes in the steps below. Notice, in particular, that the first California column almost touches the gridline marked $200,000 and that the third and fourth bars in the Hawaii category are both taller than the first two bars in the Hawaii category.

Changing worksheet data linked to a chart:

1. Scroll the worksheet so that you can see row 1 again, click cell **B4** to select it, type **108706,** and then press **Enter.** Notice that the entire chart plot area resizes as the California Shortboard chart column decreases in height

2. Click cell **C6,** type **93576,** and then press **Enter.** Notice that the third bar from the left in the Hawaii group becomes shorter

3. Click cell **C7,** type **54678,** and press **Enter.** Notice that the fourth bar from the left in the Hawaii group becomes shorter (see Figure 4.15)

FIGURE 4.15

Revised sales data and chart

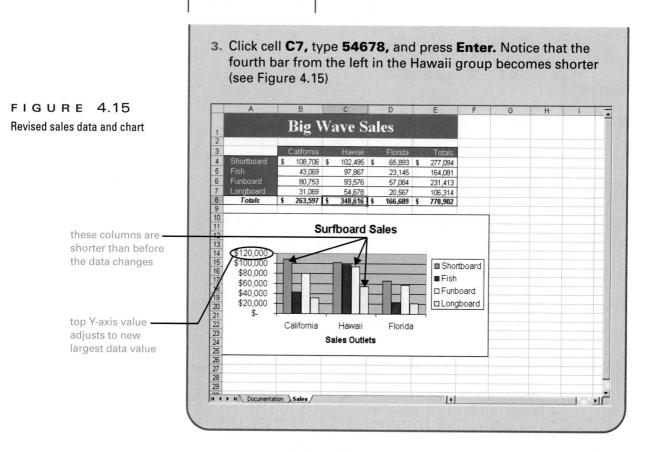

these columns are shorter than before the data changes

top Y-axis value adjusts to new largest data value

After you make changes to the data, the chart automatically changes. One of the most dramatic changes occurs when you reduce the value of the currently largest data point on the chart—the sales value for California Shortboards. The entire chart resizes automatically and the Y-axis values display new values. The embedded chart looks fine. You will make other changes to it after Keoki reviews what you have produced.

MODIFYING A CHART

You can modify every aspect of an Excel chart. For example, you can add a new data series to a chart, modify the foreground and background colors of text objects, alter the colors of data markers in a series, change the typeface of text, and reposition objects on a chart. One of the most dramatic changes you can make to a chart is to add, delete, or hide a series in the chart. You do that by adding, deleting, or hiding rows in the data range of the associated worksheet data. Keoki wants you to add a new line of surfboards to the sales totals so that he can compare their sales to the other types of surfboards.

Adding and Deleting Chart Data Series

Adding a new data series to an existing embedded chart is straightforward. There are several ways to add a series to a chart, but perhaps the simplest way is to add a row to the worksheet and then drag the new data and label cell range to the embedded chart.

You will add the new data to the worksheet. After you add the data, you can add the data series to the embedded chart.

task reference

Adding a New Data Series to an Embedded Chart

- Add the new data, both labels and values or formulas that display values, to the worksheet adjacent to existing chart data

- Select the cell range, including category labels and data, of the data series you want to add to the embedded chart

- Move the mouse to any edge of the selected worksheet cell range

- When the mouse pointer changes to an arrow, click and drag the range into the chart area and release the mouse

---

Inserting a new surfboard category and sales information into the worksheet:

1. Click cell **A8,** click **Insert** on the menu bar, and then click **Rows.** A new row 8 is inserted

2. Type **Retro** in cell A8 and press the **Tab** key

3. Type **55623;** press the **Tab** key, type **77695,** press the **Tab** key, and type **37474**

4. Click cell **E8.** Notice that Excel automatically fills in the SUM function in cell E8. Cell A8 contains a line on its top border because its format is copied from the previous cell A8, which contained "Total." Remove that line in the steps that follow

5. Click Cell **A8,** click **Format** on the menu bar, click **Cells,** and click the **Border** tab

6. Click the top line in the preview panel of the Border section. The top line in the preview panel disappears

7. Click **OK** to close the Format Cells dialog box

tip: *If a dashed line appears along the right edge of column F, Excel is indicating where a page break will occur if you print the worksheet. You can remove the line, if you wish.*

8. To remove the page break indicator, click **Tools** on the menu bar, click **Options,** click the **View** tab, click the **Page breaks** check box in the Window options panel to remove the check mark, and click **OK** to close the Options dialog box

---

Excel automatically adjusts the column sales totals located in row 9 to account for the new surfboard data you added in row 8. However, the new series is not added automatically to the chart. Now that you have added the new surfboard category and sales information for the three sales outlets to the worksheet, you can proceed to add a new series to the existing embedded column chart.

EXCEL

Adding a new series to a chart by dragging the worksheet data:

1. Drag the mouse through the cell range **A8:D8**

2. Move the mouse to the edge of the cell range until it turns into a four-headed arrow

3. Click any line surrounding the cell range, drag the cell range to anywhere in the embedded chart area, and release the mouse to create a new data series (see Figure 4.16)

FIGURE 4.16

Adding a new data series to an embedded chart

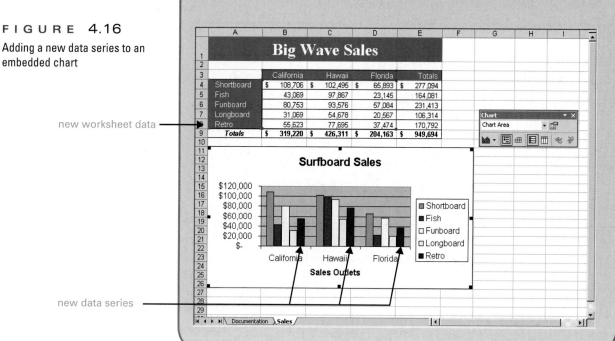

new worksheet data

new data series

After examining a chart, you may discover that you have a data series that should not be included in the chart. Similarly, you may decide that the chart should display a different data series. In either case, you can delete a series from a chart without affecting the data series in the worksheet. You can temporarily remove a data series by hiding the data in the worksheet. A more permanent solution is to delete a data series by deleting it from the chart.

task reference

Deleting a Data Series from a Chart

- Select the chart area by clicking anywhere within the chart
- Click the data marker for the series you want to delete
- Press the **Delete** key

Keoki wants to remove the Longboard from the chart but leave it in the worksheet. He asks you to show him the modified chart after you remove the series.

Deleting a data series from a chart:

1. Click the **Chart Objects list box arrow** in the Chart toolbar and then click **Chart Area** in the list to select the Chart

tip: *If the Chart floating toolbar is not visible, click inside the chart to display the Chart toolbar.*

2. Click any of the Longboard data markers (the fourth column in each group). Notice that Excel outlines the corresponding data range in the worksheet—cell range B7:D7—and that a ScreenTip appears identifying the data marker whenever you hover the mouse over it (see Figure 4.17)

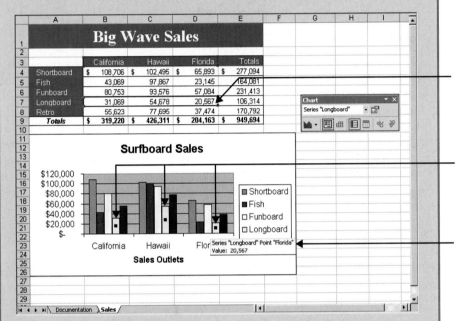

FIGURE 4.17

Selecting a data series prior to deleting it

outline indicates data associated with data markers you select

selected data markers

ScreenTip confirms which data marker is beneath the mouse pointer

3. Press the **Delete** key. The data series disappears from the chart

tip: *If you accidentally delete the wrong series, simply click the **Undo** button on the Standard toolbar, if necessary, and then select and delete the correct data series.*

Hiding Chart Data Series

An alternative to deleting a data series from a chart is hiding it. When you *hide* data (by reducing its row height to zero) in a worksheet that corresponds to a chart's data series, it is removed from the chart temporarily. Removing the data series from the chart is temporary because the data series reappears when you unhide the corresponding worksheet data row or column. Hiding data is handy when you want to print one version of a chart without a particular data series represented in the chart, for instance. Keoki wants you to show him the chart without the Fish data series included.

Hiding a data series by hiding the worksheet data:

1. Right-click the **row 5 heading label** to select row 5

2. Click **Hide** from the shortcut menu that opens. Excel hides row 5 and removes the data series corresponding to that row from the chart. You show the resulting chart to Keoki

3. Because you don't want to hide the data after Keoki examines the new chart, click the Standard toolbar **Undo** ⟲▾ button to reverse the row-hiding operation and then click any cell to deselect row 5. Row 5 reappears

Altering Chart Text

Excel charts can contain several categories of text: attached text, unattached text, and label text. ***Attached text*** includes tick mark labels, the X-axis title, and the Y-axis title. Excel initially assigns attached text to default positions in the chart area, but you can click and drag attached text to new locations. ***Unattached text*** includes objects such as comments or text boxes that you add to the chart after creating it. Add unattached text by selecting objects from the Drawing toolbar—objects such as text boxes or callouts. ***Label text*** includes text such as tick mark labels, category axis labels, data series names (the legend), and data labels. Label text is linked to cells on the worksheet used to create the chart. If you change the text of any of these items on the chart, they are no longer linked to the worksheet cells. The best way to change label text and maintain their links to worksheet cells is to edit the text on the worksheet, not on the chart.

Keoki wants you to change the chart title and add a Y-axis title. Since neither title gets its value from worksheet cells, you can alter and add them directly to the chart.

Altering the chart title:

1. Click the **Chart Title** object to select it. Selection handles and an outline appear around the chart title. The Name box displays the name "Chart Title" when you select the chart title

2. Move the I-beam-shaped mouse pointer to the end of the word "Sales" and then click the mouse to remove the selection handles. The blinking vertical bar insertion point appears to the right of the word *Sales*

3. Press the **Spacebar** and type **by Type and Outlet**

5. Click anywhere within the chart area but outside the Chart Title object to deselect it

Next, you will add a Y-axis title to identify the values on that axis.

It seems redundant to indicate in the Y-axis title that the values are in dollars and display sales with leading dollar signs in the Y-axis. You will modify the format of the Y-axis values next.

Adding a Y-axis title:

1. If necessary, select the **Chart Area.** Selection handles appear around the border of the entire chart area

2. Click **Chart** on the menu bar and then click **Chart Options** to open the Chart Options dialog box

3. Click the **Titles** tab if necessary, click the **Value (Y) axis** text box, and type **Gross Sales ($)**

4. Click **OK** to complete the process and close the Chart Options dialog box (see Figure 4.18)

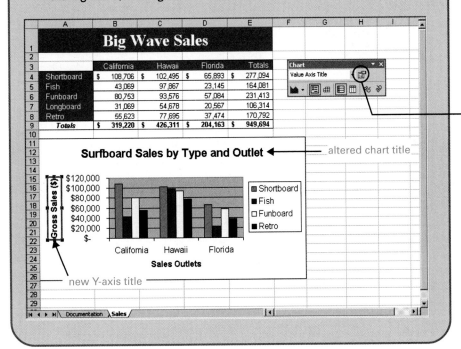

FIGURE 4.18
Chart with altered title and new Y-axis title

Format button (Format Axis, Format Chart, and so on)

Modifying the Y-axis Number Format

Excel determines the values to display on the Y-axis based on the largest and smallest values in the data series you plot. The interval between consecutive Y-axis values is uniform. Excel picks the format for Y-axis values from the formatting of the cell range represented by the data series. You can modify the Y-axis formatting using the same formats Excel provides for formatting numeric entries in a worksheet. You format the Y-axis next to remove the currency symbol, which is indicated in the Y-axis title.

Formatting the Y-axis values:

1. Click the **Y-axis** to select it. Notice that the Chart Objects list box in the Chart toolbar displays "Value Axis" when you select the Y-axis

   tip: If the Chart toolbar is not visible, click **View** on the menu bar, point to **Toolbars,** and click **Chart.**

EXCEL

2. Click **Format** on the menu bar, click **Selected Axis,** and click the **Number** tab

tip: *You can also click the **Format Axis** button on the Chart toolbar instead of Format/Selected Axis (see the Chart toolbar in Figure 4.18)*

3. Click **Number** in the Category list, type **0** in the Decimal places spin control, and check the **Use 1000 Separator** check box

4. Click **OK** to complete the formatting process. The Format Axis dialog box closes and the Y-axis values no longer display the currency symbol to the left of each value along the Y-axis. The value 0 now appears where the Y-axis intersects the X-axis

Labeling Data

While charts provide a handy way to represent numeric data that are easily understood, the exact values of significant data projected by charts is not always clear—especially when you use three-dimensional charts. It is helpful to anyone who reads your charts if you label some or all of the data markers with text that indicates their values. Look at the chart in figure 4.18, for example. If that chart were made into a transparency and presented to an audience and someone in the audience asked you, "What is the value of the gross sales of Shortboards in California?" would you be able to answer them with a precise answer? The best answer you could give is that the value is between $100,000 and $120,000. To precisely answer that question using only a chart, you need to add one or more data labels to your chart. A ***data label*** is the value or name assigned to an individual data point. Data labels are optional.

You can choose to display a data label to all data series in the chart, to one of the data series, or to a single data marker in a data series.

Keoki wants you to add a data label to the data marker corresponding to Hawaiian Shortboard sales. The data marker will indicate the exact value for gross sales represented by the marker.

task reference

Adding a Data Label to All Data Series in a Chart

- Select the chart

- Select any data series in the chart

- Click **Chart,** click **Chart Options,** click the **Data Labels** tab

- Click the **Show value** option button and then click **OK**

Adding a Data Label to a Data Series

- Select the chart

- Select the data series

- Click **Format,** click **Selected Data Series,** click the **Data Labels** tab

- Click the **Show value** option button and then click **OK**

Adding a Data Label to a Data Marker

- Select the chart
- Select the data series containing the data marker to label
- Click the data marker in the series
- Click **Format,** click **Selected Data Point,** and then click the **Data Labels** tab
- Click the **Show value** option button, and then click **OK**

Adding a data label to the Shortboard data marker for Hawaii:

1. Click the chart to select it
2. Click any **Shortboard data marker.** A single square selection handle appears in each of the three Shortboard data markers (columns)
3. Click the **Hawaii Shortboard** data marker. Eight selection handles outline the data marker
4. Click **Format** on the menu bar, click **Selected Data Point,** and click the **Data Labels** tab on the Format Data Point dialog box
5. Click the **Value** check box to place a checkmark in it (see Figure 4.19)

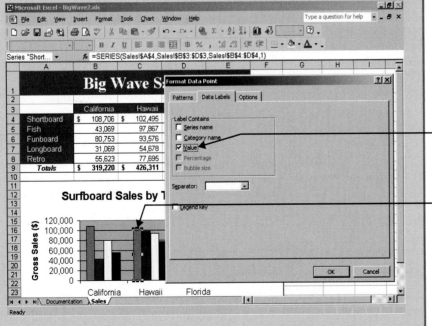

FIGURE 4.19
Adding a data label to a data marker

6. Click **OK** to compete the data label procedure, and click anywhere outside the chart to deselect the data marker (see Figure 4.20)

EXCEL

F I G U R E   4.20

Displaying a data marker's value

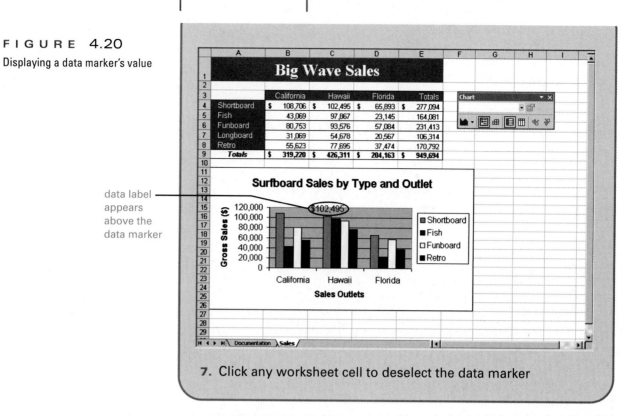

data label appears above the data marker

7. Click any worksheet cell to deselect the data marker

Keoki makes some other suggestions to you about enhancing the chart. You will apply those suggestions next.

EMBELLISHING A CHART

There are a large number of alterations or embellishments you can make to a chart. You can apply foreground and background color to any object on a chart or to the chart background itself. There is a wide selection of patterns and textures you can add to a background also. Gradients, which are color fades that change from dark to light across an object, are available. In fact, the number of enhancements you can apply to a chart is almost endless. However, be careful to not go overboard. The resulting chart can become garish and difficult to view if you use too many colors, textures, and color blends in a single chart.

Remember that not everyone has access to a color printer. Some charts printed on laser printers may yield unreadable text due to the foreground and background color and texture combinations you choose. Data markers may blend together if you choose colors that register as very similar gray-scale values on a laser printer. In other words, exercise restraint when you enhance charts with color and textures. The final result will enhance the worksheet rather than detract from it.

Adding a Text Box for Emphasis

Keoki wants you to add text to indicate that the chart belongs to the Big Wave company. The text box should contain the phrase "Copyright 2003 Big Wave" and be placed near the lower-left corner of the chart in 8-point (Arial) typeface.

Adding a text box to the embedded chart:

1. Click the **Chart Area**

2. If the Drawing toolbar is not visible, click **View** on the menu bar, point to **Toolbars,** and click **Drawing.** The Drawing toolbar appears on the screen

3. Click the **Text Box** 🖺 button on the Drawing toolbar

4. Move the mouse to the left side of the chart area near row 25 (scroll the worksheet if necessary), click the mouse to drop the text box onto the chart, and type **Copyright 2003 Big Wave**

5. With the mouse pointer in an I-beam shape, select the text inside the text box by dragging the mouse from right to left across the text within the text box until all the text is selected

tip: *Selecting text in a text box takes a little practice. If the mouse pointer becomes a four-headed arrow ✛, you are near the edge of the text box itself. In that case, move back slightly until the mouse changes to an I-beam. Then drag the I-beam mouse pointer across the text until all of it is selected.*

6. Click in the **Font Size list box** on the Formatting toolbar, type **8,** and then click outside the Chart Area (see Figure 4.21)

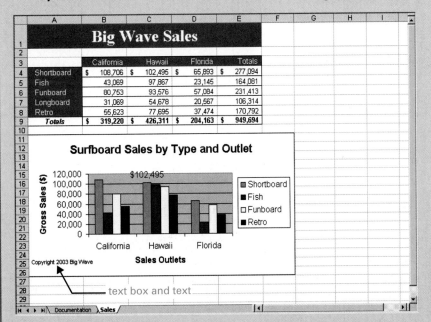

FIGURE 4.21

Adding a text box to a chart

7. If you need to adjust the position of the text box, move the mouse near the text box edge. When the mouse pointer changes to a four-headed arrow ✛, click the text box edge and drag it to the correct position within the Chart Area

8. Click **View** on the menu bar, point to **Toolbars,** and click **Drawing.** The Drawing toolbar closes

Keoki likes the text box you added, and he's satisfied that anyone viewing the chart will know it belongs to Big Wave. Next, you will add a splash of color to your chart.

Emphasizing and Enhancing with Color

There are hundreds of combinations of ways to spruce up a chart including varying the typeface, using color in the background of objects, using color in the text or foreground of objects, and adding graphics. After examining the worksheet for a few minutes, Keoki asks you to experiment with using a dark blue color for the chart title text. Keoki thinks a border or background color might be distracting, though. "Let's try using the dark blue color you will use on the chart title for the value axis title and the category axis title too," Keoki suggests. You open the worksheet and make the requested changes.

Changing the color of the chart, value axis, and category axis titles:

1. Click the **Chart Title** object. Selection handles surround the chart title

2. Click the **Format** 🖼 button on the Chart toolbar to open the Chart Title dialog box

3. Click the **Font** tab, then click the **Color list box arrow** to reveal the palette of text colors, click the **Dark Blue** square in the palette of color squares (see Figure 4.22), and click **OK** to close the Format Chart Title dialog box

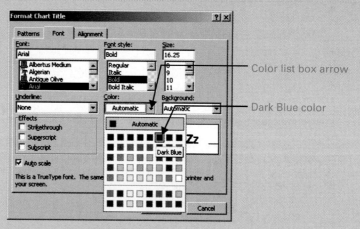

4. Select the **Value Axis Title** object and repeat steps 2 and 3 above. (The dialog box that opens is called the Format Axis Title dialog box)

5. Select the **Category Axis Title** object and repeat steps 2 and 3 above. Press the **Esc** key to deselect the category axis title. All three titles are now dark blue

---

FIGURE 4.22

Changing the chart title foreground color

Changing Patterns and Colors

Colors look great on the screen, but they may not have the same visual impact when you print a worksheet on a noncolor printer. Noncolor laser printers display colors as shades of gray, which can diminish the effectiveness of color. In the absence of color, you can use stripes or textures to differentiate elements of a chart and add impact in a noncolor printer environment. Data markers are particularly difficult to distinguish when they contain the wrong combination of colors. For example, a red data marker is almost indistinguishable from a dark blue data marker. In those cases, it is better to choose stripes and other patterns to uniquely pattern each data series.

Keoki wants you to use different patterns for each of the data markers to avoid confusion about which gross sales are due to each surfboard category.

Applying a data pattern to a data series and changing a data series color:

1. Click any **Shortboard data marker** in the series. Excel selects all data markers in the series

2. Click the **Format** 🖼 button on the Chart toolbar. The Format Data Series dialog box opens

3. Click the **Patterns** tab, if necessary, and click the **Fill Effects** button to open the like-named dialog box

4. Click the **Pattern** tab and then click the **Dark upward diagonal** pattern in the fourth row from the top, third column (see Figure 4.23). The sample pattern you select also appears in the Sample box—a larger version that is easier to view

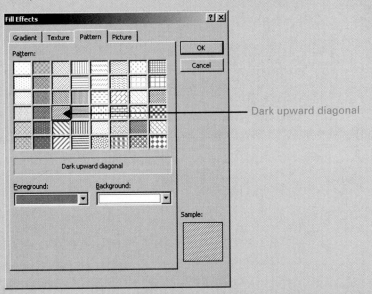

FIGURE 4.23

Fill Effects dialog box

5. Click **OK** to close the Fill Effects dialog box. Click **OK** to close the Format Data Series dialog box. The new fill pattern appears in the Shortboard data series columns

6. Click any **Fish data marker** in the series and repeat steps 2 through 5, clicking **Dark vertical** pattern (fifth row from the top, fourth column) in step 4

7. Click any **Funboard data marker** in the series, click the **Format Data Series** button on the Chart toolbar, click the **Patterns** tab, click the **Fill Effects** button, and click the **Pattern** tab

8. Click the **Foreground list box arrow** and then click the **Sea Green** square (third row from the top, fourth column) to change the series color

9. Click the **Dark downward diagonal** square (third row from the top, third column)

10. Click **OK** to close the Fill Effects dialog box and click **OK** to close the Format Data Series dialog box

11. Click any **Retro data marker** in the series and repeat steps 2 through 5, choosing **Dark horizontal** pattern (sixth row from the top, fourth column) in step 4

12. Click any worksheet cell to deselect the data marker. Each of the data series has a distinguishable pattern that will be visible even when printed on a noncolor printer (see Figure 4.24)

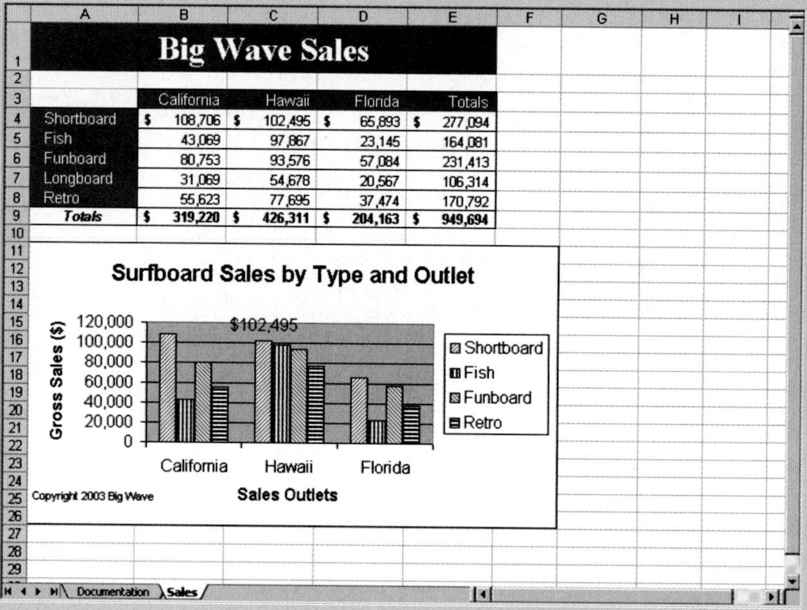

FIGURE 4.24

Data markers with patterns applied

---

anotherword

. . . on Data Series and Fill Effects

If you decide to remove all fill effects from a data series, click any marker of the data series in the chart, click **Edit** on the menu bar, point to **Clear,** and click **Formats**

PREVIEWING AND PRINTING A CHART

You know by now to preview your output before you actually print it, because you can catch small mistakes before printing too many pages. Often a multipage output can be trimmed to one or two pages simply by minimizing the margins or reorienting the output to landscape. Keoki wants you to produce two printouts. The first one is the worksheet and the embedded chart on one page. On the second printout, he wants only the chart, not the worksheet.

Previewing and Printing a Worksheet and Chart

Preview the worksheet and chart prior to printing it. Check to ensure that both the chart and worksheet fit on one page. You will do that next.

task reference

Printing a Worksheet and Embedded Chart

- Ensure that the embedded chart is not selected by clicking any worksheet cell

- Click **File** and click **Print Preview**

- Click **Print** and click **OK**

Saving, previewing, and printing the worksheet and embedded chart:

1. Click **File** and then click **Save** to save the completed worksheet and chart

2. Click cell **A2** to be doubly sure that the chart is not selected

3. Click the **Print Preview** button on the Standard toolbar to open the Print Preview window. Check to ensure that both the worksheet and chart appear on the same page.

tip: *If the entire worksheet does not appear on the first page or if both the worksheet and chart do not appear on the same page, adjust the page margins. Click the **Margins** button on the Print Preview toolbar. The margin lines appear on the preview. Drag the left and right margin lines toward the edge of the paper to decrease the margins (see Figure 4.25)*

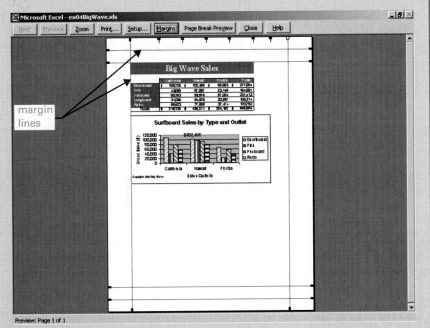

F I G U R E   4.25

Preview of worksheet and chart displaying margin lines

4. Click the **Setup** button on the Print Preview toolbar to open the Page Setup dialog box and type your name in the Right section of the header (recall that you click the **Header/Footer** tab, click the **Custom Header** button, click in the **Left section,** and then click **OK** *twice* to close two dialog boxes)

EXCEL

5. Click the **Print** `Print...` button on the Print Preview toolbar to open the Print dialog box, and then click the **OK** button to print the output

Previewing and Printing an Embedded Chart

Printing an embedded chart without the accompanying worksheet is only slightly different from printing the worksheet and chart together. The main difference between the two procedures is that you select the chart before previewing or printing it.

---

task reference

Printing an Embedded Chart

- Click the embedded chart
- Click the **Print** button on the Standard toolbar

Because Keoki wants the embedded chart printed separately, you print it next.

Printing an embedded chart only:

1. Click the **Chart Area.** Selection handles appear around it
2. Click the **Print** 🖨 button on the Standard toolbar to print the chart (see Figure 4.26)

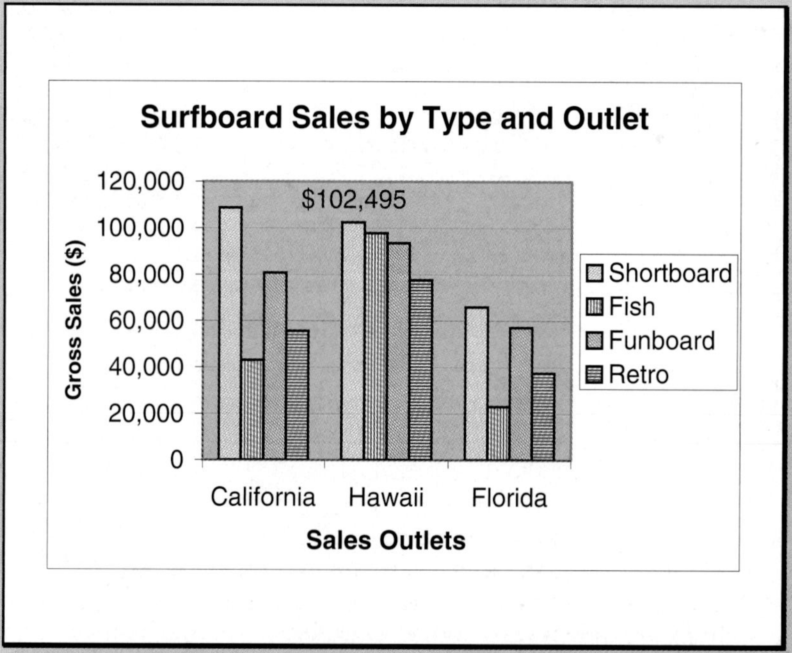

FIGURE 4.26

Embedded chart output

Surfboard Sales by Type and Outlet

Your work on the embedded chart is done. Keoki is very happy with the results. You can go on to learn about adding another type of graph to the output. This type will be a chart sheet containing a pie chart showing another aspect of Big Wave's surfboard sales.

---

making the grade   SESSION 4.1

1. A _____ _____ is a set of values that you want to chart.

2. In a column chart, the labels appearing along the X-axis are called _____ titles.

3. A chart on the same worksheet as the data it represents is called a(n) _____ chart. The other type of chart is called a _____ _____ and resides on its own sheet that is different from normal worksheets.

4. The _____ _____ helps you create a chart by displaying a series of dialog boxes that you fill in to complete the chart.

5. Modify the Big Wave worksheet you saved as **BigWave2.xls** in the following ways. Delete the Funboard data series from the chart. Modify the Y-axis title to **Sales (U.S. Dollars)** and change its point size to 14. Remove the X-axis title completely. Remove all patterns from the data markers so that they all display solid colors. Add data labels to the other two Shortboard data markers (California and Florida). Save the worksheet as **BigWaveModified.xls.** Print the worksheet and chart on one page.

SESSION 4.2 MODIFYING AND IMPROVING A CHART

In this session, you will create a pie chart and learn how to select nonadjacent data ranges for charting. You will learn about three-dimensional chart types including pie charts, exploding a pie slice to emphasize it, and the use of text and titles in three-dimensional charts. You will explore how textures can add interest to charts and learn how to create a chart sheet containing a freestanding chart. Finally, you will create a stacked column chart and learn how to format its components to highlight significant data.

CREATING A CHART IN A CHART SHEET

Keoki wants to look at a broader picture of his surfboard sales in a chart—a chart you will create in a chart sheet. He wants you to create a chart showing total sales of each surfboard type in a pie chart, based on his sketch shown in Figure 4.6. A pie chart is a good chart choice when you want to show the contribution of parts to the whole. In the case of Big Wave, the pie chart will demonstrate visually the contribution of each surfboard type to the overall sales. In a similar way, you could create a pie chart by sales outlet and examine the sales attributable to each sales outlet compared to the sum of all sales.

The pie Keoki sketched contains four slices, one for each type of surfboard. Since then, he added another surfboard to the sales summary—Retro. Therefore, the pie chart will consist of five slices. Each slice should

EXCEL

identify the surfboard type represented by the slice and indicate the percentage of sales, compared to the sum of all sales, that it represents.

Defining a Series

Creating a chart begins by first selecting the worksheet cells in the data range to be plotted. Recall that when you specified the data range for the column chart in the previous section, you simply dragged the mouse through a rectangular cell range consisting of all the rows and columns of sales, including the labels above the columns and to the left of each row. This time, the data selection process is different because you want to select two columns from a group of five columns, leaving out three columns in the middle of a range of contiguous cells. Using the sketch in Figure 4.6 as a general guideline, notice that the labels around the perimeter of the pie chart match text in worksheet cells A4 through A8 (A7, originally). Additionally, you speculate that the data represented by pie slices corresponds to the total sales of each surfboard type stored in cells E4 through E8. How do you indicate that you want to chart two noncontiguous cell ranges? The next section describes how to select cells from two noncontiguous ranges prior to calling upon the Chart Wizard.

Selecting Nonadjacent Data Ranges

Prior to launching the Chart Wizard to create a chart, select the cell range(s) that are to be charted. Because the cell ranges are in columns that are not adjacent to each other, you cannot simply drag the mouse through both ranges. Doing so would result in a chart containing two distinct types of data—sales detail information and sales sum information—that should not appear in the same chart. Selecting nonadjacent cell ranges is a common practice when creating charts. When you select nonadjacent cell ranges, each one is highlighted.

---

task reference

Selecting Nonadjacent Cell Ranges

- Click and drag the mouse through the first cell range you want to select

- Press and hold the **Ctrl** key

- Click additional cells or click and drag additional cell ranges

- When finished selecting all cells or cell ranges, release the **Ctrl** key

---

In preparation to create a pie chart, select the two cell ranges consisting of the surfboard labels in column A (cells A4 through A8) and the total sales across all three sales outlets, computed by SUM functions, in column E (cells E4 through E8).

Selecting nonadjacent data ranges in the sales worksheet:

1. If you took a break after the last session, make sure that Excel is running and open to **BigWave2.xls**

2. Click **File**, click **Save As,** type **BigWave3** in the File name list box, and click the **Save** button to preserve the work you completed in the first session

3. Click the **Sales** tab to open that worksheet, select cell range **A4:A8,** which contains names of different types of surfboards, and release the mouse

4. Press and hold the **Ctrl** key, click and drag the cell range **E4** through **E8,** and release the **Ctrl** key. The cell range E4:E8 contains the data points you want to plot on a chart and the two nonadjacent cell ranges, A4:A8 and E4:E8, are selected (see Figure 4.27)

selected, nonadjacent cell ranges

FIGURE 4.27

Selecting nonadjacent cell ranges

Creating a Three-Dimensional Pie Chart

Once you have selected the data ranges to chart, you can proceed to create the chart. Keoki wants a pie chart on a separate workbook page—a chart sheet. Charts on separate sheets are convenient to print and you can easily move chart sheets around in the workbook to reorganize their order. You can rename chart sheet tabs with meaningful names to make the charts easy to locate. If you are making a slide presentation, chart sheets are particularly convenient because you can organize the chart sheets in the same order as the slide presentation. Then you can print the chart sheets directly to a color transparency-capable printer.

Selecting nonadjacent data ranges in the sales worksheet:

1. Click the **Chart Wizard** button on the Standard toolbar to start the chart construction process

2. Click **Pie** in the Chart type list box. Several pie chart subtypes appear in the Chart subtypes panel

3. Click the **Pie with a 3-D visual effect** chart subtype (top row, second column) and then click the **Press and Hold to View Sample** button to see an example of the chart. That sample is the chart that Keoki wants. Release the **Press and Hold to View Sample** button

EXCEL

4. Click the **Next** button to proceed to Chart Wizard Step 2. Make sure that the Data range text box displays the data range value =Sales!$A$4:$A$8,Sales!$E$4:$E$8, which is a special form of the cell range notation for the two nonadjacent cell ranges you selected previously

tip: *If the Data range text box does not show the correct cell range, click the Collapse Dialog button and select the two nonadjacent data ranges A4:A8 and E4:E8 before continuing with the Chart Wizard.*

5. Click the **Next** button, click the **Titles** tab, click the **Chart Title** text box, and type **Surfboard Sales by Type**

6. Click the **Legend** tab, and click the **Show Legend** check box to clear it (see Figure 4.28)

FIGURE 4.28
Removing the chart's legend

clear to remove the chart's legend

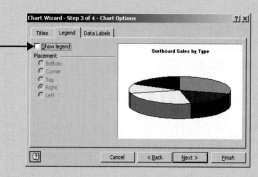

7. Click the **Data Labels** tab, click the **Category name** check box to display category names for each pie slice, and click the **Percentage** check box button to display percentages for each pie slice

8. Click the **Next** button and then click the **As new sheet** option button to create the chart as a chart sheet rather than as an embedded chart

9. Click the **Finish** button to complete the preliminary version of the three-dimensional pie chart on its own chart sheet (see Figure 4.29)

FIGURE 4.29
Preliminary 3-D pie chart

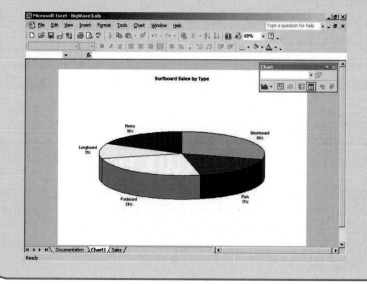

Exploding a Pie Chart Slice

Keoki gives his approval and requests that you find a way to highlight the Shortboard sales to make the data stand out to a viewer. You review several options including special colors and other methods and suggest that the best choice is to pull the Shortboard pie slice away from the rest of the chart.

Exploding a Pie Slice:

1. If necessary, click the chart sheet tab **Chart1** (your chart sheet tab may have a different name) to select the chart sheet Excel just created

2. Click the pie chart. Selection handles appear around the pie, one on each slice, and the Chart Objects list box displays "Series 1"

3. Once you have selected the entire pie, you can select one slice of it. Hover the mouse over the Shortboard pie slice. The ScreenTip "Series 1 Point "Shortboard" Value: $277,094 (30%)" appears

4. Click the **Shortboard pie slice** to select it. Selection handles disappear from all other pie slices

5. Click and drag the **Shortboard pie slice** a short distance away from the center of the pie. An outline appears and shows your progress

6. Release the mouse (see Figure 4.30)

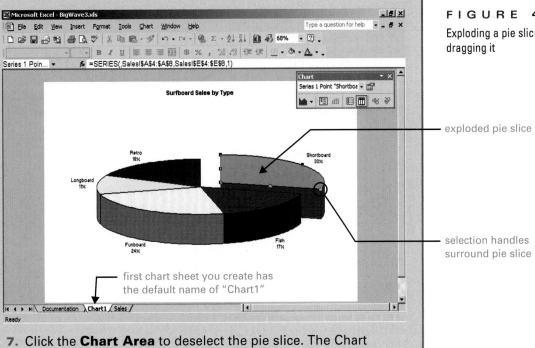

FIGURE 4.30

Exploding a pie slice by dragging it

exploded pie slice

selection handles surround pie slice

first chart sheet you create has the default name of "Chart1"

7. Click the **Chart Area** to deselect the pie slice. The Chart Objects list displays "Chart Area," confirming that you have clicked the Chart Area

EXCEL

Rotating and Elevating a Three-Dimensional Chart

While the 3-D pie chart certainly is impressive and self-explanatory, Keoki thinks the exact proportions of the pie slices are not obvious to a casual reader. He thinks that the pie chart should be tilted up, by raising the back edge, to provide a better perspective. Additionally, Keoki wants the Short-board pie slice to appear on the right side of the chart at the 3 o'clock position, considering the pie to be a clock face.

FIGURE 4.31

3-D View dialog box

Elevating and Rotating a Pie Chart:

1. With the Chart Area of the 3-D chart sheet selected, click **Chart** in the menu bar and click **3-D View.** The 3-D View dialog box opens. Notice that the Elevation text box displays 15, indicating that the entire pie chart is tilted up 15 degrees (see Figure 4.31)

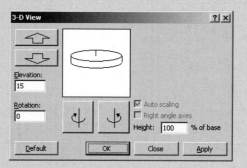

2. Double-click the **Elevation** text box, if necessary, to select its current value and then type **35**

3. Click and drag the **3-D View dialog box title bar** to move the dialog box to a corner of the screen so that you can see the Shortboard portion of pie chart

4. Double-click the **Rotation** text box to highlight its current value, type **20,** and click the 3-D View dialog box **Apply** button. Excel rotates the pie chart clockwise 20 degrees, but that is not quite enough

5. Double-click the **Rotation** text box, type **30** to rotate the pie chart clockwise 30 degrees, and click the **Apply** button. That looks just right (see Figure 4.32)

6. Click the **OK** button to complete the operation and close the 3-D View dialog box

You can see why Keoki wanted you to elevate the 3-D pie chart. It is much easier to see the pie chart and judge the size differences between the five pie slices representing total sales of the five types of surfboards.

CHANGING THE CHART TYPE

Excel has several chart types from which you can choose. You can choose a type as you create a chart. You can choose to change chart types after you have created a chart sheet or an embedded chart. With the current chart selected, you can change to a different chart type by clicking the

FIGURE 4.32

Elevating and rotating a 3-D
pie chart

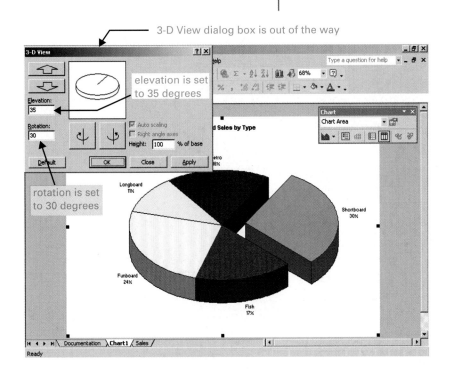

3-D View dialog box is out of the way

elevation is set
to 35 degrees

rotation is set
to 30 degrees

Chart Type command on the Chart menu or by clicking the Chart type button on the Chart toolbar. Keoki is satisfied with the 3-D pie chart you created and he does not want to change chart types. It's good to know you can
change chart types easily, though.

FORMATTING CHART TEXT

You can change the text appearing on a chart sheet the same way you
change text on an embedded chart. Recall that if you change text whose
value is part of the data range—category names, for example—the changed
text is no longer linked to the worksheet cell containing the original text.
That is, you break the link between chart text and worksheet cell text.
However, formatting chart text does not break the link between worksheet
cell source data and the chart data.

Formatting the Chart Title

You can change the font, point size, typeface, and color of text in a chart by
selecting the text and then applying the formatting changes with the
Format command or by pressing the Format button on the Chart toolbar.
Modify the pie chart title by making it bold, changing the point size to 16,
and changing the text color to dark blue.

Formatting the chart title:

1. Click the **Chart Title** object in the pie chart. Selection handles
   and a border appear around the chart title. The Name Box to
   the left of the Formula bar displays "Chart Title," confirming
   the name of the object you have selected

2. Click **Format** on the menu bar and click **Selected Chart
   Title.** The Format Chart Title dialog box appears

EXCEL

FIGURE 4.33

Format Title dialog box

3. Click the **Font** tab, click **Bold** in the Font style box, and scroll the Size list box, if necessary, until 16 comes into view

4. Click **16** in the Size box and then click the **Color list box arrow.** The color palette appears below the color list box

5. Click the **Dark Blue** color square (top row, column 6) to change the Chart Title object's text color (see Figure 4.33)

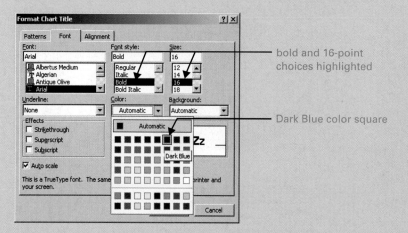

bold and 16-point choices highlighted

Dark Blue color square

6. Click **OK** to complete the chart title format operation and close the Format Title dialog box

Formatting Data Labels

You can format data labels following steps similar to the ones you followed above to format the chart title. Keoki wants the data labels to remain black, but he wants a larger point size and he wants you to bold the data labels. After looking at the chart title's size, you decide that the data labels should be slightly smaller. You choose 12-point font size for the data labels.

Formatting data labels:

1. Click any data label in the chart to select all of them. Selection handles appear around all of the data labels and the Chart Objects list box of the Chart toolbar displays "Series 1 Data Labels"

2. Click **Format** on the menu bar and click **Selected Data Labels.** The Format Data Labels dialog box appears

3. Click the **Font** tab, if necessary, and then click **Bold** in the Font style list box

5. Scroll the Size list box, if necessary, until 12 comes into view, click **12,** and then click **OK** to complete the data labels format operation. The data labels are easier to read (see Figure 4.34)

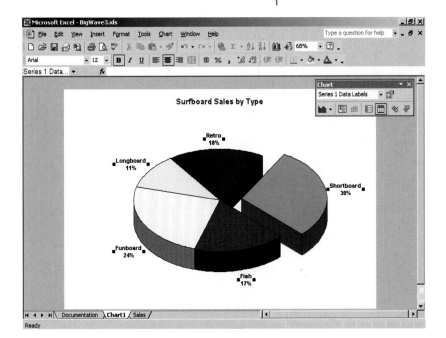

FIGURE 4.34
Pie chart with newly formatted
text

ADDING TEXTURE FOR EMPHASIS

Texture or gradient fills are applicable to the chart area, bars, and several other chart objects. When used sparingly, texture fills and gradient fills can add just the right touch to a chart to make it look professional. Because the 3-D pie chart visually represents sales of surfboards by type, Keoki wants you to add a background texture to the chart area that is related to sun, surf, or water. Doing so, he reasons, will add just the right adornment and enhance the chart's impact on all who view it.

Adding texture fill to a chart area:

1. Click the **Chart Area** object (the white area around the chart). The Chart toolbar, if visible, indicates "Chart Area" in the Chart Objects list box

2. Click **Format** on the menu bar and then click **Selected Chart Area.** The Format Chart Area dialog box appears

3. Click the **Patterns** tab, if necessary, and then click the **Fill Effects** button. The Fill Effects dialog box opens

4. Click the **Texture** tab and then click the **Texture scroll down arrow** until the Water droplets texture appears (second row from the bottom, first column)

5. Click the **Water droplets** square. The text "Water droplets" appears in the label below the Texture palette when you select the correct square (see Figure 4.35)

6. Click **OK** to close the Fill Effects dialog box and click **OK** again to close the Format Chart Area dialog box. The Water droplets texture fill appears in the chart area background (see Figure 4.36)

EXCEL

FIGURE 4.35

Selecting the Water droplets
texture

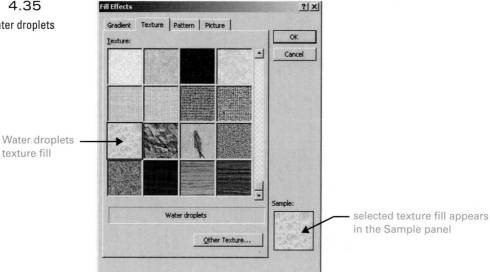

FIGURE 4.36

Chart with texture fill

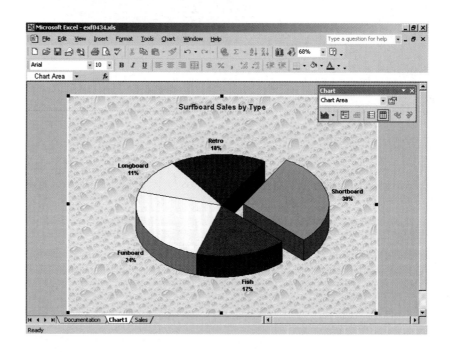

The pie chart is complete and ready to print.

anotherword

. . . on Chart Area Background Fill Effects

If you decide to remove fill effects from a chart area background, click the chart area, click **Format** on the menu bar, click **Selected Chart Area,** click **Patterns** tab, click the **None** option button in the Area panel, and click the OK button to close the Format Chart Area dialog box and remove the background texture fill from the chart area

SAVING AND PRINTING A CHART SHEET

Keoki reviews your work and is satisfied with the final result. He asks you to save the workbook and print the chart sheet. Printing chart sheets follows the same procedures as printing any worksheet. You either click the Standard toolbar print button or you click File, then Print, and set options in the Print dialog box before you click OK to print the page.

> ### Saving the workbook and printing a chart sheet:
>
> 1. Click the **Save** 🖫 button on the Standard toolbar to save your workbook
>
> 2. If necessary, click the **Chart1** sheet tab to select the chart sheet
>
> **tip:** *If you have created other chart sheets and deleted them before creating the final chart sheet, your chart sheet tab may not be called Chart1. It may have another name such as Chart2 or Chart3*
>
> 3. Click **File,** click **Page Setup,** click the **Header/Footer** tab, click the **Custom Header** button, type your name in the Right section, click **OK** to close the Header dialog box, and click **OK** to close the Page Setup dialog box
>
> 4. Click the **Print** 🖨 button to print the chart sheet. After a short pause, the chart sheet prints

DELETING CHARTS

Although you will not delete any charts you have created, you should learn how to delete both embedded charts and chart sheets in case you later need to do so. Delete an embedded chart by selecting it and then pressing the Delete key.

---

task reference

Deleting an Embedded Chart

- Click the embedded chart
- Press the **Delete** key

Deleting a chart sheet is equally simple. Be careful. Unlike deleting an embedded chart, there is no way to reverse the deletion process. You cannot undo a chart sheet deletion. If you mistakenly delete a chart sheet, your only recourse is to reconstruct the chart sheet from scratch or to open a previous version of the worksheet containing the chart sheet.

---

task reference

Deleting a Chart Sheet

- Click the tab corresponding to the chart sheet
- Click **Edit,** then click **Delete Sheet**
- Click **OK**

EXCEL

SAVING A CHART AS A WEB PAGE

Because Keoki wants to share the worksheet with his Big Wave employees in all three locations—Hawaii, California, and Florida—he asks you to create a Web page from the Excel worksheet. For now, Keoki will post the worksheet in a protected area of the Web server that only employees can access.

You can create Web pages from Excel charts about as simply as you can save a worksheet. Once you create the Web pages, make them available to anyone by posting them on a server connected to the Internet that displays Web pages. However, you do not need access to a Web server to create Web pages. You can view your Web pages on any PC that has a Web browser regardless of whether it is connected to the Internet.

---

task reference

Creating Web Pages from an Excel Chart

- Click the chart sheet tab
- Click **File** and click **Save as Web Page**
- Select a drive and folder in the Save in text box
- Click the **Selection: Chart** option
- Click the **Change Title** button, type a Web page title in the title text box, and click **OK**
- Type the Web page file name in the File name text box
- Click the **Save** button

You are ready to create a Web page from the pie chart on the chart sheet you created in this session.

Saving a Chart Sheet as a Web Page:

1. Click the **Chart1** chart sheet tab, if necessary
2. Click **File** and then click **Save as Web Page.** The Save as dialog box opens
3. Select the disk drive and folder in the Save in text box in which you want to save your Web pages
4. Click the **Selection: Chart** option
5. Click the **Change Title** button, type **Big Wave Surfboard Sales by Type** in the Title text box of the Set Title dialog box. The title you type appears in the browser's title bar whenever you open the Web page
6. Click **OK** to close the Set Title dialog box
7. Drag the mouse across the text in the File name text box and type **BigWave** to replace the Excel-suggested file name (see Figure 4.37)
8. Click the **Save** button to save the Web page

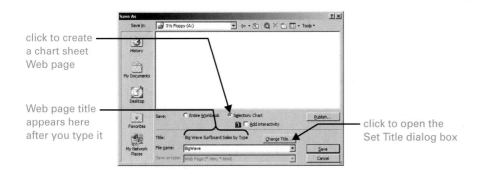

FIGURE 4.37

Saving a chart as a Web page

click to create a chart sheet Web page

Web page title appears here after you type it

click to open the Set Title dialog box

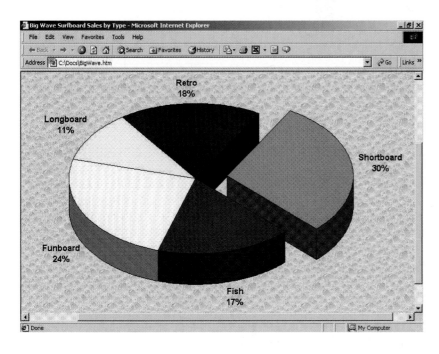

FIGURE 4.38

Big Wave Web page

If you want, you can view the Web page you just created by opening the Web page in your favorite Web browser. Figure 4.38 shows the Web page displayed with Internet Explorer.

CREATING A BAR CHART

Keoki has encouraged competition between his three Big Wave sales outlets by offering incentives if the sales outlet reaches or exceeds selected gross sales goals. He expects gross sales at each outlet to exceed $200,000 per year—the amount he calculates he must make just to keep the sales outlet open. Keoki is pleased when annual sales exceed $200,000 in any sales outlet. He pays a bonus to sales associates in those regions. For sales outlets selling more than $300,000 in one year, Keoki promises a double bonus for the sales associates in those regions.

Keoki thinks that a bar graph is the best way to show the progress of each sales outlet and to display the annual totals to every Big Wave salesperson. Keoki asks you to figure out a way to color-code each segment of a bar so that it colorfully indicates when the sales region reaches the next sales goal.

A bar chart is similar to a column chart and can be used interchangeably. Bar charts can illustrate competitions slightly better than column charts because bar charts are drawn from left to right and resemble progress toward a goal or a race proceeding from left to right. Bar charts

EXCEL

Bar chart with color-coded value alerts

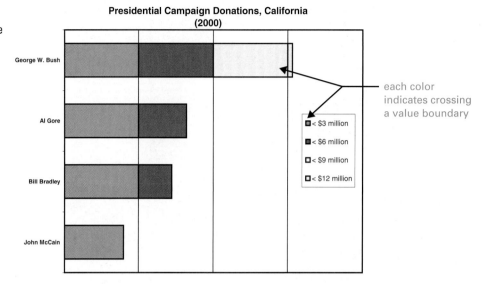

Presidential Campaign Donations, California (2000)

each color indicates crossing a value boundary

□ < $3 million
■ < $6 million
□ < $9 million
□ < $12 million

are often used to highlight values that exceed a critical level—blood pressure is too high, temperatures are reaching a critical value, or fuel reserves are below a safety point. One way to highlight critical goals or value points with a bar chart is to color-code a data marker to indicate when the data marker has surpassed one or more critical points. Figure 4.39 illustrates this concept. Each segment of a bar is color coded to indicate when campaign funds for each candidate exceed successive $3 million boundaries. Color codes help a reader quickly grasp the big picture—only George W. Bush raised more than $9 million in California. The paragraphs that follow explain how to create color-coded value alerts using a special type of bar chart.

The ***stacked bar chart,*** a subtype of the bar chart, combines the data markers in a data series together to form one bar, placing each marker at the end of the preceding one in the same data series. A stacked bar chart is particularly well suited in situations that Figure 4.39 illustrates—when data series comprise a category and you are interested in viewing the sum of the data values in the series. You will use a stacked bar chart to vividly illustrate sales from each sales region that exceed particular milestones. The key is not in the chart but in the data. To create a stacked bar chart similar to the one in Figure 4.39 for Big Wave surfboards, you will create new data and then chart the data.

Creating data series for a stacked bar chart:

1. Click the **Sales** sheet tab to select the worksheet containing the sales data

2. Click cell **G5** and type **California,** click cell **G6** and type **Hawaii,** and click cell **G7** and type **Florida**

3. Click cell **H5**, type **=MIN(B9,200000),** click cell **H6,** type **=MIN(C9,200000),** click cell **H7,** type **=MIN(D9,200000),** and then press **Enter.** These formulas calculate values that

represent the first segment—up to $200,000—of the sales for each sales outlet. Next, you will add another data marker that represents the value between $200,000 and $300,000

tip: *You may want to widen columns H, I, and J, as necessary, to view the results of the formulas.*

4. Click cell **I5,** type **=MIN(B9-H5,100000),** click cell **I6,** type **=MIN(C9-H6,100000),** click cell **I7,** type **=MIN(D9-H7,100000),** and then press **Enter.** These formulas calculate values that represent the second segment—from $200,000 to $300,000— of the sales for each sales outlet

5. Click cell **J5,** type **=B9-H5-I5,** click cell **J6,** type **=C9-H6-I6,** click cell **J7,** type **=D9-H7-I7,** and then press **Enter.** These formulas calculate values that represent the final segment— above $300,000—for each sales outlet (see Figure 4.40)

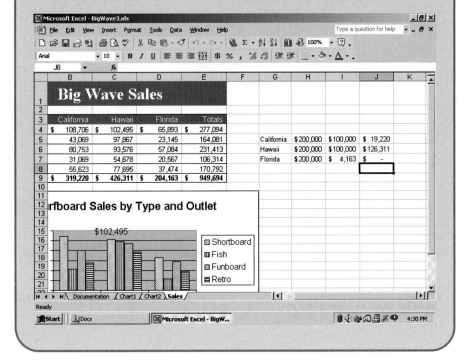

FIGURE 4.40

Creating new data for a stacked bar chart

The new data show the sales for each sales outlet broken down into three segments: 0 to $200,000, $200,001 to $300,000, and greater than $300,000. Using this new data, you can create a stacked bar graph that shows how each series' segment contributes to the total sales represented by a bar in the bar chart. You create the chart next.

Creating a stacked bar chart:

1. Click and drag the cell range **G5:J7**

2. Click the **Chart Wizard** button, click **Bar** in the Chart type list box, click the **Stacked Bar** square in the Chart subtype panel (top row, second column), and click the **Next** button to go to the next Chart Wizard step

EXCEL

3. Click the **Columns** option button and click the **Next** button

4. Click the **Titles** tab, if necessary, and then click the **Chart title** text box and type **Critical Sales Boundaries**

5. Click the **Legend** tab, click the **Show Legend** check box to remove the checkmark, and click **Next**

6. Click the **As new sheet** option button and then click the **Finish** button. The stacked bar chart appears in its own chart sheet, Chart2, following the Chart1 chart sheet (see Figure 4.41)

F I G U R E   4.41

Stacked bar sales chart

Critical Sales Boundaries

bar color change indicates bonus range

color change indicates upper bonus range

Keoki couldn't be happier. He's pleased with all three charts and sends you a nice e-mail expressing how much he appreciates your hard work.

Saving the workbook:

1. Click the **Documentation** sheet tab to make it the active sheet

2. Click **File** on the menu bar, click **Save as,** type **BigWave4.xls** in the File name text box of the Save As dialog box, and click the **Save** button to save the final version of your worksheet to disk under a new name

3. Click **File** and then click **Exit** to exit Excel

You have completed your work in this chapter and have created an embedded chart and two chart sheets.

making the grade

1. You select nonadjacent cell ranges by selecting the first cell range, pressing the _____ key, and selecting the second cell range.

2. A(n) _____ chart resides on a worksheet page, whereas a(n) _____ _____ is on a separate sheet.

3. A _____ chart is a good choice when you want to depict contribution of parts to a whole.

4. You can _____ a three-dimensional pie chart to get a better perspective of it.

5. Open up the original worksheet, **ex04BigWave.xls,** and save it as **BigWave5.xls.** Next, create data similar to that you created in the exercise entitled "Creating data series for a stacked bar chart" above. Click the **Sales** worksheet tab to open that worksheet. Type **Shortboard, Fish, Funboard,** and **Longboard** into cells A11 through A14, respectively. Type the following in the indicated cells:

   Cell B11: **=MIN(E4,100000)**

   Cell C11: **=MIN(E4-B11,100000)**

   Cell D11: **= E4-B11-C11**

   Select cell range **B11:D11** and copy it to cell range **B12:D14** to complete the data area you will chart. Create a three-dimensional stacked bar chart in a chart sheet based on the data in cell range B11:D14 using the Chart Wizard. If necessary, click the Columns option in the Data range panel. Eliminate the legend in Chart Wizard step 3 of 4 and title the chart appropriately. Add your name in the chart sheet header. The chart shows bar color changes when the bars cross $100,000 and $200,000. Click the Documentation tab to make that sheet active and save the worksheet. Print the stacked bar chart sheet and the Sales worksheet. Close Excel.

SESSION 4.3 SUMMARY

Excel charts pictorially display values and provide a graphic way for viewers to easily understand the magnitude or change in data values. You can create either two-dimensional or three-dimensional charts including column, bar, line, pie, scatter, area, and doughnut. For each chart type, you can choose from several chart subtypes. Column subtype charts include simple column, stacked column, and stacked column with a 3-D visual effect. Chart data is called data series—the set of values you chart. Categories organize values in the data series. The X-axis in a column chart displays category names.

Choosing the correct type of chart to display your data is important. Each chart has a different purpose. A pie chart best displays the contribution of parts to the whole—how much of your tax dollar goes to education, for example. Line charts are a good choice to show trends. The plot area contains the chart and other elements surrounding the chart include the chart title, category names, and the X- and Y-axes. Excel supports both embedded charts and chart sheets. Embedded charts appear on a worksheet along with data and float on a layer above the worksheet. A chart sheet is a separate sheet that contains a chart but does not contain worksheet data. Embedded charts and chart sheets are otherwise exactly the same—both types can display any of the Excel chart types.

Chart data—the values represented by the data series—are linked to the data markers. This dynamic relationship means that you can change the value of worksheet data and the chart will automatically adjust to reflect the changes. Category names are linked to worksheet cells too, though they typically display text.

You can modify every aspect of a chart including the overall chart type, the format (color, typeface, and size) of any text or numeric value on a chart, the background color of the plot area or chart area, the color or existence of gridlines and data labels, the format and scaling of Y-axis values, and whether a legend appears on the chart.

Delete data series from a chart by hiding the data in the worksheet (hide the row or column) or by selecting the data series and pressing the Delete key. Print an embedded chart by printing the worksheet on which it resides. Alternatively, click an embedded chart to print just the embedded chart.

Tilt or rotate three-dimensional pie charts until the perspective is just right. Explode a pie slice for emphasis by clicking the pie and then clicking the pie slice. Then drag the pie slice away from the center. Data labels for pie slices can be category names, category names and values, or percentages. You can apply a texture to several chart elements including pie slices, bars, columns, the plot area, or the chart area to add interest and vitality to a chart. You can save an Excel chart as a Web page with the Save As Web Page command in the File menu. After saving the Web pages on your computer disk, you can upload them to an Internet-connected computer so that the world can view your creation.

With a few simple formulas, you can create stacked bar or stacked column charts that display different data segments in a different color to emphasize crossing significant numeric boundaries or goals. Using the MIN function, you can dissect a value into parts that you can chart as a bar with a different color or pattern for each segment that is part of the bar or column.

MOUS OBJECTIVES SUMMARY

- Create an embedded chart and a chart sheet (MOUS Ex2002-6-1)
- Modify an existing chart by revising data, altering chart text, and labeling data (MOUS Ex2002-6-1)
- Use color and patterns to embellish a chart (MOUS Ex2002-6-1)
- Add a new data series to a chart (MOUS Ex2002-6-2)
- Alter a chart type and create a three-dimensional chart (MOUS Ex2002-6-1)
- Create a pie chart with a title, exploding slice, labels, and floating text (MOUS Ex2002-6-1)
- Add texture to a chart (MOUS Ex2002-6-1)
- Delete embedded charts and chart sheets (MOUS Ex2002-4-1)

task reference summary

Task	Page #	Recommended Method
Creating a Chart	EX 4.9	• Select data cell range Click the **Chart Wizard** button
		• Respond to the series of Chart Wizard dialog box choices
Snapping an embedded chart into place	EX 4.13	• Select the chart
		• Press and hold the **Alt** key
		• Drag a chart left, right, up, or down until the chart edge snaps to a cell boundary
		• Release the mouse and Alt key
Adding a new data series to an embedded chart	EX 4.17	• Select the cell range of the data series you want to add
		• Move the mouse to any edge of the selected worksheet cell range
		• When the mouse pointer changes to an arrow, click and drag the range into the chart area and release the mouse
Deleting a data series from a chart	EX 4.18	• Select the data marker
		• Press **Delete**
Adding a data label to all data series in a chart	EX 4.22	• Select a data series
		• Click **Chart**, click **Chart Options**, click the **Data Labels** tab
		• Click the **Show value** option, click **OK**
Adding a data label to a data series	EX 4.22	• Select the data series
		• Click **Format**, click **Selected Data Series**, click the **Data Labels** tab
		• Click the **Show value** option, click **OK**
Add a data label to a data marker	EX 4.23	• Select the data series, click the data marker in the series
		• Click **Format**, click **Selected Data Point**, click the **Data Labels** tab
		• Click the **Show value** option, click **OK**
Printing a worksheet and embedded chart	EX 4.29	• Click any worksheet cell
		• Click the **Print** button
Printing an embedded chart	EX 4.30	• Click the chart
		• Click the **Print** button

EXCEL

task reference summary

Task	Page #	Recommended Method
Selecting nonadjacent cell ranges	EX 4.32	• Select the first cell range
		• Press and hold the **Ctrl** key
		• Select additional cells or cell ranges
		• When finished selecting cells, release the **Ctrl** key
Deleting an embedded chart	EX 4.41	• Click the embedded chart
		• Press the **Delete** key
Deleting a chart sheet	EX 4.41	• Click the chart sheet tab
		• Click **Edit**, click **Delete** Sheet, click **OK**
Creating Web pages from an Excel chart	EX 4.42	• Click the chart or chart sheet tab
		• Click **File**, click **Save as Web Page**
		• Select a drive and folder
		• Click the **Selection: Chart** option
		• Optionally type a page title and click **OK**
		• Click **Save**

CROSSWORD PUZZLE

Across

1. A chart _____ resides on its own workbook page
7. _____ text includes tick mark labels and the X-axis title
8. The _____ area contains all the chart elements
9. A chart's _____ appears above the chart and labels it
10. A(n) _____ chart resides on a worksheet
12. Each data series in a chart can have up to 32,000 values or data _____
13. A data _____ is a graphic representation of the value of a data point
14. A data _____ is the value or name assigned to an individual data point

Down

2. _____ the data in a worksheet, but not delete it, to remove it from a chart
3. _____ marks are small lines uniformly spaced along the axis
4. Organizes the values in one data series under a name
5. Click and drag a _____ handle to resize a chart or other object
6. A _____ is an extension of a tick mark and helps identify the value of data markers
11. A data _____ is a set of values that you want to chart
12. The _____ area is bounded by the X-axis and the Y-axis
15. A line that contains a measurement by which you compare plotted values

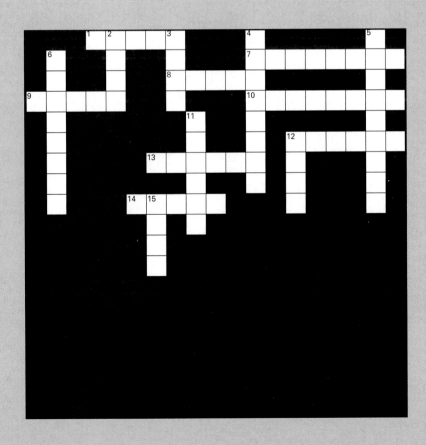

FILL-IN

1. A _____ _____ is a set of values that you chart.

2. The values in a data series are named by a _____.

3. The _____ area of a chart is bounded by the X-axis and the Y-axis.

4. What object in a chart identifies which data marker represents each series when you chart multiple series?

5. A _____ chart is a better choice than a pie chart to represent the daily average temperature in a city for a month.

6. The _____ box is a drawing object into which you can type text and place on a chart to highlight a feature.

REVIEW QUESTIONS

1. Suppose you create a column chart using data from the Big Wave surfboard data in which each row is a data series and row totals are in the rightmost column. You select the cells to plot, but you accidentally include the totals column. The totals are plotted as a separate series in the chart. Explain how to remove the totals column from the chart and still display the totals column in the worksheet.

2. Explain briefly how to remove dollar signs from the Y-axis values in a column chart.

3. The legend Excel created is too small. Legend names are difficult to read. How do you increase the size of the legend? What do you do to make the labels inside the legend larger?

4. You click a chart sheet tab and then click Edit, Delete Sheet, and click OK. You realize you deleted the wrong chart sheet. How do you recover the accidentally deleted chart sheet?

CREATE THE QUESTION

For each of the following answers, create an appropriate, short question.

ANSWER	QUESTION
1. Click Edit and then click Delete Sheet	_____
2. One of the set of values being charted	_____
3. Extensions of tick marks that help identify the value of data markers	_____
4. Click and drag one of these to resize an embedded chart	_____
5. They display the numeric value of a data marker	_____
6. Click this button on the Chart toolbar to change a pie chart into a bar chart	_____

1. Charting Olympic Gold, Silver, and Bronze Medals

Olsen, Kramer, and Shubert (OKS) is a public relations firm that has been hired to do post-Olympic analysis of the games. They have hired Alison Najir and you to produce statistics about the competition and graph the results. In particular, OKS wants you to produce a chart of the medals that competing countries have won. They think a three-dimensional stacked bar chart showing bronze, silver, and gold medals in a single bar for each country would be a good way to chart the results. There are too many countries winning medals to conveniently represent each one, so the company asks you to produce a chart sheet showing the number of medals won by teams winning at least 10 medals total. You have done your Web research and prepared a list of medal winnings—bronze, silver, and gold—in descending order by total medals won. You proceed to produce the chart.

1. Open the workbook **ex04Olympics.xls** and use the Save As command in the File menu to save the workbook under the name **Olympics2.xls**
2. Click the **Medal Data** tab and then drag the mouse to select the cell range **A3:D14** (to include in the chart all countries winning at least 10 medals and the column title row)
3. Click the **Chart Wizard** button, click **Bar** in the Chart type, click the **Stacked bar with 3-D visual effect** in the Chart subtype panel, click **Next** to go to Step 2, and click **Next** again to go to Step 3
4. Click the **Chart title** text box and type **Top Medal Winners, 2000 Olympics**
5. Click the **Value (Z) axis** text box and type **Medals**
6. Click the **Data Labels tab,** click the **Value** check box, and then click **Next**
7. Click the **As new sheet** option button and then click the **Finish** button
8. In the Chart toolbar, click the Chart Objects list arrow, scroll the list, click any **Series "Bronze"** to select all Bronze data markers, click the **Format Data Series** button in the

Chart toolbar, click the **Patterns** tab, and click the **Brown** square (top row, second column) in the Area frame, and click **OK**

tip: Be careful when selecting a data marker not to select the data label inside a data marker. You select a data marker when the Chart toolbar Chart Object list box contains "Series. . . ."

9. Repeat Step 8 for the **Silver data marker** (second from the left in any bar), but this time select the **Gary-40%** color square on the Patterns tab (third row from the top, column eight), and then click **OK**
10. Repeat Step 8 for the **Gold data marker** (third from the left in any bar), but this time select the **Light Yellow** square (fifth row from the top, column three) and then click **OK**
11. Place your name in the chart sheet header, click the **Cover Sheet** tab and type your name next to the label "Workbook designer," and enter today's date next to the "Design date" label
12. Print the Cover Sheet and the Chart1 chart sheet, save the workbook, and exit Excel

2. Mapping Rainfall in Hawaii

The field office of the Hawaii visitor's bureau in Kauai, Hawaii, wants you to produce a line chart of the average rainfall for the previous year—January through December. A line chart is the best way to represent this data because it shows trends for each of the five regions. Follow these steps to produce and print the chart.

1. Open **ex04Rainfall.xls**, type your name in the Designer line, type the current date in the Design Date line, and save the file as **Rainfall2.xls** (click **File**, click **Save As,** type the new name, and click the **Save** button)
2. Click the **Rainfall Averages** tab, click cell **A2,** and type your first and last names
3. Click and drag the mouse to select the cell range **A3:M8** and click the **Chart Wizard** button
4. Click **Line** in the Chart type list box and click **Next**

5. Click **Next** again, click the **Chart title** text box, and type **Average Rainfall, Kauai, Hawaii,** click the **Value (Y) axis** and type **Inches,** click **Next**, and click **Finish**

6. Drag the embedded chart until its upper left-corner covers cell A10

7. Click the **chart selection handle** in the lower-right corner of the chart area and drag it down and to the right until the lower-right corner of the chart area just covers cell M30. (Remember, you can press the Alt key as you drag the corner to snap it to exact cell boundaries)

8. Click cell **A1** to deselect the embedded chart

9. Save the workbook again, print the Rainfall Averages worksheet, and then click the **Documentation** tab, print the Documentation worksheet, and exit Excel

challenge!

1. Charting California's Expenditures

The Director of Finance for the State of California, G. Timothy Gage, has collected data about the 2001–2002 Expenditures by fund source for the State of California. The data are in a workbook called **ex04California.xls.** He wants you to help him get the data into shape. Specifically, he wants you to do two things for him. First, he wants you to format the worksheet data so that it looks better—currently it is in raw form and difficult to read. Second, he wants you to produce a two-dimensional pie chart showing the percentage contribution to the total 2001–2002 expenditures. He wants the chart to display a legend and the chart title to be "California Expenditures (2001–2002)." While he leaves other chart formatting details to you, he insists that you emphasize the Education pie slice by exploding it out from the rest of the chart, and he wants the chart on its own chart sheet.

Figure 4.42 shows one way you can format the worksheet. Hint: It is formatted using Merge and Center for the title and subtitle, colors, bold-face, background color, and a shadow around the table. Column A is wide enough to display the widest text in its column.

Start by loading **ex04California.xls** and save the worksheet as **California2.xls.** Then type your name on the Documentation worksheet to the right of the "Designer:" text. Type the current date in cell C8. On the Expenditures worksheet, place your name in the worksheet header. Do the same for the Chart1 chart sheet page. Print all three pages.

2. Charting the Rental Car Market

Herb Klein is researching the U.S. rental car market. He conducted part of his research on the Web and through professional magazines. One Web site, Auto Rental News, is chock full of car rental statistics (www.autorentalnews.com) that have helped Herb understand the magnitude of the rental car market. While Herb is a marketing wizard and understands Excel enough to enter data, he has difficulty understanding how to chart the data. He wants you to help him by producing two charts of the data he has collected in a worksheet called **ex04RentalCar.xls.**

Two charts interest Herb. The first one will be a chart sheet column chart showing the estimated U.S. rental revenue by each of nine top car rental companies. The second chart will be an embedded two-dimensional pie chart showing the number of cars in service of each company in comparison to the total cars in service. Start by opening **ex04RentalCar.xls** and immediately save it under the new name, **RentalCar2.xls.** Here are the details of what he wants.

The chart sheet column chart, when completed, will show car rental companies in the X-axis as categories. The Y-axis values should not show currency symbols and should be expressed in whole dollars. The chart title is "U.S. Rental Revenue Est. (Millions)" and is 16-point bold text. The Y-axis title is "Revenue (Millions)" with default formatting. Add data labels to two columns—the highest revenue and the lowest revenue—so those

FIGURE 4.42

Example of formatted Expenditures worksheet

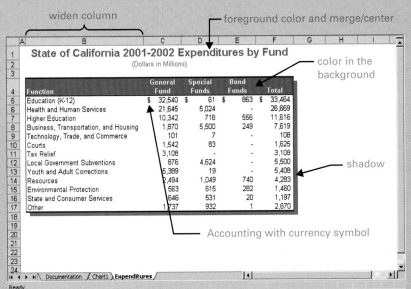

widen column			foreground color and merge/center						
	A	B	C	D	E	F	G	H	I
1	State of California 2001-2002 Expenditures by Fund								
2		(Dollars in Millions)							
3									
4	Function		General Fund	Special Funds	Bond Funds	Total			
5	Education (K-12)		$ 32,540	$ 61	$ 863	$ 33,464			
6	Health and Human Services		21,645	5,024	-	26,669			
7	Higher Education		10,342	718	556	11,616			
8	Business, Transportation, and Housing		1,870	5,500	249	7,619			
9	Technology, Trade, and Commerce		101	7	-	108			
10	Courts		1,542	83	-	1,625			
11	Tax Relief		3,108	-	-	3,108			
12	Local Government Subventions		876	4,624	-	5,500			
13	Youth and Adult Corrections		5,389	19	-	5,408			
14	Resources		2,494	1,049	740	4,283			
15	Environmental Protection		563	615	282	1,460			
16	State and Consumer Services		646	531	20	1,197			
17	Other		1,737	932	1	2,670			

color in the background

shadow

Accounting with currency symbol

Documentation / Chart1 \ Expenditures /

Ready

two columns display the amount at their column tops. Place in your name in the chart sheet page header's left section.

Embed the second chart, a two-dimensional pie chart, on the same page as the worksheet data. The chart area should occupy cells A14 through G36. Display values only on the pie segments, display the legend on the left side of the chart area, and create a chart title "Cars in Service" formatted bold and 16-point typeface. Place your name in the page header's left section.

On the Documentation page, type your name and the current date in the underlined areas to the right of Designer and Design Date, respectively. Modify the worksheet data page, called Car Rental Statistics, any way you want or not at all. Print all three worksheets.

1. Graphing Agricultural Production Values

Terry Branson is the county agent for Lancaster County, Nebraska, and is responsible for aiding citizens of the county and state of Nebraska with agricultural questions. Most of the inquiries he receives are from the farming community, and questions range from what type of feed is best for farmers' livestock to which fertilizer is best for tulips. Lately, Terry has been getting a number of inquiries about crop production in Nebraska and neighboring states. Several farmers in the region have been growing sugar beets and alfalfa with some success, but the prices in both those products have been poor in recent years. Many of the questions have been about alternative crops and their viability in Nebraska. Some farming individuals and corporations have asked Terry to research crops such as corn, sorghum, and soybeans and to report to them the average yield of these products per acre in Nebraska. In order to give the farmers the big picture, Terry wants to include productivity rates, measured in bushels per acre, for Kansas, Oklahoma, and Texas as well as for Nebraska. Because Terry does not have these statistics at his fingertips, he asks you to use the Internet to look up statistics about corn, sorghum, and soybean production and produce a graph.

The graph will use a column chart listing the three crops along the X-axis as categories and the bushels per acre plotted along the Y-axis. The four data series will correspond to states. Include a legend listing the four states of Kansas, Nebraska, Oklahoma, and Texas. The chart title should be "Crop Production per Acre," the Y-axis title should be "Bushels/Acre," and the X-axis title should be "Crops." Change the color of all three titles to a dark green, and resize and reposition the chart so that the embedded chart covers the cell range A10 through F30.

Begin by opening **ex04Crop.xls.** Fill in cells B5:E7 with the values for bushels per acre for the crops in the corresponding states. Graph the cell range A4:E7. Here's how you find the bushels per acre values required to complete this assignment: Launch your Web browser and to go www.fedstats.gov and locate the MapStats section of the home page. Start with Kansas. Click the list box arrow beneath MapStats, click **Kansas** in the list (see Figure 4.43), and then click the **Submit** button to the right of the list box. Ensure that the list box for Kansas says "State level only" and click the **Get Profile** button. When the next page appears, click the **Field Crops** link under the Agriculture heading near the top of the page. A *Field Crops in Kansas* page opens. On this page is a table containing crops and their bushels per acre values (in a column labeled "Yield per harvested acre (bushels)"). Write down the values from that column for corn, sorghum, and soybeans. Click the **Fedstats home page** link to return to the FedStats home page. Repeat this Web search procedure for Nebraska, Oklahoma, and Texas. After you gather the twelve values, close your browser, fill in the values in the worksheet, create an embedded column graph, insert your name in the worksheet header, and print the worksheet.

FIGURE 4.43

FedStats home page

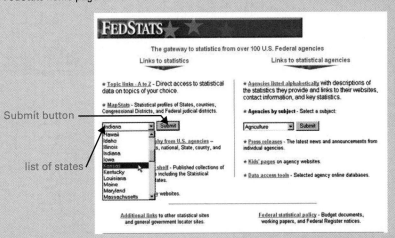

e-business

1. Researching the Largest Coffee Exporting Countries

Jehad Nasser wants to open a Web store to sell coffee beans and coffee supplies. He wants to know which countries export the most coffee and then determine from which countries he will purchase raw coffee beans. To start his research, he has asked you to search the Web for information on coffee bean production and export. One of his acquaintances from Java, Indonesia, suggests Jehad investigate Web sites such as the International Coffee Organization (www.ico.org) to locate statistics on coffee production and export. Jehad has done some work and collected data from the Web including production and export values for 45 coffee-producing nations. He wants you to produce a pie chart showing the percentage of production by the top six coffee exporters. The top six exporters are those who export the largest number of bags of coffee per year. Fortunately, Jehad has gone to the trouble of sorting the list he produced in descending order by the number of bags each country exports.

To accomplish this task, Jehad wants you to complete the Documentation worksheet by doing the following. Start by opening Jehad's preliminary worksheet called **ex04ExportCoffee.xls**. Then add a label such as **Designed by:** and fill in your name. Add a label "Design date:" and fill in the current date next to it. Add a title at the top of the Documentation worksheet that describes, in three or four words, the title of the worksheet. Finally, add a **Purpose:** label and a sentence describing what the workbook contains. Print the documentation in landscape orientation.

Create a two-dimensional pie chart on a chart sheet showing the export percentages of the top six countries and that of all other coffee-producing countries. The "all others" category is the *sum* of export bags for all other countries. (Hint: You will want to add a row after the sixth country that sums the 7th through 45th countries' exports.) In other words, the pie chart will have seven slices. The pie chart data labels should show the percent and the country names. Delete the legend. Title the chart, in 14-point bold typeface, "Top Six Coffee Exporters." Explode the pie slice of the largest exporter, Brazil. Include your name in the header of the chart worksheet.

The Coffee Production and Export worksheet contains the data you will chart. Place your name in the worksheet header. Next, open up a row below the entry for Mexico, place all others in cell B12, and sum up production and export values for Uganda through Benin, placing the sum of production in cell C12 and the sum of export in cell D12. Chart the export values of Brazil through "all others," including the country names as category along with the export values. Set the Coffee Production and Export print range to the first 12 rows (the title through the "all others" row). Save the completed workbook as **ExportCoffee2.xls.** Print the entire workbook.

around the world

1. Charting Hourly Compensation Rates around the World

The Bureau of Labor Statistics (www.bls.gov) maintains tables comparing hourly compensation rates, in U.S. dollars, for the employees in the manufacturing sector for several countries. Melissa Franklin, your supervisor at Applied Economics, Inc., wants you to produce a chart of the data that she can present at a talk she is giving to a group of businesspersons next week in Atlanta. The raw data, shown in Figure 4.44, shows the hourly compensation values for seven countries for selected years between 1975 and 1999. Hourly compensation includes wages, bonuses, vacation, holidays, premiums, insurance, and benefit plans.

Begin by loading the worksheet, called **ex04HourlyLabor.xls.** Format the worksheet so that the column labels and the numbers are attractive and easy to read. Then create a chart in a chart sheet that is well labeled and displays, in the best form possible, the information in a chart. Which chart type is best to display the changes in the hourly compensation for a country? Use that chart type choice for all countries. Add a text box displaying your name in the lower-right corner of the chart. Save the workbook and then print the worksheet and the chart.

2. Charting Unemployment Rates around the World

The U.S. Bureau of Labor Statistics (BLS) collects all sorts of information about the U.S. labor force and provides statistical summaries. In addition to tracking the U.S. labor force, the BLS provides comparisons of U.S. labor segments with foreign countries and provides the information in various types of tables. The BLS maintains a large Web site at www.bls.gov and you can use your browser to go to that location and view some of their

reports. (Most reports are in PDF, or portable document format, that are rendered using the free software product called Acrobat Reader.)

Janet Morrison, the Sonoma County chief of labor statistics, is interested in charting unemployment rate trends between the United States and France during the 1960s as an embedded chart. She would like to compare the United States and France to see if there is a trend both for each country and between the two countries. She wants you to produce a line chart of the unemployment rates with the 1960s along the X-axis and unemployment rates along the Y-axis. Change the color of the chart title, Y-axis label, X-axis label, and X-axis category names to dark blue. Place the chart after the last data row so that it will fit along with the worksheet data on one printed page. Add the appropriate chart title and axes titles.

Start by loading the unemployment worksheet called **ex04Unemployment.xls.** Before you make any changes to the worksheet, save it under the new name **Unemployment2.xls** to preserve the original worksheet. To identify the chart as yours, place a text box containing your first and last names somewhere on the chart. Print the chart and be sure to save the altered worksheet before leaving Excel.

FIGURE 4.44

Hourly compensation comparison

	A	B	C	D	E	F	G	H
1	Hourly compensation costs in U.S. dollars for production workers in manufacturing							
2								
3		1975	1980	1985	1990	1995	1999	
4	Canada	5.96	8.67	10.95	15.95	16.1	15.6	
5	France	4.52	8.94	7.52	15.49	20.01	17.98	
6	Italy	4.67	8.15	7.63	17.45	16.22	16.6	
7	Japan	3	5.52	6.34	12.8	23.82	20.89	
8	Spain	2.53	5.89	4.66	11.38	12.88	12.11	
9	Sweden	7.18	12.51	9.66	20.93	21.44	21.58	
10	United States	6.36	9.87	13.01	14.91	17.19	19.2	
11								

running project

Pampered Paws

Grace Jackson, Pampered Paws' owner, wants you to chart the sales of dog food and cat food for the first six months of her business. She has gathered sales information about four of her most popular dog foods and four of the most popular cat foods in a workbook called **ex04Paws.xls.** Grace wants you to create two chart sheets.

The first chart sheet is a stacked column chart sheet showing sales of each of the four dog foods. Each column represents a month, and the four data markers in each column are the sales of each type of dog food. When completed, the stacked column chart sheet will display six columns, one for each sales month. Type the chart title **Dog Food Sales** for the column chart. The legend displays a different color for each dog food brand. The Y-axis displays sales, and values display the currency symbol.

The second chart sheet is a three-dimensional pie chart showing the percent of the total cat food sales each brand contributes. Tilt the 3-D chart 45 degrees and explode the Iams Lamb/Rice pie slice. Title the chart **Cat Food Sales.** Display a legend and label each slice with the percent (only) of each product's sales.

Begin by loading the worksheet called **ex04Paws.xls.** Then write expressions to sum each row's sales beneath the Total column for both dog and cat products. Subtotal dog food sales in the cell next to the label "Subtotal" and do the same for cat food sales. Sum the two subtotals in the cell H16.

Reorient the worksheet containing sales data so that it prints in landscape orientation. Place a page header on all three sheets containing your name in the center section. Print the two chart sheets and the worksheet.

reference 1

Excel *file finder*

Location in Chapter	Data File to Use	Student Saves Data File as
CHAPTER 1		
Opening a workbook	ex01Scrip.xls	
Saving a workbook	ex01Scrip.xls	ex01Scrip.xls
Saving a workbook / new name	ex01Scrip.xls	Scrip2.xls
Clearing several cells' contents	Scrip2.xls	Scrip3.xls
Closing a workbook	Scrip3.xls	Scrip3.xls
Formulas	ex01Income.xls	Income2.xls
Protected cells	ex01Timecard.xls	
Label	ex01Johnsons.xls	
Entering values	ex01Computer.xls	Computer2.xls
Cell references	ex01GNP.xls	GNP2.xls
CHAPTER 2		
Saving a worksheet		Recycle.xls
Saving modified workbook	Recycle.xls	Recycle.xls
Setting print margins	Recycle.xls	Recycle.xls
Insert comments in cell	Recycle.xls	Recycle.xls
Autoformat	Recycle.xls	Recycle2.xls
Insert	ex02Wages.xls	Wages2.xls
Creating an invoice	ex02Randys.xls	Randys2.xls
Comment indicator	ex02Payroll.xls	Payroll2.xls
Sorting		Brokerage2.xls
Comparing records	ex02E-Merchant.xls	E-Merchant2.xls
CHAPTER 3		
Start Excel	ex03Fruit.xls	ExoticFruit.xls
Indenting Text	ExoticFruit.xls	ExoticFruit.xls
Save workbook / new name	ExoticFruit.xls	ExoticFruit2.xls
Formatting	ExoticFruit2.xls	ExoticFruitModified.xls
Increasing row height	ExoticFruit2.xls	

REF 1.1

REFERENCE

Location in Chapter	Data File to Use	Student Saves Data File as
Remove drawing toolbar	ExoticFruit2.xls	ExoticFruit2.xls
Save workbook	ExoticFruit2.xls	ExoticFruit2.xls
Header	ExoticFruit2.xls	ExoticFruit3.xls
Cell formatting	ex03Bookstore.xls	Bookstore2.xls
Create business card		BusinessCard
Formatting	ex03Schedule.xls	
Formatting	ex03Payment.xls	
Comparing data	ex03Headphones.xls	headphones2.xls
Formatting	ex03Rowing.xls	
Borders	ex03Paws.xls	Paws33.xls
CHAPTER 4		
Opening a worksheet	ex04BigWave.xls	BigWave2.xls
Saving, previewing, and printing	BigWave2.xls	BigWave2.xls
Modifying a chart	BigWave2.xls	BigWaveModified.xls
Selecting nonadjacent data ranges	BigWave2.xls	BigWave3
Saving and printing	BigWave3	BigWave3
Creating Web pages	BigWave3	[web page name]
Saving workbook	BigWave3	BigWave4.xls
Stacked bar chart	ex04BigWave.xls	BigWave5.xls
3-D chart	ex04Olympics.xls	Olympics2.xls
Selection handle	ex04Rainfall.xls	Rainfall2.xls
Headers	ex04California.xls	California2.xls
Pie chart	ex04RentalCar.xls	RentalCar2.xls
Column graph	ex04Crop.xls	
Pie chart	ex04ExportCoffee.xls	ExportCoffee2.xls
Formatting	ex04HourlyLabor.xls	
Labeling	ex04Unemployment.xls	Unemployment2.xls
Chart comparison	ex04Paws.xls	

reference

MOUS Certification Guide

MOUS Objective	Task	Session Location	End-of-Chapter Location
Note: MOUS objectives do not apply to Chapter 1			
CHAPTER 2 EX2002-1-1	**Planning and Creating a Worksheet** Move text, values, and formulas	2.1	EX 2.48
EX2002-3-1	Format cells	2.2	EX 2.48
EX2002-3-2	Insert and delete rows and columns, adjust column width	2.2	EX 2.48
EX2002-3-7	Set a print area	2.2	EX 2.48
EX2002-5-1	Create formulas containing cell references and mathematical operators	2.1	EX 2.48
EX2002-5-1	Differentiate between absolute, mixed and relative cell reference	2.1	EX 2.48
EX2002-7-3	Create cell comments	2.2	EX 2.48
CHAPTER 3 EX2002-1-2	**Formatting a Worksheet** Clear all formatting from selected cells	3.1	EX 3.48
EX2002-3-1	Applying currency and accounting formats to numbers	3.1	EX 3.48
EX2002-3-1	Modify the typeface and point size of text and numbers	3.1	EX 3.48
EX2002-3-1	Apply boldface, italics, and underlines to cells	3.1	EX 3.48
EX2002-3-1	Left-, center-, and right align text	3.1	EX 3.48
EX2002-3-1	Clear all formatting from selected cells	3.2	EX 3.48
EX2002-3-2	Hide and reveal rows and columns	3.2	EX 3.48
EX2002-3-7	Modify the worksheet's print characteristics	3.2	EX 3.48
CHAPTER 4 EX2002-4-1	**Creating Charts** Delete embedded charts and chart sheets	4.1	EX 4.48
EX2002-6-1	Create an embedded chart and chart sheet	4.1	EX 4.48
EX2002-6-1	Modify an existing chart by revising date, altering chart text and labeling data	4.1	EX 4.48
EX2002-6-1	Use color and patterns to embellish a chart	4.1	EX 4.48
EX2002-6-1	Alter a chart type and create a three-dimensional chart	4.2	EX 4.48
EX2002-6-1	Create a pie chart with a title, exploding slice, labels and floating text	4.2	EX 4.48
EX2002-6-1	Add texture to chart	4.2	EX 4.48
EX2002-6-2	Add a new data series to a chart	4.1	EX 4.48

reference 3

reference roundup

Task	Page #	Preferred Method
Worrkbook, open	EX 1.11	• Click **File**, click **Open**, click workbook's name, click the **Open** 🖼 button
Formula, entering	EX 1.17	• Select cell, type **=**, type formula, press **Enter**
Sum function, entering	EX 1.20	• Select cell, type **=SUM(**, type cell range, type **)**, and press **Enter**
Editing cell	EX 1.22	• Select cell, click formula bar, make changes, press **Enter**
Workbook, saving	EX 1.24	• Click **File**, click **Save As**, type file name, click **Save** 💾 button
Help, obtaining	EX 1.25	• Click the **Microsoft Excel Help** command from the **Help** menu (or click the Microsoft Excel **Help** 🔲 button on the Standard toolbar)
		• Click the **Answer Wizard** tab
		• In the *What would you like to do* text box, type an English-language question (replacing the words displayed and highlighted in blue) on the topic with which you need help and click the **Search** button
Contents, clearing	EX 1.27	• Click cell, press **Delete** keyboard key
Header/Footer, creating	EX 1.31	• Click **View**, click **Header and Footer**, click **Custom Header** or **Custom Footer**, select section, type header/footer text, click the **OK** button, and click the **OK** button
Printing worksheet	EX 1.33	• Click **File**, click **Print**, click the **OK** button
Worksheet formulas, printing	EX 1.36	• Click **Tools**, click **Options**, Click the **View** tab, click **Formulas** check box, click **OK**, click **File**, click **Print**, click the **OK** button
Workbook, closing	EX 1.37	• Click **File**, click **Close**, click **Yes** to save (if necessary)
Writing formulas	EX 2.9	• Select a cell, type **5**, type the formula, press **Enter**
Modifying an AutoSum cell range by pointing	EX 2.11	• Press an arrow key repeatedly to select leftmost or topmost cell in range, press and hold **Shift**, select cell range with arrow keys, release **Shift**, press **Enter**
Writing a function using the Paste Function button	EX 2.17	• Select a cell, click **Paste Function**, click a function category, click a function name, click **OK**, complete the formula palette dialog box, click **OK**
Copying and pasting a cell or range of cells	EX 2.21	• Select source cell(s), click **Edit**, click **Copy**, select target cell(s), click **Edit**, click **Paste**
Copying cell contents using a cell's fill handle	EX 2.23	• Select source cell(s), drag the fill handle to the source cell(s) range, release the mouse button
Changing relative references to absolute or mixed references	EX 2.27	• Double-click the cell, move insertion point to the cell reference, press **F4** repeatedly as needed, press **Enter**
Moving cells' contents	EX 2.29	• Select the cell(s), move the mouse pointer to an edge of the selected range, click the edge of the selected cell or cell range, drag the outline to the destination location, release the mouse

Task reference roundup

Task	Page #	Preferred Method
Spell-checking a worksheet	EX 2.31	• Click cell **A1**, click the **Spelling** button, correct any mistakes, click **OK**
Inserting rows	EX 2.34	• Click a cell, click **Insert**, click **Rows**
Inserting columns	EX 2.34	• Click a cell, click **Insert**, click **Columns**
Applying AutoFormat to cells	EX 2.36	• Select a cell range, click **Format**, click **AutoFormat**, select a format style, click **OK**
Modifying a column's width	EX 2.39	• Select the column heading(s), click **Format**, point to **Column**, click **Width**, type column width, and click **OK**
Inserting a comment	EX 2.45	• Click a cell, click **Insert**, click **Comment**, type a comment, and click another cell
Formatting numbers	EX 3.7	• Select cell(s)
		• Click **Format**, click **Cells**, click **Number**
		• Click format category and select options
		• Click **OK**
Copying a cell format to a cell or cell range	EX 3.10	• Select the cell whose format you want to copy
		• Click the **Format Painter** button
		• Click (click/drag) the target cell(s)
Wrapping long text within a cell	EX 3.17	• Select the cell or cell range to which you will apply a format
		• Click **Format**, click **Cells**, and click the **Alignment** tab
		• Click the **Wrap text** check box
		• Click **OK**
Applying fonts and font characteristics	EX 3.18	• Select the cell or cell range that you want to format
		• Click **Format**, click **Cells**, and click the **Font** tab
		• Select a typeface from the Font list box
		• Select a font style and a font size
		• Click **OK**
Clearing formats from a cell, cell selection, rows, or columns	EX 3.21	• Select the cell, cell range, rows, or columns
		• Click **Edit**, point to **Clear**, and click **Formats**
Modifying a row's height	EX 3.23	• Click the row heading
		• Click **Format**, point to **Row**, and click **Height**
		• Type the row height in the Row height text box
		• Click **OK**

Task reference roundup

Task	Page #	Preferred Method
Add a border to a cell	EX 3.25	• Click the cell to which you want to add a border
		• Click the Formatting toolbar **Borders list box arrow**, and click the border you want
Activating/removing a toolbar	EX 3.27	• **Right-click** the menu bar
		• Click the name of the toolbar you want to activate or remove
Adding a text box to a worksheet	EX 3.28	• Activate the Drawing toolbar
		• Click the **Text Box** button
		• Click the worksheet in the location where you want the text box
		• Drag an outline away from the initial point until the text box outline is the right size and shape
		• Type the text you want to appear in the text box
Hiding rows or columns	EX 3.34	• Select the rows or columns
		• Click **Format**, point to **Row** (or **Column**), and click **Hide**
Applying color or patterns to worksheet cells	EX 3.35	• Select the cells to which you want to apply a color or pattern
		• Click **Format**, click **Cells**, and click the **Patterns** tab in the Format Cells dialog box
		• If you want to apply a pattern, then click a pattern from the Pattern list box
		• If you want the pattern to appear in color, then click the Pattern list box again and click a color from the Pattern palette
		• If you want to apply a colored background, then click a color in the Cell shading color palette in the Format Cells dialog box
Printing multiple worksheets	EX 3.45	• Ctrl-click the sheet tabs of each sheet you want to print
		• Click the **Print** button
Creating a Chart	EX 4.9	• Select data cell range Click the **Chart Wizard** button
		• Respond to the series of Chart Wizard dialog box choices
Snapping an embedded chart into place	EX 4.13	• Select the chart
		• Press and hold the **Alt** key
		• Drag a chart left, right, up, or down until the chart edge snaps to a cell boundary
		• Release the mouse and Alt key
Adding a new data series to an embedded chart	EX 4.17	• Select the cell range of the data series you want to add

Task reference roundup

Task	Page #	Preferred Method
		• Move the mouse to any edge of the selected worksheet cell range
		• When the mouse pointer changes to an arrow, click and drag the range into the chart area and release the mouse
Deleting a data series from a chart	EX 4.18	• Select the data marker
		• Press **Delete**
Adding a data label to all data series in a chart	EX 4.22	• Select a data series
		• Click **Chart**, click **Chart Options**, click the **Data Labels** tab
		• Click the **Show value** option, click **OK**
Adding a data label to a data series	EX 4.22	• Select the data series
		• Click **Format**, click **Selected Data Series**, click the **Data Labels** tab
		• Click the **Show value** option, click **OK**
Add a data label to a data marker	EX 4.23	• Select the data series, click the data marker in the series
		• Click **Format**, click **Selected Data Point**, click the **Data Labels** tab
		• Click the **Show value** option, click **OK**
Printing a worksheet and embedded chart	EX 4.29	• Click any worksheet cell
		• Click the **Print** button
Printing an embedded chart	EX 4.30	• Click the chart
		• Click the **Print** button
Selecting nonadjacent cell ranges	EX 4.32	• Select the first cell range
		• Press and hold the **Ctrl** key
		• Select additional cells or cell ranges
		• When finished selecting cells, release the **Ctrl** key
Deleting an embedded chart	EX 4.41	• Click the embedded chart
		• Press the **Delete** key
Deleting a chart sheet	EX 4.41	• Click the chart sheet tab
		• Click **Edit**, click **Delete** Sheet, click **OK**

Task reference roundup

Task	Page #	Preferred Method
Creating Web pages from an Excel chart	EX 4.42	• Click the chart or chart sheet tab
		• Click **File**, click **Save as Web Page**
		• Select a drive and folder
		• Click the **Selection: Chart** option
		• Optionally type a page title and click **OK**
		• Click **Save**

reference 4

making the grade

CHAPTER 1

SESSION 1.1

1. Spreadsheet
2. What-if
3. Workbook, worksheets
4. Standard, formatting
5. Active

SESSION 1.2

1. Function
2. a. Formula
   b. Value
   c. Text
   d. Text
   e. Text
   f. Text
   g. Value
3. =Sum(B4:C6)
4. Save, Save As
5. Clear Contents
6. What-if
7. Header
8. See solution file **ex01scrip-solution.xls**

CHAPTER 2

SESSION 2.1

1. AutoSum automatically creates a sum formula with selected cells adjacent to it in its argument list. An AutoSum on the right end of a row contains the sum of the row, whereas an AutoSum below a column includes all the contiguous cells above it in the argument list. Sometimes AutoSum guesses the range incorrectly. In that case, you have to adjust the cell range.

2. Because an equal sign (=) does not precede the formula, Excel creates a text entry that is "D5+F5."
3. Fill handle
4. Order of precedence consists of rules that govern the order in which Excel evaluates mathematical operators in an expression. Excel first evaluates D5*D6 and then adds that product to D4 to produce the result. In other words, multiplication occurs first in the expression =D4+D5*D6 because multiplication has precedence over addition, the first operator in the formula.
5. You can produce the average of a range by dividing its sum by the number of elements in the range. The equivalent of the formula =AVERAGE(A1:B25) is =SUM(A1:B25)/50

SESSION 2.2

1. Test a worksheet by entering zero to observe the computed values. Use a calculator to compare one or two worksheet formula results with the calculator's answers.
2. Undo, Edit
3. c
4. b
5. See the file **Recycle2.xls**

CHAPTER 3

SESSION 3.1

1. Formatting does not change the *contents* of a cell. It changes the *appearance* of a cell's displayed results.
2. The General format is the default Excel cell format
3. right; left
4. currency; decimal places
5. Solution file is **ex03ExoticFruitMTG31.xls**

SESSION 3.2

1. Select a row by clicking its row heading. Then click Format, Row, Height, type in the height, and click OK.
2. Border (not Borders)
3. toolbar; Menu
4. selection handles
5. Solution file is **ex03ExoticFruitMTG32.xls**

CHAPTER 4

SESSION 4.1

1. data series
2. category
3. embedded; chart sheet
4. chart wizard
5. Solution file is **ex04BigWaveMTG41.xls**

SESSION 4.2

1. Ctrl
2. embedded; chart sheet
3. pie
4. elevate
5. Solution file is **ex04BigWaveMTG42.xls**

REF 4.1

glossary

Absolute cell reference: A cell reference in which a dollar sign ($) precedes both the column and row portions of the cell reference.

Activating (toolbar): Making a toolbar appear on the desktop.

Active cell: The cell in which you are currently working.

Active sheets: Sheets that are selected.

Alignment: The position of the data relative to the sides of a cell.

Argument list: The collection of cells, cell ranges, and values listed in the comma-separated list between a function's parentheses.

Argument list, function: The data that a function requires to compute an answer, in which commas separate individual list entries.

Arguments, function: They specify the value that the function uses to compute an answer and comprise the argument list that can be values, cell references, expressions, a function, or an arbitrarily complex combination of the preceding that results in a value.

Assumption cells: Cells upon which other formulas depend and whose values can be changed to observe their effect on a worksheet's entries.

Attached text: Chart objects such as X-axis title, Y-axis title, and tick marks

AutoComplete: Excel offers to fill in the remainder of the cell with information that matches your partial entry from another cell in the same column.

Axis: line that contains a measurement by which you compare plotted values.

Bottom margin: Area at the bottom of the page between the bottommost portion of the print area and the bottom edge of the page.

Categories: Organizes values in a data series.

Category names: Correspond to worksheet text you use to label data.

Cell: The Excel worksheet element located at the intersection of a row and a column and identified by a cell reference.

Cell border: Format that applies lines of various types to one or more edges of cells (left, right, top, bottom) of the selected cell(s)

Cell contents: The text, formulas, or numbers you type into a cell.

Cell range: One or more cells that form a rectangular group.

Cell reference: A cell's identification consisting of its column letter(s) followed by its row number.

Chart area: Area in which all chart elements reside.

Chart sheet: Chart on a separate sheet.

Chart title: Labels the entire chart.

Charts: Sometimes called graphs, they are a graphical representation of data.

Comments: Worksheet cell notes that are particularly helpful to indicate special instructions about the contents or formatting of individual cells.

Data label: Value or name assigned to an individual data point.

Data marker: Graphic representation of the value of a data point in a chart.

Data points: Values that comprise a data series.

Data series: Set of values that you want to chart.

Dock (toolbar): Toolbar adheres to one of the four edges of the window.

Drop shadow: Shadow cast by an object.

Editing: Modifying the contents of a cell.

Embedded chart: Chart on a worksheet near the data you are charting.

Error value: Special Excel constant that indicates something is wrong with the formula or one of its components.

Fixed pitch (font): Every character is the same width.

Floating (toolbar): Toolbar that can appear anywhere on the work surface.

Font: Combination of typeface and qualities including character size, character pitch, and spacing.

Footer: Text that appears automatically at the bottom of each printed page in the footer margin.

Format: Cosmetic changes to a worksheet that make the text and numbers appear different.

Formatting: Process of altering the appearance of data in one or more worksheet cells.

Formula: Expression that begins with an equal sign and consists of cell references, arithmetic operators, values, and Excel built-in functions (see Chapter 6) that result in calculated value.

Formula bar: Appears below the menu bar and displays the active cell's contents.

Function: A built-in or prerecorded formula that provides a shortcut for complex calculations.

General (format): Formatting that aligns numbers on the right side of a cell, aligns text on the left side, indicates negative numbers with a minus sign on the left side of a number, and displays as many digits in a number as a cell's width allows.

Gridlines: Extensions of tick marks that help identify the value of the data markers.

Grouping: Joining two objects into one object.

Header: Text that appears automatically at the top of each printed page in the header margin.

Hide (data): Reduce a row's height to zero.

Label text: Chart text such as tick mark labels, category axis labels, and data series names.

Landscape: Print orientation in which the width is greater than the length.

Left margin: Defines the size of the white space between a page's left edge and the leftmost edge of the print area.

Legend: Indicates which data marker represents each series when you chart multiple series.

Mathematical operator: Symbol that represents an arithmetic operation.

Menu bar: Contains Excel menus.

Mixed cell reference: Cell reference in which either the column or the row is never adjusted if the formula containing it is copied to another location.

Mouse pointer: Indicates the current position of the mouse.

Name box: Appears on the left of the formula bar and displays either the active cell's address or its assigned name.

Pitch: Number of characters per horizontal inch.

Plot area Rectangular area bounded by the X-axis on the left and the Y-axis on the bottom.

Point: Height of characters in a typeface; equal to 1/72 of an inch.

Pointing: Using the mouse to select a cell range while writing a formula.

Portrait: Print orientation in which the length is greater than the width.

Precedence order: Determines the order to calculate each part of the formula—which mathematical operators to evaluate first, which to evaluate second, and so on.

Precedent cell: Cell upon which a formula depends.

Properties dialog box: Contains several text boxes that you can fill in with helpful information including the fields Title, Subject, Author, Manager, Company, Category, Keywords, and Comments.

Proportional (font): Each character's pitch varies by character.

Range Finder: Feature that color-codes an outline surrounding each cell referenced by a formula.

Relative cell reference: Cell references in formulas that change when Excel copies them to another location.

Right margin: Defines the white space between the print area's rightmost position and the right edge of a printed page.

Selection handles: Small white squares that appear around an object that is selected.

Series in: Option that establishes the way the data series is represented—either by rows or by columns.

Sheet tab: Contains the sheet's name.

Sheet tab scroll buttons: The buttons you click to scroll through an Excel workbook's sheet tabs.

Sizing handles: (*see* "selection handles")

Source cell(s): The copied cell(s).

Spreadsheet: A popular program used to analyze numeric information and help make meaningful business decisions based on the analysis.

Stacked bar chart: Subtype of the bar chart, combines the data markers in a data series together to form one bar, placing each marker at the end of the preceding one in the same data series.

Standard toolbar: Contains buttons that execute popular menu bar commands such as Print, Cut, and Insert Table.

Status bar: Bar appearing at the bottom of the display that shows general information about the worksheet and selected keyboard keys.

Syntax: Rules governing the way you write Excel functions.

Target cell(s): Cell or cells to which the contents are copied.

Task Pane: A dialog window that provides a convenient way to use commands, gather information, and modify Excel documents.

Text (entry): Any combination of characters that you can type on the keyboard including symbols.

Text box: Rectangular-shaped drawing object that contains text.

Tick marks: Small lines, similar to marks on a ruler, that are uniformly spaced along each axis and identify the position of category names or values.

Top margin: Area between the top of page and topmost edge of the print area.

Unattached text: Chart objects such as comments or text boxes.

Value (entry): Numbers that represent a quantity, date, or time.

What-if analysis: Making changes to spreadsheets and reviewing their effect on other values.

Workbook: Collection of one or more individual work-sheets.

Workbook window: Document window open in Excel.

Worksheet: They resemble pages in a spiral-bound workbook like the ones you purchase and use to take class notes.

Wrap text: Formatting that continues long text on multiple lines within a cell.

X-axis: Contains markers denoting category values.

X-axis title: Briefly describes the X-axis categories.

Y-axis: Contains the value of data being plotted.

Y-axis title: Identifies the values being plotted on the Y-axis.

Glossary for Common Microsoft Office XP Features

Access 2002: Relational database tool that can be used to collect, organize, and retrieve large amounts of data. With a database you can manipulate the data into useful information using tables, forms, queries, and reports.

Answer Wizard: Located in the Microsoft Help dialog box, it provides another means of requesting help through your application.

Application: A program that is designed to help you accomplish a particular task, such as creating a slide show presentation or creating a budget.

Ask a Question: A text box located in the top right corner of your window, it is perhaps the most convenient method for getting help.

Clipboard: A temporary storage location for up to 24 items of selected text that has been cut or copied.

Clippit: The paper clip office assistant.

Excel 2002: An electronic spreadsheet tool that can be used to input, organize, calculate, analyze, and display business data.

F1: The robot office assistant.

Formatting toolbar: A collection of buttons that allows you to change the appearance of text, such as bold, italicize, or underline.

FrontPage 2002: A powerful Web publishing tool that provides everything needed to create, edit, and manage a personal or corporate Web site, without having to learn HTML.

Integrated application suite: A collection of application programs bundled together and designed to allow the user to effortlessly share information from one application to the next.

Links: The Cat office assistant.

Menu bar: Displays a list of key menu options available to you for that particular program.

Office Assistant: Character that will appear ready to help you with your question.

Office XP: The newest version of the popular Microsoft integrated application suite series that has helped personal computer users around the world to be productive and creative.

Outlook 2002: A desktop information management tool that allows you to send and receive e-mail, maintain a personal calendar of appointments, schedule meetings with co-workers, create to-do lists, and store address information about business/personal contacts.

Paste Options button: Button that appears when you paste into your document. It will prompt the user when clicked with additional features such as allowing you to paste with or without the original text formatting.

PowerPoint 2002: A popular presentation tool that allows users to create overhead transparencies and powerful multimedia slide shows.

Professional edition: Office XP version that includes Access, in addition to the Standard version of Word, Excel, PowerPoint, and Outlook.

Professional Special edition: Office XP version that includes Access, FrontPage, and Publisher, in addition to the Standard version of Word, Excel, PowerPoint, and Outlook.

Publisher 2002: A desktop publishing tool that provides individual users the capability to create professional-looking flyers, brochures, and newsletters.

Rocky: The dog office assistant.

Smart tag button: Buttons that appear as needed to provide options for completing a task quickly.

Standard edition: Office XP version that consists of Word, Excel, PowerPoint, and Outlook.

Standard toolbar: A collection of buttons that contains the popular icons such as Cut, Copy, and Paste.

Task pane: This window allows you to access important tasks from a single, convenient location, while still working on your document.

Title bar: Located at the top of each screen, it displays the application's icon, the title of the document you are working on, and the name of the application program you are using.

Toolbar: A collection of commonly used shortcut buttons.

Word 2002: A general-purpose word-processing tool that allows users to create primarily text-based documents, such as letters, résumés, research papers, and even Web pages.

index